Russian Monks
on Mount Athos

Russian Monks
on Mount Athos

THE THOUSAND YEAR HISTORY
OF ST PANTELEIMON'S

NICHOLAS FENNELL

HOLY TRINITY PUBLICATIONS
Holy Trinity Seminary Press
Holy Trinity Monastery
Jordanville, New York
2021

Printed with the blessing of His Eminence,
Metropolitan Hilarion First Hierarch
of the Russian Orthodox Church Outside of Russia

HOLY TRINITY
SEMINARY PRESS

An imprint of

HOLY TRINITY PUBLICATIONS
Holy Trinity Monastery
Jordanville, New York 13361-0036
www.holytrinitypublications.com

ISBN: 978-1-942699-30-9 (paperback)
ISBN: 978-1-942699-42-2 (ePub)
ISBN: 978-1-942699-43-9 (Kindle)

Library of Congress Control Number: 2021936518

Cover Photo: "Mount Athos, St Panteleimon Monastery." Photograph by
Anya Ivanova. Source: dreamstime.com: 22512111.

The sources for the internal photos and illustrations are found on page 226.

New Testament Scripture passages taken from the New King James Version.
Copyright © 1982 by Thomas Nelson, Inc. Used by permission.

Dedicated to the Mother of God
and written for Marina, John and Donya, and Alexandra

Contents

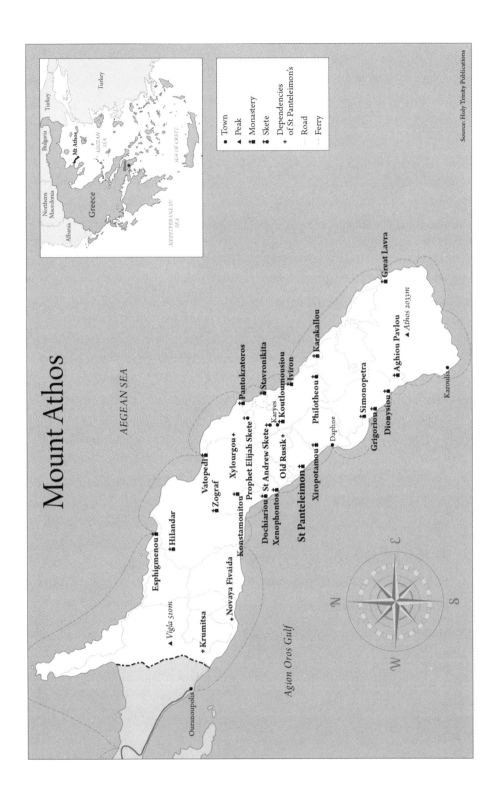

Mount Athos

AEGEAN SEA

Agion Oros Gulf

Ouranoupolis

Esphigmenou ‡
▲ Vigla 510m
+ Novaya Fivaida
+ Krumitsa

‡ Hilandar

Vatopedi ‡
‡ Zograf
Xylourgou +
Prophet Elijah Skete ●
Konstamonitou ‡
Dochiariou ‡ St Andrew Skete ‡
Xenophontos ‡ Old Rusik +
Karyes
St Panteleimon ‡

‡ Pantokratoros
‡ Stavronikita
Koutloumousiou ‡
‡ Iviron

Xiropotamou ‡
Philotheou ‡
‡ Karakallou

Daphne ●

Grigoriou ‡
‡ Simonopetra
Dionysiou ‡
‡ Aghiou Pavlou

‡ Great Lavra
▲ Athos 2033m

Karoulia ●

● Town
▲ Peak
‡ Monastery
● Skete
+ Dependencies of St Panteleimon's
-- Road
-- Ferry

Source: Holy Trinity Publications

Turkey
Bulgaria
Northern Macedonia
Albania
Greece
Turkey
AEGEAN SEA
Mt Athos
MEDITERRANEAN SEA
SEA OF CRETE

N W S E

The Russian Monastery on Mount Athos

General Introduction

Mount Athos, also known as the Holy Mountain, is a self-governing Eastern Orthodox monastic enclave of Greece. It occupies the north-easternmost prong of the
Halkidiki peninsula. Its shoreline, harbors, and land border with mainland Greece
are closed to females, and entry to males is restricted. The entire territory of Athos
is divided between twenty Christian Orthodox monasteries. They are *stavropegic*,
a privileged status conferred on them by the spiritual head of the Holy Mountain,
the Ecumenical Patriarch; their abbots are independent of any other episcopal jurisdiction. They are also *kyriarchic* / self-administrating and autonomous because as a
body the Twenty govern the Holy Mountain, and each administers the houses and
properties belonging to them both on Athos and outside. Since all twenty have had
chrysoboulla from crowned patrons—initially Byzantine emperors and then rulers
of Serbia, Bulgaria, and the Danubian Principalities—they have the royal title of
Vasiliki / Imperial.

All of the twenty monasteries are cenobitic: the brethren of each monastery
pledge total obedience to the abbot, who is appointed for life; all monastic property
and duties are shared; the brethren worship together at all services and eat together
in the refectory. Formerly many of the Twenty were idiorrhythmic: they were loose-
knit communities of semi-independent monks who earned their keep living each
according to his wealth, but not eating together. By the eighteenth century, idiorrhythm was becoming the norm on Mount Athos, even though all the twenty monasteries had cenobitic rules from their founders, often with curses on those who dared
to violate them. In the nineteenth and twentieth centuries, many of the Twenty were
idiorrhythmic. The last such monastery was Pantokratoros; it became a cenobium
in 1992.

All property on Athos belongs to or is leased from the Twenty. They also possess dependencies outside Athos. On their Athonite land the Twenty house various

organizations which are dependent on them yet outside their monastic walls. These organizations fall broadly into two categories. In the first is the *kellion (plur. kellia) /* cell, a general term embracing a variety of dwelling places, such as *isihastiria, kathismata,* and *kalyves.*[1] The *kellia* house from one to twelve monks and often contain a chapel. To the second category belong the *sketes.* These are traditionally an idiorrhythmic collection of *kellia,* built round a central church. Each skete has its own autonomous, internal administration run by the skete's head, the prior. As in all cenobia, the prior (or, in the case of a monastery, the abbot) rules in conjunction with his Council of Elders, known as the *Synaxis* in Greek or *Sobor* in Russian. The skete also has its own patriarchal charter, which defines the details of its internal life and of its relationship with its governing monastery. The Russian Prophet Elijah Skete was the first Athonite cenobitic skete: it was therefore a monastery-within-a-monastery. Currently, there are twelve sketes, of which the Prophet Elijah Skete and three others are cenobia. The rest are of traditional idiorrhythmic form. Until the 1960s there used to be itinerant Athonites who had no fixed abode, known in Russian as *siromakhi.*

Each of the twenty monasteries has a representative in the *Iera Koinotis,* the Athonite ruling council or Sacred Community, which sits in Karyes, the capital of Athos. This Council meets twice a week to deal with routine business, and at other times as necessary. Biennially, and on other occasions should the need arise, a Double Synaxis is convoked, composed of the twenty representatives and the twenty abbots. All decisions are carried in the *Koinotis* by a two-thirds majority vote. The Twenty are divided into five groups, each of which serves for five years as the *Iera Epistasia /* the Executive Committee of the Council. This committee is chaired by the *Protepistatis* or *Protos* and is renewed yearly on a rotational basis on July 1.[2] The Greek government is represented by the *Politikos Dioikitis /* Civil Governor, who is answerable to the Greek Foreign Ministry. One of his functions is to administer the police of the peninsula.

In three of the monasteries services are conducted in Slavonic: in Hilandar, which is traditionally Serbian, Zograf, which is Bulgarian, and in the Russian monastery of St Panteleimon, also known in Greek as the Rossikon or, in Russian, as Rusik.[3] The language of the other seventeen is Greek and nearly all their brethren are Greeks. The Twenty are in a strict—*ametavliti /* immutable—hierarchical order confirmed by patriarchal decrees in 1877 and 1911. The first and most senior monastery is the Great Lavra, founded in 963. The other monasteries in order of seniority are: Vatopedi, Iviron, Hilandar, Dionysiou, Koutloumousiou, Pantokratoros, Xiropotamou,

Zograf, Dochiariou, Karakallou, Philotheou, Simonopetra, Aghiou Pavlou, Stavron-ikita, Xenophontos, Grigoriou, Esphigmenou, St Panteleimon, and Konstamonitou. The Russian monastery continues to be only nineteenth on the ladder, yet it is one of the oldest. At the beginning of the twentieth century it was much the largest; its vast brotherhood was altogether anomalous in the Orthodox world[4] and is today again one of the most numerous.

The Holy Mountain is located next to some of the most wealthy and popular resorts of the Mediterranean. It has become a fashionable destination for the adventurous traveler undeterred by the bureaucratic obstacles aimed at controlling visitor numbers.[5]

The Russian Orthodox visit in great numbers and are sometimes more numerous than Greeks. Ouranoupolis, the main Athonite pilgrim port on the mainland, welcomes them: prices are high and business is thriving; and most restaurant, shop, and hotel signs are in (often incorrect) Russian, as well as Greek and English. On the Mountain itself, Russian is spoken almost everywhere—by monastery guest masters, shopkeepers in Karyes, and taxi drivers. Today's Russian influx is a relatively recent phenomenon, which started about a decade after the collapse of the USSR. On the eve of the First World War, almost half of the Holy Mountain's population was Russian, notwithstanding the expulsion of some thousand dissenters in 1913, as we shall see in Chapter 9; and Russian pilgrims arrived in their thousands.

At the last stop of the Ouranoupolis ferry before the main Athonite port of Daphne the Russian Monastery of St Panteleimon towers over its quay. Its imposing buildings, nearly all of which have been restored and which once housed almost five thousand (well over 1,500 monks plus three thousand lay visitors and workers), dwarf those of any of the other monasteries. The main guest quarters alone can accommodate six hundred in comfort. Yet of the ninety-odd pilgrims that disembark at the monastery quay nearly every day in the summer only a handful are Westerners or Greeks. St Panteleimon Monastery and Russian Athos are a closed book for those who do not understand Russian.

Demystifying Russian Athos

Until the end of the twentieth century little information was available to those interested in Russian Athos, except to the few who had access to the academic libraries and archives of Russia. No serious study had been written in any Western language. The library of St Panteleimon Monastery remained inaccessible. Until sometime in the 1970s, however, the eminent Greek researcher of Russian Athos, Professor A.-E. Tachiaos of Thessaloniki University (1931–2018), was granted free access to the monastery's archives and manuscripts; but then inexplicably its doors closed.[6] Even in the nineteenth century, when St Panteleimon's was at its apogee and its library was both expanding and being widely used by the Russian brethren, outsiders were not welcome in the library. Professor Aleksey Afanas'evich Dmitrievsky, author of the seminal monograph *Russkie na Afone: ocherk zhizni i deatel'nosti igumena svyaschennoarkhimandrita Makariya (Sushkina) / The Russians on Athos: a Study of the Life and Work of Abbot and Archimandrite Makary (Sushkin)*, 1895, which is generally accepted to contain the authoritative biography of St Panteleimon's first Russian abbot, was not allowed in the library:

> The main repository of these documents is the archive of the Russian St Panteleimon Monastery on Athos; it has hitherto not been sorted out and tidied. For all our desire to gain access, we were firmly refused permission, so we had to make do with merely those documents which *happened* to be in the hands of private individuals.[7]

Working in the UK, the few texts I had access to were housed in the British Library, the Bodleian, and the Cambridge University Library. It was only thanks to the generous loan by Tachiaos of the Dmitrievsky book and other key texts, and his permission to use the Slavonic section of the Thessaloniki University library that I was able to embark on my own research at the end of the 1980s. Over the past twenty years, however, there has been an explosion of literature published in Russian about the Holy Mountain. This includes reprints of Russian Athonite primary sources written from the eighteenth century to 1917, travelogues, and histories. Many of these are freely available on the internet. The most important online source in Russian about Mount Athos is the journal *Russky Afon, Pravoslavny dukhovno-prosvetitel'ny portal o russkom monashestve na Svyatoy Gore Afon / The Orthodox Spiritual and Educational Portal about Russian Monasticism on Mount Athos*, published by the Ukrainian researcher S. V. Shumilo on http://afonit.info. Its bulletins about the Holy Mountain appeared monthly and sometimes more frequently until late 2018, when the website ran out of funds. The bulletins then appeared sporadically and eventually stopped being issued; let us hope they will not one day disappear from the web. They are mainly based on extracts from the books being printed by St Panteleimon Monastery, and on reports from the daily life of the monastery and the Mountain in general.

The major scholarly works to be printed on Russian Athos include the series *Russky Afon / Russian Athos*, first published in Moscow by Indrik in 2006. It currently runs to twelve volumes, the last of which came out in 2017. Volume 6 is a reprint of Dmitrievsky's *Russkie na Afone*; the rest are by other Athonite scholars over the past two centuries. In 2011, the then president of the Russian Federation, D. A. Medvedev, together with Patriarch Kirill of Moscow, held a meeting to establish for St Panteleimon Monastery a "fund dedicated to the restoration of [its] dilapidated buildings and the refurbishment of those in use."[8] Thanks to this initiative, the monastery library was restored and modernized, and publication of what was intended to be the authoritative history of St Panteleimon's and of Russian Athos was embarked upon. An ambitious series of books was planned, entitled *Seriya: Russky Afon XIX– XX vekov / Russian Athos in the Nineteenth and Twentieth Centuries Series.*

The first volume, *Russky Afonsky otechnik XIX–XX vekov* (the full title translates as *The Russian Athonite Gerontikon, or Select Biographies of the Russian Elders and Ascetics living on Athos in the XIX–XX Centuries*), came out in 2012.[9] It is anonymous and, most unusually for any Russian publication to appear since the 1960s, in pre-revolutionary script.[10] The language, however, is decidedly contemporary. The other publications of the series are in modern script. Although volume 1, like the others, is a magnificent, heavy hardback, with expensive paper and lavish illustrations, and handsomely bound in red and gold, its value as source material is limited. The footnotes are informative, but the scope of the book is unclear: on the one hand, much of its material is interesting and detailed, although the text is clearly aimed at the pious reader rather than the scholar; on the other, the list of elders and ascetics described is by no means exhaustive. Names are unhelpfully given in chronological order at the back rather than as an alphabetical index.

Subsequent volumes of the series have appeared in rapid succession. In 2013, the second volume was published: the *Monahologion of St Panteleimon Monastery*, a compilation of brief biographies of over four thousand of the brethren who lived in the monastery from 1803 to 2003.[11] Also in 2013, part 1 of volume 7 was published, the catalogue of the library's Russian and Slav manuscripts.[12] This is a fine edition containing hundreds of photographs of the MS samples and precise details about each of the 1,435 texts. It was presented by the then monastery librarian, Monk Ermolay (Chezhiya), at the *Afon i slavyansky mir / Athos and the Slav World* Conference held in Kiev in May 2014. He gave each of the fifty or so delegates a copy—a handsome present.

Fr Ermolay spoke of the ambitious publishing program for the series. He hoped that one day the Russian and Slav manuscripts would be available online, with a URL attached to each one, thus allowing the public to click on and view in full any of the texts. Summing up, he said:

> This ... project will allow us at last to lift the veil of ignorance about the Russian Athonite population, which has been unjustly forgotten in our motherland during the years of the suppression of the faith by atheists ... To this day nearly all Russian Athonite spiritual treasures have been inaccessible to our compatriots ... The series will be made up of twenty-five volumes, certain of which will be sub-divided into separate books—from two to four. Thus the total number of volumes in the series will exceed thirty.[13]

Fr Ermolay set the bar impossibly high. He promised that the second part of volume 7, the catalogue of Greek MS and those in other languages, would come out in May 2015, and apologized that he was not able to bring it with him to Kiev. He then set out a road map for the publication of the rest of the twenty-five volumes. Ten of them were promised for 2014 and 2015. He himself was in danger of burning up. As librarian, he was sent to one conference after another to publicize the series and speak about the monastery's renovation in preparation for the millennial celebrations of the Russian presence on Athos, planned for 2016. Not only was he the principal author and editor of the volume 7 editions, and one of the chief overseers of the library's refurbishment, but he was also responsible for the distribution of the series, as well as for the reception of pilgrims at the monastery, the allocation of whose accommodation he oversaw. By 2017 he had relinquished his responsibilities and retired from the monastery to an isolated *kellion* / hermitage.

Publication of subsequent additions to the series continued apace, but in seemingly random order. The first history of the monastery, from its beginnings to 1725, was promised for 2014, but came out a year later.[14] Ninety percent of the text is by D. B. Zubov, one of the three directors of Institut russkogo Afona.[15] It has just eighty-nine footnotes for 386 pages of text. The last third of the book, pp. 387–602, is entitled "Russky afonsky Paterik" / "The Russian Athonite Paterikon;" it is made up of hagiographies of the Russian Athonite saints and ascetics who lived on the Holy Mountain or in Russia. This is a rehash of the last third of *SRA 1*, the first volume of the St Panteleimon series.[16]

The second history of the monastery to be published covers the years 1912 to 2015.[17] A little over a hundred pages are by O. E. Petrunina of Moscow State University. She writes an excellent introduction to Russian Athos and the political situation in the Near East from the end of the nineteenth century, and during the first quarter of the twentieth century. The other seven hundred pages are by the Ukrainian academic, Professor M. V. Shkarovsky, who bases his text mainly on hundreds of unpublished documents from the St Panteleimon archive. He writes in painstaking detail, but his narrative occasionally loses chronological sequence and repeats itself. The much-awaited earlier history, covering the years 1725–1912, came out several months later, at the end of 2015.[18] It is a compilation of chapters and sections by no fewer than twelve authors, including Petrunina, Shkarovsky, and Monk Ermolay. The quality of the writing is variable, but much is excellent, especially the contributions of Petrunina, of the historian L. A. Gerd, of K. A. Vakh, general editor of the Indrik series, and of Igumen Pyotr (Pigol'), principal editor of the independent church journal specializing in Russian Athonite matters, *K Svetu.*

Although many of the volumes Fr Ermolay promised have appeared in print, the St Panteleimon library is becoming inaccessible again. He was succeeded by Monk Martiry, who proved helpful and cooperative. Unfortunately, in 2018 the latter was also replaced, at the same time as Fr Makary (Makienko) was removed to Karyes.[19] The wonderful prospect of the 1,435 Russian and Slav MS of volume 7/1 being freely available with individual URLs on the internet has not been realized. Perhaps it never will be, now that Fr Ermolay has gone. Most of the first ten volumes used to be available on the internet as downloadable Adobe documents, but in around 2017 the links to the Adobe documents were removed. Furthermore, printed copies of the volumes are difficult to buy. A couple have been on sale at St Panteleimon Monastery for a very reasonable 50 euros each, and they could be bought in the St Panteleimon Dependency bookshop in Moscow; but their supply has been unreliable. Volume 5, however, was for a long time available nowhere, not even in the monastery itself.[20]

Clearly, even to the Russian reader much of the history of St Panteleimon Monastery and of Russian Athos is hard to access. Nothing seems to have proceeded according to plan. Like Fr Ermolay's projects, Medvedev and Patriarch Kirill's fine initiative ran out of steam: "unfortunately, the Fund ... did not meet the expectations of Russian Athonites."[21] Medvedev's committee met again in January 2014, but then folded. The rest of the St Panteleimon refurbishment continued at the expense of wealthy individuals, such as the oligarch, Oleg Deripaska, and organizations like Fond Andreya Pervozvannogo. No doubt the rest of the series will be published, although Russian books and their availability tend to be less predictable than schemes involving bricks and mortar.

CHAPTER 1

The Monastery's Early History: From Xylourgou to the Old Mountain Rusik

The history of the Russian monastery on Athos can be divided into three stages, which Priest-Monk Kirion (Ol′khovik), the former St Panteleimon representative in Karyes, defines as follows:

> From the tenth to the twelfth centuries Russian Athonites inhabited the ancient Russian Lavra of the Mother of God, also known as Xylourgou. From 1169 to [the 1760s] the ancient Monastery of St Panteleimon was the Russian house on Athos, more commonly referred to as *Nagorny* or *Stary Rusik* / Mountain or Old Rusik / Russian Monastery.[1] For the last two hundred years, Russian Athonites have occupied the present-day St Panteleimon Monastery by the sea … Xylourgou and *Stary Rusik*, are today the sketes of St Panteleimon.[2]

Although Russian monks are believed to have been on Athos previously, the first verifiable document mentioning Russian Athonites dates to the beginning of the eleventh century.[3] This manuscript belongs not to the St Panteleimon archive, but to that of the Great Lavra. Owing to the Russian monastery's numerous fires and dilapidation, the paucity of ancient acts in its archive had long cast doubt on Russian Athonite tradition, according to which the first Russian monastery had been established on the Holy Mountain by the reign of Prince Vladimir of Kiev (980–1015). The earliest acts in its possession are from 1030 and 1048. In 1932, however, the French Byzantinist Paul Lemerle and his team unearthed in the Great Lavra archive (Drawer 1, Document 173) an act dated February 1016. It was signed by twenty-one abbots; the thirteenth signature reads: "Monk Gerasimos, presbyter by the grace of God and abbot of the monastery of the Ros … he appends his personal signature as witness."[4]

The thirteenth position of Abbot Gerasimos's signature indicates the relative seniority of his monastery. By 1031 Xylourgou had become a fully fledged monastery.[5]

9

A Chrysobull of Constantine IX Monomachos dated 1048 conferred on it royal lavra status. S. V. Shumilo observes:

> The ancient Russian monastery reached its apogee in the reign of Vladimir's son, Prince Yaroslav the Wise .... It had the right in disputes to address the emperor directly without having to go through the Protaton [the governing body of the Koinotis or Sacred Community in Karyes], which was forbidden to other Athonite houses. By this time, Xylourgou was a well-run house with hired workmen. It had its own wharf, vessels, cornfields, mill and road joining the monastery to the wharf.[6]

St Anthony Pechersky came to Xylourgou as a pilgrim from Kiev and was tonsured in the monastery in 1051. He then went back to Kiev, where he founded the Kievo-Pecherskaya Lavra, the first monastery of Rus'. St Anthony was the founder of Russian monasticism.[7]

It is important to note that Xylourgou was a distinctly Russian monastery. One of its inventories dated 1142 mentions forty-nine "Russian books," but none in Greek. This, Shumilo points out, "indicates both the nationality of the brethren and their work as copiers."[8] According to A.-E. Tachiaos:

> Without doubt we have here proof of the existence a Russian monastery on the Holy Mountain. At the time the Greeks designated the Russian people and its country with the indeclinable proper noun *Ros* ($ʿΡῶς$). They had first been referred to thus ... by Photios, Patriarch of Constantinople in 867.[9]

The move to Mountain Rusik happened in the reign of Abbot Lavrenty, in 1161, because Xylourgou was too small for the expanding brotherhood. The new house was now also called the Monastery St Panteleimon, as its *katholikon* / central church was dedicated to the Great Martyr. In the next five hundred years, the monastery's fortunes fluctuated. It did not attain the level of prosperity enjoyed by Xylourgou in the twelfth century. Interpreting what happened to Mountain Rusik until the eighteenth century is largely guess-work, owing to the paucity and unreliability of written records. It is believed that links with Russia were severed after the fall of Kiev and during the Mongol period. Whereas overseas pilgrimage from Kiev had reached its acme in the eleventh century, "the conquest of Rus' by the Golden Horde in the thirteenth century indubitably affected pilgrimage .... The journeyings [abroad] of Russian pilgrims were noticeably reduced, but did not cease completely."[10]

Shortly after the move to Mountain Rusik, Rastko Nemanja, the future St Savva, Enlightener of the Serbs, was born (between 1169 and 1175) to Stefan II Nemanja *Župan* / Ruler of Serbia (1170–1196). In 1191, longing for the monastic life, the young man fled from his father's house to Athos. According to legend, the distraught *Župan* sent his voivodes in pursuit. They found him at St Panteleimon's in the Mountains. There, while the soldiers were asleep during a nocturnal service, the young man was tonsured with the monastic name of Savva in the monastery tower. From there "he threw down his layman's clothes, and a letter addressed to his father, whereupon his pursuers, realizing that he had become a monk and was beyond their reach, returned home empty-handed."[11]

Over the next two centuries the main Athonite benefactors were the Serbian rulers, of whom Stefan IV Dušan (1331–1355) was the most powerful. He became the principal Athonite *ktitor* / founder and benefactor.[12] From August 1347 to April 1348, he, his wife Elena, and his whole family stayed on the Mountain visiting all the monasteries and generously endowing them.

> It was then that [Stefan] gave St Panteleimon's its greatest holy treasure— the sacred skull of the Great Martyr and Healer Panteleimon along with a Chrysobull in Greek .… The Russian monastery itself, in which Serbs made up most of the brotherhood, became almost officially the second most important Serbian monastery [on the Mountain], and was called "Russian" only because of its past history.[13]

The internecine squabbles following the death of Stefan Dušan marked the end of Serbian protection of the Holy Mountain. On June 6, 1466, an agreement was signed between Abbot Averky of St Panteleimon and the Bulgarian monastery in Rila. This cemented the Slav confraternity of the two monasteries and facilitated the transfer of monks between them.[14] St Panteleimon's now looked to Muscovy for benefaction.

The earliest record of alms-gathering in the Moscow court is in 1497, when Abbot Paisy and three elders appeared before Ivan III, who gave them gifts for St Panteleimon's and other Athonite monasteries. In the following century, Russian Athonites returned to their home country to gather alms. In 1533 Grand-Prince Vasily III of Moscow gave St Panteleimon's Abbot Gavriil a substantial donation of fifteen thousand gold coins for the Athonite monasteries houses. Gavriil made his way back to the Mountain via Minsk, where he lost the money to thieves.[15] Interestingly, the Grand-Prince's gift was not exclusively to the Russian monastery. The Serbian researcher, A. Fotić, comments:

It seems that in the difficult times of Ottoman rule … the Russian rulers did not think of using their wealth to make [St Panteleimon's] a leading Athonite monastery. The most important place among the [Slav] monasteries … was always reserved for the Serbian monastery of Hilandar. From the mid-sixteenth century even the Russian rulers themselves, when periodically setting down the amount of financial aid and gifts for some of the Athonite monasteries, invariably and unambiguously gave precedence to … Hilandar over their own [Russian Monastery]. The reason undoubtedly was the high regard Hilandar enjoyed not only on Mount Athos, but also in the Balkan hinterland and across the Orthodox world.[16]

In 1555, Ivan IV was told that St Panteleimon was "very much in debt."[17] He responded, but "the 500 rubles sent by Tsar Ivan found no recipient."[18]

In 1568, the Porte decreed that all real estate on Athos and the mainland belonging to the monasteries be confiscated. The houses needed to raise fourteen thousand gold pieces to buy back their property—a sum ironically similar to Vasily III's generous donation. The amount was so great that they had to take out loans from Jewish moneylenders in Sidrekapsi and Thessaloniki at extortionate rates of interest. The larger and wealthier monasteries took decades to repay the debt; St Panteleimon's was ruined. In March 1571, Ivan IV granted 500 rubles to Hilandar, but only 350 to St Panteleimon's.

At some point after that date, the [St Panteleimon] monks locked their monastery up and dispersed into the surrounding *kellia*. In order to prevent their treasury from being seized by the unforgiving moneylenders, the Russian monks entrusted all their valuables, such as church vessels and vestments, to the monks of Hilandar for safekeeping. It is known that in 1582, Ivan [Meshenikov, the tsar's emissary,] did not disburse the aid of 500 rubles intended for [the Russian house] because the monastery had been deserted.[19]

Commenting on Meshenikov's mission to Athos, the Athonite historian, Priest-Monk Ioanniky (Abernethy) observes:

When … Meshenikov, was sent to the East in 1582 to hand out alms to monks, he came back to Moscow with a deed signed by Pachomios, the Protos of the Holy Mountain, testifying that "the monastery of St Panteleimon has been already empty for ten years following the death of Matfey the Builder, and there is no one to whom to give the money intended for him."[20]

The general pattern of the monastery's fortunes from the sixteenth to the eighteenth centuries was one of hardship and decline. On October 18, 1635, the Roman Catholic Apostolic Missionary to Athos, Nicola Rossi, wrote to his bishop that the monastery had been built "by a Russian king" and that it was inhabited by some 150 monks, most of whom were Russians. Where, when, and how so many monks from Russia happened to be living there, whereas some fifty years earlier the monastery had been deserted for ten years, is a mystery. As Fr Ioanniky repeats several times with reference to Russian Athonite monasticism in the sixteenth and seventeenth centuries, "history is silent about this." Writing four years later, Rossi reported that the monastery's brethren comprised Ruthenians (Little Russians from Transcarpathia. Little Russians originated from the equivalent of modern-day Ukraine and Belarus), Bulgarians, and mostly Greeks.[21] It seems that the Russians were unable to survive long without help from outside. Indeed, all Athonite monasteries depended on outside patronage, which was originally provided by the Byzantine emperors, and Serbian and Bulgarian monarchs, and later by the Danubian *gospodars* / princes. The Turks imposed the *harach*. This head-tax was hard to bear and would not have been met without the help of royal patronage, which was also always at hand to restore buildings damaged by natural disasters such as fire. The Russians were far from home; they were in a more vulnerable position than other Athonites, who were largely Balkan peasants, too poor and probably unsympathetic to help. The Russians, needing to gather alms, frequently came home to collect the riches they needed, and the tsars were usually the most generous givers.

In 1626, Archimandrite Filaret came from St Panteleimon's to Mikhail Fyodorovich with a document signed by Patriarch Cyril I of Constantinople testifying that the monastery was seriously in debt. The tsar, on the Patriarch's recommendation, arranged alms-gathering missions in Russia every four years.[22] The Greek Athonite historian, Monk Dorotheos (Vatopedinos), comments that overall in the seventeenth century:

> The situation did not improve. A letter by Patriarch Cyril I (Loukaris) ... states that "the monastery has fallen into ruin and debt." Thus towards the end of the [seventeenth] century the prolonged parlous state of the house obliged the Sacred Community to place it under the trusteeship of the other [Athonite] monasteries.[23]

There was a rare glimmer of hope in 1709, when Priest-Monk Ippolit Vishensky, visiting Mount Athos from the monastery of Saints Boris and Gleb in Chernigov, reported that the Russian monastery was thriving, and that just outside it lived only Russians, and not Greeks.

For the rest of the eighteenth century the monastery's fortunes continued to decline. Vasily Grigorovich-Barsky, the renowned Little Russian author, who illustrated his own book of travels in Athos and the Near East, found on his first visit to the Holy Mountain in 1725 that the monastery's brethren numbered only four, of whom two were Russian.

The position of the Russians on Athos was insecure owing to the frequent Russo-Turkish wars.[24] A Greek manuscript records that in May 1730: "The monks were chased out of the Monastery called the *Great Rosi*, [for] the Ishmaelites encamped in it and set up a minaret in its church."[25] On his second visit to the Mountain, in 1744, Barsky found that "The number of Russian monks having dwindled away, now that they were unable to go abroad from their country, the monastery was taken over by the Greeks, who possess it to this day."[26]

According to a new "civil law in Russia, letters of introduction were no longer issued and Russians ceased to travel freely abroad."[27] Furthermore, owing to Peter I's reforms aimed at secularizing Russia:

> the ... monastery was forgotten by the fatherland ... For three generations, not a single [pilgrim] came to settle in the Russian monastery. In 1735 the last Russian monk died in the monastery, which was inhabited by Greeks. Mountain *Rusik* was empty by the 1760s because of its distance from the sea ... A strong earthquake in 1790 reduced the Old Mountain Monastery to rubble.[28]

There ensued what one modern Russian historian terms a "dark period," until 1803.[29] Barsky sums up the sorry state of the Russian Athonites, who were:

> wandering hither and thither in the hills, in great need and feeding themselves by the sweat of their brows, and being despised by all. I felt sorry for them, for foxes have holes and birds nests, but the Russians have nowhere to rest their heads ... for in the Greek monasteries they are unable to communicate on account of the incompatibility of language, rules and temperament, and with the Serbs and Bulgarians [there is no common tongue] because of the above-mentioned good reasons.[30]

During the monastery's "dark period," there was no written account of its state other than official deeds and acts. Barsky's was the only eye-witness description of the plight of Russian Athonites, who had lost their monastic home. Now that the St Panteleimon brethren were almost exclusively Greek, the monastery was Russian only in name.

Greek Athos, on the other hand, was undergoing a renaissance: in the latter half of the eighteenth century the revivers of hesychasm, Saints Nikodemos of the Holy Mountain and Makarios of Corinth, were engaged in the Kollyvades dispute.[31] St Paisy Velichkovsky, their contemporary supporter in the dispute, founded the Prophet Elijah Skete, in 1757.[32] This was a house of Slav and Romanian speakers. Those of the Great and Little Russians not living in isolated *kellia* or Karyes gravitated to it.[33] The skete became the only Russian Athonite house in the dark period, and continued thus after St Paisy's departure from Athos in 1763. By now, Bulgarians inhabited Xylourgou.

During the Russians' absence from it, Mountain Rusik was not forgotten by benefactors. The Danubian gospodars gave it as a dependency the Doamna Monastery in Botoşani in 1709. In 1744, when much of Constantinople's population was dying from the plague, St Panteleimon's skull was brought from Athos and effected miraculous cures. The stricken household of Gospodar Ioannis Nikolau Kallimakh of Moldavia was visited by the relic:

> Nobody [in the household] died of the deadly buboes. The Gospodar, upon seeing such a godly blessing and numerous miracles in other houses, took in his care the Monastery of St Panteleimon, bestowing upon it a substantial sum of money, and in July 1744 he granted it his Chrysobull.[34]

From then onward the monastery received from the gospodars yearly grants: initially 100 leva, which was increased to 150 leva in 1750, and 250 at the end of the century. In 1750 Monk Meletios brought the skull to the household of Gospodar Constantin Rakovitsa, and in the following year his wife, Sultana, had the relic encased in gold. The skull was eventually housed in a silver reliquary.[35] There were other gifts from the gospodars: in 1760 Gospodar Alexander Kallimakh gave the monastery as a dependency from his Bogdan-Serai Palace in Constantinople the Church of St Nicholas and its surrounds; and his wife, Roxandra, gave a fine *epitaphion* / Holy Friday burial shroud embroidered in silver and gold.

The monastery also found special favor with the patriarchs of Constantinople. In 1752 Kyrillos V gave it as a dependency land in Kalamaria outside Thessaloniki.

In 1762 Ioannikios III intervened on behalf of St Panteleimon's in a dispute with Vatopedi over a *konaki* / house in Karyes.

Yet despite the aid it was receiving from its powerful patrons, St Panteleimon Monastery continued to deteriorate. By the 1760s, the monastery's mountainous location was proving inconvenient because of its distance from the sea and the rugged terrain which made the delivery of supplies difficult. Cenobitic rule was abandoned in favor of a laxer idiorrhythmic regime. A fire destroyed the central church, dedicated to St Panteleimon, in 1773. Mountain Rusik's empty buildings and surrounding forest became home to a herd of some three thousand goats and their herders. The brethren now made their third and final move, to the *Kellion* of the Resurrection on the south-eastern shore, where the present-day monastery is located.[36] Bishop Christophoros of Ierissos had acquired the *kellion* in 1677. As Patriarch Dionysios IV had granted it stavropegic status, the *kellion* was exempt of tax and independent of the ruling monasteries. How the *kellion* came into the possession of the St Panteleimon brethren is uncertain, but it is likely that the bishop left it in his will to them.[37]

In 1776 Patriarch Sophronios II granted the monastery's *skevophylax* / sacristan, Fr Vasileios, and an accompanying monk leave to go on an alms-gathering mission with the skull of St Panteleimon and a portion of the True Cross. In 1778, Abbot Elisaios went to St Petersburg to ask for the thirty-five rubles owed to the monastery by the Palestinskie Shtaty.[38] His request was refused because he had arrived without the necessary papers from the patriarch:

> It is likely … that Abbot Elisaios undertook such a distant and risky journey because of the extraordinary straits the Russian house found itself in at the time. The situation of St Panteleimon Monastery in about 1778 was probably somewhat uncertain: having abandoned their old house, the monks had not yet settled into their new one. Furthermore, this great change in the life of the monastery had not yet been confirmed.[39]

At the end of the eighteenth century, St Panteleimon's was suffering great material hardship. Along with Konstamonitou, Esphigmenou, and Dionysiou, it owed the Turkish authorities 100,000 piasters[40] in dues. St Panteleimon's was also embroiled in boundary disputes with Xenophontos. Patriarch Gerasimos III intervened on behalf of the former, but the disputes flared up again and in 1801 the sultan himself intervened on behalf of St Panteleimon's. Nevertheless, disarray and poverty continued to blight the monastery, and squabbles broke out among the brethren. Eventually the Sacred Community proposed to liquidate St Panteleimon's and strike it off the list of the Twenty.

Chapter 2

From Abbot Savvas to Abbot Gerasimos

In 1803 the Sacred Community proposed to Patriarch Kallinikos V (1801–1806, 1808–1809) that the St Panteleimon's be struck off the list of the ruling monasteries, and that its lands and chattels be sold to pay off its debts. As it was unable to raise even 20 piasters,[1] the other houses plundered it. Idiorrhythm was the root cause of its ruin:

> Multiple authority ... whereby [the house] was run by periodically elected leaders hindered the wellbeing of monasteries. This led to ... the decline of [our house's] material fortunes and strict monastic discipline, giving rise instead to internal disorders and ructions, which prevented [its] proper and peaceful development.[2]

Patriarch Kallinikos V, however, ensured that the monastery survived. He issued a *syngilion* / charter in 1803 declaring that the Russian house should not be liquidated, now that Russian victories over the Turks were helping Ottoman Christians. He stipulated that St Panteleimon's must become a cenobium and appointed as its new abbot Priest-Monk Savvas (Peloponneseos), a renowned ascetic living in a *kellion* / hermitage belonging to Xenophontos Monastery, which had recently adopted cenobitic rule. The appointment was approved by the Sacred Community, but Savvas himself was not consulted. The ascetic declined the honor three times; on the fourth he reluctantly accepted.

Fr Savvas worried about the considerable sums needed for the new buildings of the impoverished monastery, which he intended to establish some fifty paces from the *Kellion* / Hermitage of the Resurrection.[3] All the bequests from the Kallimakh family had already been spent, but "in no way on the monastery itself."[4] Patriarch Kallinikos promised money from his patriarchal funds, which were limited, and summoned Savvas to Constantinople. Exhausted by his journey from the Mountain, the future abbot, now in his nineties, had to rest for two days upon his arrival. News quickly spread that the ascetic and the wonderworking remains of St Panteleimon were in the capital. On the fourth day Fr Savvas appeared at the *Phanar* / the patriar-chal quarter in Constantinople, and was troubled when the patriarch and members of the Synod greeted him by kissing his hand.

Fr Savvas was granted leave to stay four years in the city to gather alms. In 1806 the patriarchal treasury was locked, owing to the renewal of hostilities between Russia and Turkey. The old man, who was confirmed by patriarchal *syngilion* / char-ter as abbot of St Panteleimon in the same year, realized that he still had insufficient funds. When all hope seemed to be lost, Skarlat, another member of the Kallimakh dynasty, fell ill. He was the grand dragoman to the Sublime Porte, grandson of Alexan-der, and son of Ioannis, both of whom had been cured by the relics of St Panteleimon. Thus: "The ailing gospodar himself solemnly declared that if only the Holy Great Martyr [Panteleimon] would heal him from his mortal sickness, he would promise to become the benefactor of the Athonite monastery dedicated to that saint."[5] Savvas infused Athonite herbs in water sanctified on the relics of St Panteleimon and made Skarlat drink the potion. A miraculous cure was effected.

Now at last Savvas had enough money. Not only did the gospodar handsomely endow the Athonite house, and thus "religiously carry out his promise,"[6] but in 1811 Savvas arranged for the sale of Doamna Monastery for 200,000 piastri.[7] St Pantelei-mon's now had five sources of income:

1. money from the Kallimakhs;
2. modest grants from the Imperial Russian *Palestinskiye Shtaty;*
3. income from the Kallimakh Bogdan-Sarai Palace Church of St Nicholas in Constantinople;
4. income from the monastery's dependencies on Athos and elsewhere;
5. rent from *kellia* belonging to the monastery.

From 1812–1821 the monastery was built from scratch. In 1815 Patriarch Grigorios V consecrated the new *katholikon* / central church dedicated to St Panteleimon. As in Old Mountain Rusik, the monastery's other main church was dedicated to the Dor-mition. Water was supplied to all buildings, which included living quarters, a bakery, an olive press, and a refectory.

The nonagenarian abbot worked with tireless energy. As well as managing the finances and building projects, he had to deal with disputes with the Bulgarian inhab-itants of Xylourgou, who stubbornly refused to adopt cenobitic rule. Although the skete was a dependency of St Panteleimon's, it was supported by Bulgarian benefactors and its brethren maintained close ties with Zograf. News of the disobedience reached Constantinople. In 1815 Patriarch Kyrillos VI (1813–1818) asked Grigorios V (1793–1798, 1806–1808, and 1818–1821), who was in temporary retirement on Athos, to intervene. Nevertheless, the brotherhood of Xylourgou refused to comply until 1833, when the skete became cenobitic.

Abbot Savvas had also to sort out boundary disputes with the monastery's neighbors, Xenophontos, Xiropotamou, and Koutloumousiou. The disagreement with the first of these must have been personally embarrassing for Savvas, a former Xenophontos *kelliot* / hermit. He also had to deal with legal wrangles over the *Kellion* / Hermitage of the Anapavseon and the monastery's dependency on Kassandra, the first of the three Halkidiki peninsulas. Finally, St Panteleimon Monastery and Great Lavra quarreled over the ownership of the St George *Kellion* / Hermitage in Karyes. Grigorios V intervened and all the disputes were settled in favor of St Panteleimon's.

Although successive patriarchs were not in a position to help St Panteleimon's materially, they were keenly interested in its fate and unfailingly defended it. Initially patriarchal support was perhaps due to the special stavropegic status granted to the Resurrection *Kellion* / Hermitage. Later, Kallinikos V hoped that St Panteleimon's would serve as an example of cenobitic rule to the many idiorrhythmic monasteries. Grigorios V's special interest in St Panteleimon's, however, may also have been influenced by the momentous changes happening in the Balkans in the first quarter of the nineteenth century.

The successive defeats of Turkey at the hands of Russia as well as romantic ideals inspired by the French Revolution were a catalyst for these changes. After the Treaty of Kuchuk-Kainarji (1774) at the conclusion of its 1768–1774 war with Turkey, Russia was free to intervene in favor of Orthodox Christians in the Ottoman Empire. The Straits[8] were open for Russia and irredentist uprisings were sparked off, in particular the first Serbian uprising (1804–1813). Russian prestige was at its peak in 1812, thanks not only to the defeat of Turkey in the 1806–1812 war, but also to the victory over Napoleon. In 1812 the sultan recognized the autonomy of Serbia, which was supported by Russia. After the second Serbian uprising (1815–1817) the Porte increased the autonomy of the Serbs. In the words of the Russian historian O. E. Petrunina:

> The victory of Russia over Napoleon and its support for the Serbs created a profound impression on the Orthodox East. The Christian subjects of the Ottoman Sultan laid their hopes on the Russian tsar, who had, to quote Pushkin, become "the chief of tsars." Some [of these subjects], for example, were

members of secret Greek societies; they expected military and political support from him. Others, such as the eastern patriarchs and Athonite monks, [were hoping for] material support.[9]

The French Revolution that began in 1789 had already stirred the Balkan peoples, especially the Greeks. In 1814 Greek merchants in Odessa founded the Philiki Hetaireia to overthrow Ottoman rule and establish a Greek independent state. Some believed that the Russian foreign minister, the Greek Count Ioannis Kapodistrias, secretly directed the society, but in 1820 it was led by Alexander Ypsilantis, a Greek general in the Russian army. In 1821 he invaded the Danubian Principalities of Moldavia and Wallachia in a bid to overthrow Turkish rule there and eventually in Greece. His campaign was unsuccessful, but it sparked off the uprising in the Peloponnese in the same year. Following Russia's defeat of the Turks in the 1828–1829 war, the Kingdom of the Hellenes was formed in 1830. The Porte now recognized the autonomy of Wallachia and Moldavia under Russian tutelage.

The 1821 Peloponnese uprising heralded a troubled period on Athos. In a single month St Panteleimon Monastery lost its abbot, who had painstakingly built it up from scratch, and its royal defender and benefactor. On April 14, Abbot Savvas died aged 103.[10] Skarlat Kallimakh had been gospodar of Wallachia, but was suspected by the Porte of collaborating with the Greek irredentists. He was hanged in Constantinople on April 21, 1821. A similar fate befell Grigorios V, who was martyred on Easter Sunday that year. He was canonized by the Church of Greece a century later and by the Moscow Patriarchate in 2000.

Meanwhile, the rest of the Athonite community was in a revolutionary fever. The Philiki Hetaireia, supported by the Church, was spreading propaganda in Macedonia, most of whose bishops belonged to the society. Serres in North-East Macedonia and the Holy Mountain were insurgent hotbeds. Some of the Athonite monasteries had arms caches. Inspired no doubt by the revolutionary ardor of Ypsilantis who had departed for the Danubian Principalities, the prominent Hetaerist warrior, Emmanouil Pappas, sailed in a ship laden with arms from Serres to Athos in March 1821. Some two thousand young Athonite monks rallied to his support, eager to fight. His campaign in Halkidiki initially met with success, but by June the Turkish army had the upper hand; the insurgents were besieged and broken. Fifty thousand refugees fled from the Turks in the hope of finding succor on the Holy Mountain. They received none. The insurgents were heavily defeated at the Battle of Kassandra (Halkidiki) on October 30, 1821, by the Pasha of Thessaloniki, Mehmet

Emin Abulubud. Athonite revolutionary ardor was extinguished; the young monks returned to the contemplative life. In December 1821 Pappas fled by ship for Hydra and died on the way.

On December 15, 1821, Turkish troops invaded Athos. The monasteries were plundered and suspected insurrectionists were deported to Thessaloniki, where many died. There remained on the Holy Mountain a three thousand-strong task-force, whose upkeep was forced upon the monasteries. Most of the troops left in the spring of 1822; a garrison of forty men stayed behind for the next eight years. During the occupation, the Athonite population was drastically diminished.[11] The Russian Monastery was plunged once again into debt: it owed 100,000 silver kuruş. Most of the St Panteleimon brethren fled to the Peloponnese. The last of the Turkish troops went away and the relative autonomy of Athos was restored following the victory of Russia over the Ottomans in the 1828–1829 war.

Thanks perhaps to these repeated military triumphs by Russia, St Panteleimon Monastery continued to be known as the Russian Monastery, the Rusik, or Rossikon, as the Greeks called it. Nonetheless, its brethren, as we have seen, had been Greek since the end of the eighteenth century: "the [monastery] is Russian only in name— for Russians did indeed once live in it," testified the Russian prince, Archimandrite Anikita (Shirinsky-Shikhmatov), who visited it in 1835.[12] Ten years later, the author of the first complete scholarly history of Mount Athos, Archimandrite Porfiry (Uspensky), mooted that the "age-old conviction that St Panteleimon Monastery belongs to us Russians [is] false." He also believed that since the sixteenth century the monastery "received insubstantial alms from Moscow, but our monks did not live in it and would have long ago disappeared from Athos had not [the monastery] been supported by the Moldavian Gospodars and Greek monks."[13]

Greek historians have been at pains to claim that the monastery was no longer Russian even in name. According to Monk Dorotheos, it became known as *Avthentikon Koinovion ton Kallimahidon ... Kathargoumenis tis tou Rosikou prosigorias* / "The True Cenobium of the Kallimakhs ... the former Russian appellation having been abolished."[14] The Russian historian, O. A. Rodionov, explains that this renaming was first brought to light by the patriarchal archivist, Archimandrite Kallinikos (Delikanis, 1855–1932), in his description of Athonite monasteries 1630–1863.[15] Kallinikos quotes two patriarchal syngilia, of 1806 and 1807, as proof of the monastery's change of name.

Rodionov points out that the archimandrite merely summarized the two syngilia but did not quote them in full; furthermore, later syngilia by the same patriarchs,

Grigorios V and Kallinikos V, refer to St Panteleimon Monastery simply as the *Rossikon* / Russian Monastery. In view of Russia's beneficially influential role in the Balkans, the patriarchs, from the eighteenth century to Grigorios V and Kallinikos V, were keen to promote the interests of the Rossikon.

From the latter quarter of the nineteenth century some Greeks have contin-ued to maintain that St Panteleimon Monastery had never been Russian, despite the fact that it was and is still known as *Rossikon* / the Russian Monastery, or *Ton Ros* / [Belonging to] the Russians. N. Mylonakos, a one-time policeman serving in Karyes, claimed that the Rossikon had always been called Russian because pious Greek Athonite monks insist on sticking to traditional names; and that the name does not denote whom the monastery belonged to, as in the case of Iviron, which is only nominally *Iberian* [Georgian] because the last of the Georgians lived in it in the fourteenth century.[16] According to a report written in 1926 by the Athenian Profes-sors Alivisatos and Petrakakos, who were commissioned by the Greek government to prepare new statutes for Mount Athos, St Panteleimon's was known as *Rossikon* / the Russian Monastery, or *Ton Ros* / [Belonging to] the Russians because at some unspecified date in the past it was inhabited by Slavs from a Dalmatian town called Rosa. In 1874, in the Constantinople anti-Russian journal *I Thraki*, it was reported that the name Rossikon or *Roussikon* is based on the surname of the monastery's unknown founder, who came from Thessaloniki.[17]

The Greek theories about the renaming of St Panteleimon's and about its ethnic origins betray a hostile rivalry toward Russian Athonites. To this day, this enmity has periodically resurfaced. In the past decade some members of the Sacred Community have been saying that St Panteleimon's became Russian only after the 1830s. All that is certain is that from the end of the eighteenth century the monastery had been in Greek hands.

The next abbot after Savvas was perhaps the first non-Greek in charge of St Pan-teleimon Monastery by the sea. Before his death Savvas had chosen two successors: Priest-Schema-Monk Gerasimos and Deacon-Monk Venedictos, a Greek. The eth-nicity of Gerasimos is uncertain. The eminent Greek historian of Athos, Monk Ger-asimos (Smyrnakis) Esphigmenitis, calls him "the monastery's last Greek abbot"[18]; in the "Monahologion of St Panteleimon Monastery" he is also billed as a Greek,[19] but the Russian writer, Fr Serafim (Vesnin), who joined the brotherhood under Gerasi-mos in 1843 and wrote under the pseudonym of Svyatogorets, calls him Bulgarian.[20] Archimandrite Porfiry (Uspensky) observed: "He looks Slav. I was told that he is not a Greek but a Bulgarian."[21] Gerasimos was a native of Macedonia; he hailed from the village of Evdomista (Tur. Kioup-Kioi), now known as Ano Vrondou, in the district of Serres. He spoke or had a working knowledge of several languages—probably Turkish, Bulgarian, Russian, and his native Macedonian Slav dialect, as well as Greek.

Fr Gerasimos was born Georgy, son of Vasily, in 1772. His surname is unknown. He was made a *rasofor* monk at the age of twenty-eight. In 1804 he joined the Greek Athonite Aghia Anna Skete, where he was tonsured with the name of Gavriil. After a year spent in the St Nicholas *Kellion* / Hermitage belonging to Koutloumousiou, he joined St Panteleimon Monastery. He was tonsured to the Great Schema with the name of Gerasimos in 1821. He and most of the brethren left for the comparative safety of the Morea when the troubles began later that year. He was elected abbot upon his return to St Panteleimon Monastery in 1830; his appointment was confirmed by Patriarch Konstantios two years later.[22]

Fig 1.1 Xylourgou, the first Russian Athonite monastery (1016–1161).

Fig 1.2 St Panteleimon in the Mountains or the Old Mountain Rusik (1161–1773). Illustrated by Vasily Grigorovich-Barsky, 1744.

St Panteleimon's-by-the-Sea

Fig 1.3 The St Panteleimon Monastery by the sea before the 1830s.

Fig 1.4 A view from a hill above Saint Panteleimon Monastery on the Athos peninsula.

Fig 1.5 Elder Arseny, spiritual father to all Russian Athos; on the Mountain from 1821; died in 1846.

Fig 1.6 Archimandrite Anikita, invited to found the Russian brotherhood of St Panteleimon's and failed to do so; at the monastery 1835–1836; died in 1837.

Fig 1.7 Spiritual Father Pavel, in charge of the Russian brotherhood from 1839; died in 1840.

Fig 1.8 Elder and Spiritual Father Ieronim, in charge of the Russian brotherhood 1840; died in 1885.

Abbots of St-Panteleimon's-by-the-Sea

Fig 1.9 Abbot Savvas
(1803–1821)

Fig 1.10 Abbot Gerasimos
(1833–1875)

Fig 1.11 Abbot Makary
(1875–1889)

Fig 1.12 Abbot Andrey
(1889–1903)

Fig 1.13 Abbot Nifont
(1903–1905)

Fig 1.14 Abbot Misail
(1905–1940)

Fig 1.15 Abbot Iustin
(1940–1958)

Fig 1.16 Abbot Ilian
(1958–1971)

Fig 1.17 Abbot Gavriil
(1971–1975)

Fig 1.18 Abbot Avel´
(1975–1978)

Fig 1.19 Abbot Ieremiya
(1978–2016)

Fig 1.20 Abbot Evlogy
(2016—)

Fig 1.21 Count N. P. Ignat´ev (1832–1908), Imperial Ambassador to the Porte 1864–1877; instrumental in securing the Ecumenical Patriarch's blessing for Archimandrite Makary (Sushkin)'s appointment as St Panteleimon Monastery's first Russian abbot in 1875.

Fig 1.22 Archimandrite Makary (Sushkin).

Fig 1.23 Krumitsa vineyards. The skete was financed and built between 1840–1874 by Abbot Makary and to this day produces grapes for Tsantali wines.

Fig 1.24 The planned new Central Church of the Holy Trinity, a vast expansion to which Tsar Nicholas II was invited. Nothing came of the grandiose project.

Fig 1.25

The Monastery of St Simon the Canaanite

Fig 1.26 The Caucasian New Athonite Monastery of St Simon the Canaanite: founded in 1875, destroyed by the Turks in 1876, rebuilt from 1878, closed in 1924, and briefly reopened in 1994.

Fig 1.27 Fr Arseny (Minin) (1823–1875) The first abbot of the New Athonite Monastery of St Simon the Canaanite. An influential author, he went on the first very successful alms-gathering missions to Russia; he and Svyatogorets brought St Panteleimon's to the attention of the Russian public.

Fig 1.28 Archimandrite Ieron (Nosov) (1829–1912), the second abbot of the New Athonite Monastery of St Simon the Canaanite arrived in 1875.

Fig 1.29 Fr Serafim Svyatogorets (Vesnin), tonsured to the Great Schema with the name of Sergy (1814–1853: on Athos from 1843); author of the immensely popular and influential *Pis´ma k druz´yam svoim o Svyatoy Gore Afon* [*Letters to my Friends about Holy Mount Athos*].

CHAPTER 3

The Return of the Russians in the Reign of Abbot Gerasimos

Archimandrite Anikita's Failed Mission

The ground was prepared for the relinquishing of Greek ownership of St Panteleimon Monastery during the reign of its new, Slav-speaking abbot. Archimandrite Gerasimos made the transition possible because of his linguistic gifts and ability to understand the character of brethren of different nationalities. His brotherhood contained a handful of non-Greeks, perhaps Bulgarians, Serbs, and even one or two Russians; and a senior St Panteleimon monk, Archimandrite Prokopios (Dendrinos) from Odessa, was also a Slav-speaker. Writing in 1843, the popular Athonite author, Serafim Svyatogorets[1] (Vesnin) observed:

> At the moment the entire brotherhood amounts to as much as two hundred, among whom is the Greek section, and Bulgarians, Serbs and Moldavians, and one Christianized Jew. Do not think that the multi-ethnicity and multi-linguistic makeup of the brotherhood can shatter the unity of spirit and tranquility of life—on the contrary! Having one goal beyond the grave, one desire and singleness of purpose, all of us make up a single flock under the leadership of our modest yet experienced pastor and elder [Gerasimos].[2]

Abbot Gerasimos, whose succession to Savvas had patriarchal backing at a time when idiorrhythm was being discouraged on the Holy Mountain, was a model cenobitic leader. In the 1830s he was responsible for a brotherhood small enough for him to be in close contact with each of his charges. The ascetic and author of *Skazanie o stranstvii i puteshestvii po Rossii, Moldavii, Turtsii i Svyatoy Zemle / The Tale of Wanderings and Journeyings through Russia, Moldavia, Turkey and the Holy Land*, Monk Parfeny (Ageev), knew him personally:

> He has an amazing gift of discernment. He looks after two hundred spiritual children, all of whom he directs not authoritatively but paternally. Some he punishes, others he teaches, and others he admonishes with tears. All he loves

25

and cherishes as a loving father. His cell is a place of healing and is never shut, and all the brethren, his spiritual children, both well and sick, hasten to their pastor and spiritual physician …. Having attended to all, he leaves his cell. First he visits the ailing brethren, then each of the cells, and then he visits all the workmen and craftsmen; afterwards he goes out of the monastery to all the brethren working at their various obediences and toils with them …. He never forces a brother to work, but rather restrains him and often orders him to take a rest …. Betimes in the refectory he decries a brother's weaknesses and failings, but only indirectly and never naming the culprit. He always speaks with tears and fatherly love, and reduces all the brethren to tears …. And every one of them loves him as a father …. Throughout the Holy Mountain he is revered as a strict keeper of the cenobitic monastic rule.[3]

As the head of a model cenobium Gerasimos was pragmatic about money. He knew its worth but was an ascetic and non-possessor.[4] Since the death of its benefactor, Skarlat Kallimakh, the monastery was very poor. Monk Parfeny (Ageev) tells of Artemy, a Russian monk who came to St Panteleimon's asking to be accepted into the brotherhood in return for 20,000 leva. Artemy hoped that the money would excuse him from doing any kind of obedience. The abbot explained:

> We live in a monastery; we do not collect money but save souls. Should anyone offer money we shall not refuse, but shall use it for the monastery's needs. The offerer, however, must submit to all the monastery's rules and renounce his free will.[5]

As if in answer to Abbot Gerasimos's prayers, Archimandrite Anikita arrived on the Holy Mountain. A prince, minor poet, and scholar, Anikita was a member of the wealthy and influential Shikhmatov-Shirinsky family.[6] Although he had renounced his worldly goods, fasted zealously, and longed for the ascetic life, he came laden with valuables and a large sum of money. On June 9, 1835, he landed at Xiropotamou Monastery, his ship having been blown off course from the Dardanelles. Thence he went by mule to the Prophet Elijah Skete, which was at the time the center of the Russian Athonite community. The prior, Priest-Monk Parfeny, offered the visitor his own cell, which had once housed St Paisy (Velichkovsky), the skete's founder. On June 11 Anikita had confession with the prior, with whose blessing he served his first liturgy on Athos.

On June 13, 1835, Anikita visited Pantokrator, the skete's ruling monastery. From there he went to Iviron, arriving on the evening of June 15. The next day, Sunday, after matins in the monastery, he went to the Iviron church of St John the Forerunner on the seashore:

> To the ineffable joy of my heart I was made worthy of serving the Divine Liturgy (in Slavonic) in front of a sizeable congregation of ascetics, both Greeks from the monastery (among whom was the Archimandrite himself) and Russian anchorite *kelliots*.[7]

Here he might have met the Elder Arseny, who had been living with his brother in Christ, Schema-Monk Nikolay, in one of the Iviron *kellia*. According to Parfeny (Ageev), Anikita became a spiritual son of the elder—as Parfeny himself had done. Anikita's own diaries, however, make no mention of Arseny. Indeed, the archimandrite refers to the prior of the Prophet Elijah Skete, as "the builder [of the house], ... my spiritual father."[8]

On June 18, 1835, Anikita writes:

> I set off in the early morning for the Russian Monastery of St Panteleimon, whence on the day before Monk Nikifor had been sent to me with mules. I arrived at the monastery by midday .... It is one of the best Athonite cenobia for the strictness of its monastic life. Its Abbot, Elder Gerasimos, and the most pious *Daskalos* / Teacher [Deacon Venediktos], who are in truth men of God, received me with great love despite my many sins.[9]

On June 20, having served a liturgy in Slavonic he set off on a monastery boat to visit the coastal monasteries south of St Panteleimon's. He was accompanied by the Russian *Dukhovnik* / Spiritual Father Priest-Monk Prokopy and a few of his compatriots from the St Panteleimon brethren.[10] On June 22 he returned to the Prophet Elijah Skete, where he took all the services, including those of the Feast of the Translation of the Relics of St Mitrofan of Voronezh, on June 25. Anikita had celebrated the feast twelve months previously in Voronezh where he had been commissioned by Antony, the local Bishop, to write a revised version of the saint's life (canonized in 1831). Anikita brought with him to Athos a precise copy of the wonderworking saint's icon, painted by the artist of the original. St Mitrofan was Anikita's talisman, to whom he fervently prayed for deliverance from his chronic sickness and for protection during his voyage to the East.

On July 2 Anikita visited St Panteleimon's a second time. His party arrived in the afternoon on mules sent by the monastery and "was met with genuine love."[11] He handed over the money he had collected for the building of a church dedicated to

St Mitrofan, the blueprint of which had already been drawn up, no doubt during his first visit in June. He finalized the setup of the church with the St Panteleimon fathers and on July 4 left on another tour of the Holy Mountain. On July 7 he was back at the Prophet Elijah Skete, which he now considered his Athonite home: "I returned safely to my skete."[12] He stayed there until the 29, when he went to St Panteleimon's a third time "with all my chattels on ponies sent from the monastery, accompanied by Frs Nikita and Fyodor and others."[13] The next day he embarked on a Greek ship for Thessaloniki, and thence to Palestine.

According to Parfeny (Ageev), Anikita took Elder Arseny and Monk Nikolay with him on the pilgrimage. Anikita's diary, however, makes no mention of these venerable traveling companions, although Arseny and Nikolay certainly visited the Holy Land: the elder later told Parfeny that he and Nikolay, having spent many years in eremitical seclusion, found the hubbub and crowds most trying, and they suffered numerous tribulations while maintaining their harshly ascetic fasting regime. Anikita would have been a difficult and unlikely traveling companion. How would accommodation arrangements on board ship have been arranged? Anikita traveled in his own cabin, while the rest of his party had cheaper quarters.[14] As a prince and scholar the archimandrite was feted at every stage of the pilgrimage by diplomats and senior clergy; the pious flocked to his liturgies, which he often celebrated in Greek: his fame sat uneasily with his strict fasting and the austere way of life he aspired to.

Anikita spent forty days in prayer at the Holy Sepulcher, where he solemnly vowed to serve forty liturgies known as a Sorokoust[15] upon his return to Panteleimon's, in the Church of St Mitrofan. Having overwintered in the Holy Land, where he was informed that he had been appointed chaplain to the Russian embassy church in Athens, he returned to the Holy Mountain via Cyprus, Rhodes, and Patmos.

On the Feast of St Nicholas, May 9, 1836, Archimandrite Anikita's ship anchored off the St Panteleimon quay. The day began inauspiciously: "At first I was not let into the holy house, owing to a false rumor about the plague supposedly raging in Jerusalem."[16] He celebrated the liturgy in the monastery's St Nicholas Church the next day and left for Iviron and the Prophet Elijah Skete on May 13.

On May 15, 1836, he returned to St Panteleimon's intending to fulfil his promise of celebrating the forty liturgies. It is strange that during his May 9–13 stay at the monastery he had not taken a look at the new chapel; indeed, he did not do so until May 18, three days after his return to St Panteleimon's. What he discovered came as an unpleasant shock. His diary, which is for the most part a dull mixture of dates, place names, and pious reflections, becomes uncharacteristically animated:

> I found that the saint's church, by the mysterious ways of God, was unfinished, or rather abandoned …. I was grieved to discover that my dream had not been fulfilled. God from on high condescended that Satan hinder the well-laid plans and stir up the monastery elders by making them fear that which posed no threat. As a result, notwithstanding their promise, they completely broke their word and utterly refused to build a church in their monastery for the great St Mitrofan.[17]

Anikita laid the blame on the Greeks. He did not wish to admit this in his diary, but the accusation in a letter to a friend in Odessa is unequivocal and bitter:

> Our great wonderworker St Mitrofan did not deign to accept my initial proposal to have his church in the so-called Russian monastery, which was inhabited by Greek fathers. Instead, he wished to be housed among his compatriot venerators in the Russian Skete of the Prophet Elijah …. The most venerable fathers of the Russian monastery, spurred on by the Enemy and with God's condescension, allowed their initial zeal for our saint to cool somewhat, and the cooling of their ardor caused the saint to depart from them.[18]

On the other hand, Parfeny (Ageev), who had not yet arrived on the Mountain and whose account is therefore second-hand, says that the Russians were responsible for the fiasco:

> The Russians [in the monastery] were a motley collection unused to living under authority. They began to disrespect and disobey the Greeks. They opposed the Greeks, whom they threatened, saying that the monastery belonged to us Russians, and our leader is a prince, and we'll chase you out. At this point all the Greek brethren were in turmoil, and suffered daily tribulations and temptations. When their fine cenobitic way of life began to fall apart, they said to Abbot Gerasimos and Elder Venediktos that we cannot live with the Russians and do not want their riches. We'd do better feeding on rusks and water, and being on our own: the Russians have destroyed our life.[19]

According to Parfeny (Ageev), Anikita upbraided Priest-Monk Prokopy, who had, as we have seen, traveled with him on June 20 the year before: "Yours is to be not a spiritual father, but a shepherd boy." Dismissing the other Russians in his party, the archimandrite said: "Go, brethren, each of you where he will. I am no longer your leader. You could not live in the monastery; now wander off."[20]

The archimandrite was now in a hurry. He had been summoned to Athens, but would not break his forty-liturgy promise. He celebrated the first in the Monastery's St Nicholas Church on May 17, Pentecost Sunday, and continued his daily obedience in the monastery for another three weeks. On July 8, 1836, he departed for the skete, where he was to complete the rest of the forty. He left behind in the monastery vestments, icons, ecclesiastical treasures, and Russian books.

The archimandrite and the other Priest-Monks with him vested themselves and sang a *moleben* / short service of intercession to St Mitrofan. They then bore the great icon of St Mitrofan in solemn procession all the way to the skete via Karyes. On the ascent to the capital he stopped at the ruins of Old Mountain Rusik where he served a *panikhida* / memorial for "our brethren, up to thirty in number, who lived in this very monastery and were slaughtered by their fellow Greek brethren."[21] The trek impressed Greek observers, whose story Parfeny (Ageev) relates thus:

> Having selected the brethren, the prince himself and two Priest-Monks, in priestly vestments, took the icon of St Mitrofan and set off on foot with the rest of the brethren following them … for twenty versts. When they passed through Karyes a Greek merchant mocked the Russians and St Mitrofan, but the Lord punished him. His skins of vegetable oil all burst and the oil ran down the street. Upon perceiving that God's punishment had befallen him, he stopped the prince with the icon, tearfully asked for forgiveness and kissed the icon.[22]

Before he left for Athens, Fr Anikita entrusted the St Mitrofan icon and a large sum of money to the skete's *dukhovnik* / spiritual father, Priest of the Great Schema Pavel.

Another account, written by one Monk Ignaty in 1860, describes Anikita's departure from St Panteleimon Monastery thus:

> [after the liturgy] Fr Anikita came out of the church in his *epitrachelion* and *phelonion* / priestly vestments bearing on his breast the great icon of St Mitrofan of Voronezh …. He was accompanied by the Russians movingly singing the *troparion* and *kontakion* / hymns to the saint. On leaving the monastery gates, he set off up the road to Karyes. On seeing this the Greeks were troubled and told Abbot Gerasimos, who gestured despairingly and said: "Alas, we are in the wrong. We treated this famous man badly and shall pay for this."[23]

The Return of the Russians

It seemed that St Panteleimon Monastery was destined to remain in Greek hands after all. The ground for the permanent settlement of the Russians in their monastery, however, had already been prepared. Priest-Monk of the Great Schema Elder Arseny was to become the spiritual father and founder of the new Russian community on Athos. As we have seen, he and his brother in Christ, Monk Nikolay, initially inhabited one of the Iviron *kellia*. This they had had to rebuild from ruins. They lived a life of self-sufficiency and poverty, growing their own food and carving wooden spoons. They gave away anything they did not need. Elder Arseny's non-possession was so great that even Fr Nikolay protested. Arseny explained:

> When are we to become true monks? The Lord has led us through so many tribulations, but you still protest. At the worst of times the Lord fed us; can He not do so now? Now, thank God, [we can] sell our wares; and we shall work and sell again, and give away what we need not, thereby investing in God. Why hold on to what is alien [and] distracts our minds from God?[24]

Monk Parfeny (Ageev), who tried to emulate them, emphasizes three things about the two ascetics: their complete dependence on God, both spiritual and material; their unswerving obedience to God and to each other; and, above all, their rigorous non-possession. Parfeny himself benefited from the generosity of Arseny, who gave him all he had so that he, Parfeny, could start living on the Mountain self-sufficiently. Whoever came to the elder was always asked: "Well, have you enough? Do you need anything?"[25] Arseny did not expect of anyone else the degree of asceticism he and Nikolay had attained. Many, including Parfeny (Ageev), wished to become his disciples and live in the same *kellion*, but were turned away.[26] The elder demanded of his spiritual children only complete obedience, which was hard to follow. Arseny had warned Parfeny:

> My decisions will accord not with your wish and desire, nor with my human whims, but with God's will … I shall lead you along a narrow, dolorous path, according to God's will, but it will seem to you cruel and unbearable.[27]

According to Parfeny, not only disobedience, but also not asking for the elder's blessing spelled disaster. Parfeny ascribes Archimandrite Anikita's unsuccessful mission to reestablish a Russian brotherhood in St Panteleimon Monastery to his failure to consult the elder: "He made a grave error because he had not asked the blessing of *Dukhovnik* / Spiritual Father Fr Arseny."[28] As we have seen, Parfeny based this on hearsay, for Anikita's visit was before his time.

Parfeny did, however, witness the arrival of Priest of the Great Schema Pavel and his group of Russian monks at St Panteleimon's. This was the same Pavel to whom Archimandrite Anikita had entrusted the money for the completion of the Church of St Mitrofan in the Prophet Elijah Skete.

In the same year that Anikita left for Athens, 1836, the Prophet Elijah Skete was infected by the plague. Most of the brethren died, including Prior Parfeny. Pavel selflessly cared for his ailing brothers, survived the infection, and was appointed Parfeny's successor. The priorate was a poisoned chalice. The skete's Little Russian brethren quarreled with the Great Russian brethren. Pavel, a Great Russian, was accused of "weakness of character" and "love of wealth."[29] He was also blamed for the loss of precious syngilia and charters, which Pantokratoros (the ruling monastery) confiscated. Pavel was deposed three times; Anikita was invited to take his place, but died in 1837 on his way back to the Mountain from Athens; and even Elder Arseny was asked to take over, which he did for a short while before returning to his eremitical life because "the unsavory Little Russians did not cease to stir up and shatter the peaceful life … of the skete."[30]

In 1839, having been part of its brethren for thirty-five years, Fr Pavel was expelled from the skete and moved to Karyes with a group of Great Russians. The monks of St Panteleimon Monastery, meanwhile, were bitterly regretting Anikita's departure. They therefore asked for Elder Arseny's blessing to beg Pavel to take Anikita's place. A delegation headed by Archimandrite Prokopios (Dendrinos) was dispatched to the capital. They pleaded with Pavel and his followers to join the monastery. He was reluctant, but acceded once Arseny had given his blessing.[31]

On November 21, 1839, on the day of the Entry into the Temple of the Mother of God, the Russians were solemnly received for the second and last time at the gates of St Panteleimon's. Monk Parfeny (Ageev), who had arrived on Mount Athos earlier in the same year, was present. He describes the event with his characteristic blend of drama and pious emotion:

> On the 21st day of November [1839] twenty mules were sent early in the morning to Karyes from the Russian monastery to fetch Fr Pavel with his brotherhood and all his belongings, and [the party] set off for the Russian monastery and arrived at the gates. Fr Pavel dismounted, put on his *epitrachelion* and *phelonion* / priestly vestments, and carrying the icon of St Mitrofan the Voronezh

Wonderworker, which he had brought with him, entered the monastery gates. The Abbot and brethren struck up [a] *stichera* / hymn for the Feast of the Entry of the Mother of God into the Temple, and processed straight to the great *Katholikon* / Central Church of the Holy Great Martyr Panteleimon …. They placed the icon of St Mitrofan upon a lectern and brought out from the sanctuary the skull of St Panteleimon, which they put on an adjacent lectern … and brought out of the sanctuary [a piece of] the Lord's True Cross, which they placed on a third lectern. Then Fr Pavel [having venerated the Cross, skull and icon], came out into the middle of the church and prostrated himself thrice. Then he went up to Abbot Gerasimos and prostrated himself. The abbot wept and prostrated himself in turn, and each kissed the other on the hands and on the lips [*sic*] …. And there was in the church great joy and gladness, and each one prostrated himself to the ground before the other, the Russians before the Greeks and the Greeks before the Russians, and all celebrated.[32]

Parfeny comments with unwitting foresight: "Never had there been such joy in the Russian monastery; yes, and perhaps there never will be."[33] Everyone wept copiously.[34] The festivities were concluded with a speech of exhortation and instruction by Gerasimos first to the Greeks and then to the Russians. He warned that the Greeks were a volatile and choleric people and exhorted the Russians to follow the Greeks' example of cenobitic rule. With characteristic pragmatism he touched on the material benefits the new brethren would bring:

Let me say again: how many times we would sit down in the refectory with practically no bread but just moldy crusts [to eat]! …. If the Russians are to live forever here, just as our house is now poor and bare and trampled on by all other Athonite houses, so will it be wealthy, in good order and adorned, and it will be renowned both all over the Holy Mountain and throughout the world: for the Russians come from a prosperous land, glorious and wealthy Russia.[35]

Parfeny imaginatively and with some relish transcribes more speeches. Those of Deacon Venediktos and Archimandrite Prokopios were in Greek, which neither Parfeny nor the Russians could understand: "When he said this the Greeks all stood and looked at him, but the Russians understood little …. I cannot remember [what was said] word for word, for Greek was spoken."[36] The joy of Venediktos was mixed with relief. He blamed himself for Anikita's departure, which had lain on his conscience for three years, and admitted that Abbot Gerasimos alone had opposed the quarrel of the Greek brethren with Anikita. Now at last, declared the 106-year-old Greek *daskalos* / teacher, he could die in peace. He recited the *nunc dimittis*, was led back to his cell where he confined himself and died on December 11, 1840.[37]

The Russians were given two chapels, as well as a separate, five-story building to live in, on the third floor of which they were to have their own St Mitrofan *Katholikon* / Central Church. Pavel was assigned the cell next to the church. All monastic duties were to be done by Greeks and Russians together, confession was to be daily and Communion would be taken weekly.

The seeds of the ethnic discord to follow were unwittingly sown. Although Gerasimos insisted that Russians and Greeks perform their monastic duties together, the former were assigned separate living quarters and separate places of worship. The monastery was thus already physically divided. Gerasimos was also undermining his own authority by appointing Pavel as father-confessor and de facto leader of the Russians. In the short term, the Russians' wealth saved the monastery from debt and decay. But riches and the monastic life do not go together; and when the well-off live in close proximity with the poor, envy, greed, and pride are bound to flourish. Elder Arseny's non-possession was impossible to follow in St Panteleimon Monastery.

On July 29, 1840, two days after the Feast of St Panteleimon, Pavel fell ill. He died on August 2.

CHAPTER 4

The New Spiritual Father and Leader of the Russian Brotherhood Is Chosen

F r Pavel was sorely missed. He and Abbot Gerasimos had been able to run the Russian and Greek brotherhoods harmoniously:

> The brethren formerly belonging to the Prophet Elijah Skete enjoyed special privileges in the monastery: whilst being subservient to the abbot, they were directly under the authority of their spiritual father, Priest of the Great Schema Pavel. The Russians received their own church for services in Slavonic and were generally independent. Initially it was difficult to house in one monastery two brotherhoods which were in fact independent … Nonetheless, … Frs Gerasimos and Pavel managed to prevent clashes. Despite the peaceful coexistence [of the two brotherhoods], the Greeks of the other monasteries harshly criticized Fr Gerasimos for taking on the Russians.[1]

The abbot set about looking for someone to replace Fr Pavel. Apart from Elder Arseny, the only Russian Athonite considered to be suitable was one Monk Ioanniky (Solomentsov), who, although only relatively recently settled on the Mountain, had already gained the reputation of an exemplary ascetic.

His father was a merchant. Those from mercantile backgrounds were playing a vital part in establishing a strong Russian presence in the Orthodox Near East, and eventually in increasing the stability and wealth of the Russian Athonite houses. These *kuptsy* / merchants were zealously charitable Orthodox pioneers and builders. They formed the "powerful class of Russian merchants and entrepreneurial factory owners—the Russian 'businessmen' who were famous everywhere for their honesty … and, above all, for their prayerful piety."[2]

Fr Ioanniky (Solomentsov) was born in 1805 with the baptismal name of Ivan. His native town was Stary Oskol, whose citizens were zealously church-going.[3] His family was well-to-do and extremely pious. Ivan's eldest brother became a monk and his sister an abbess, in whose nunnery their own mother was tonsured to the Great

Schema. Encouraged by his grandmother, Ivan became a proficient church reader at an early age. The whole family loved church services:

> Often on feast days or Sundays we'd all gather in the hall, light incense and the icon lamp, and start singing …. We would … sing to our hearts' content for three to four hours …. During the visits of our aunts, who were nuns at Orlovsky Monastery, our house practically became a church: … singing, reading, and prayers happened every day.[4]

By the age of six Ivan was serving in the sanctuary and had become an expert campanologist. He had longed to become a monk from the age of five. He was not allowed to forget, however, his filial duty and his place in the Solomentsov firm. He persuaded his sister, who had as many as twenty suitors at the age of sixteen, to take the veil. Ivan's father asked him to stay at home as compensation for the loss of his daughter. They haggled over the length of time Ivan was to remain at home, and settled for two years beyond his sister's departure.

Ivan's prolonged stay was hard: "I suffered harsh trials and nearly perished."[5] He refused to accept the wealthy brides his parents lined up for him and fought manfully against earthly temptations. He spent a night on his knees under a pear tree, praying for strength; in the morning the devilish torments left him, and he went to matins with a light heart, but the tree withered and died. All the while, he worked in his family's tannery business. He sold their wares at local fairs and markets with singular success.

At last he was free to go. In 1831 he set off with his brother in Christ, Nikolay Goncharov. They sought "a place suitable for the ascetic life where they could find what they longed for: silence and cenobitic discipline, away from the female sex, and an escape from ordination to the priesthood."[6] No suitable monastery was found. In 1834 a friend advised them: "In Russia you will find nowhere closed to the female sex. Such a place, and the only one in the Orthodox Church, is to be found solely on the Holy Mountain of Athos."[7] The pair returned to Stary Oskol to obtain foreign travel passports. They left Russia in 1835, but had to return home once they reached Constantinople, where the plague had broken out. From Odessa they went to Voronezh to venerate the relics of St Mitrofan. There they met a fool in Christ, who predicted: "You, my brother Ivan, will arrive on Athos; you'll set up your hive and will be letting swarms fly from it."[8] It was only in 1836, with a group of friends from Stary Oskol, that they reached the Holy Mountain.

Upon his arrival, Ivan chose as his spiritual father Elder Arseny, who tonsured him a monk with the name Ioanniky. On his advice Monk Ioanniky took on two novices and bought the Prophet Elijah *Kellion* / Hermitage belonging to Stavronikita Monastery. There he stayed in eremitical seclusion for four years. Monk Parfeny (Ageev) joined them to work as a cook, baker, church reader, and *kanonarchis* / choir master.[9]

A delegation of Russian brethren was sent to Fr Ioanniky entreating him to come to St Panteleimon Monastery, but he refused to leave his *kellion*. Next Elder Arseny was begged to come to St Panteleimon's, but unsurprisingly he also refused. The delegation again went to Fr Ioanniky, but the young hermit declined the invitation: "Although I love your holy house for the strictness of its life, I can in no way agree to come and live with you. I have left Russia so as to avoid being ordained. Furthermore, I cannot endure your severe cenobitic rule on account of my ill health."[10]

In despair the Russians asked the elder what to do. He advised them to fast and say special prayers for a week, and then return to him. At last Fr Arseny received them and joyfully proclaimed: "It is God's will that Fr Ioanniky be in the Russian monastery."[11]

Parfeny (Ageev) recalls how Fr Ioanniky's brotherhood was taken by surprise:

We … along with our [Fr] Ioanniky, knew nothing [of this]. Suddenly a note was delivered to us from the [elder] requesting that all three of us go to see him. We were amazed, for why should he summon all three of us at once? When we arrived … he told us to go to the church; he put on his *epitracheilion* / stole, and began thus: "Fr Ioanniky, the Lord blesses you to enter the Russian cenobitic monastery with your disciples. Sell your *kellion* / hermitage."[12]

With characteristic emotion Ageev describes how all three burst into tears and fell to the ground begging the elder to relent. Fr Ioanniky protested that he had left Russia with the express intention of avoiding ordination—for he knew that if he were to enter the monastery, he would become *dukhovnik* / spiritual father to the Russians and therefore would have to become a priest. He also protested that his health was too weak "to endure Greek food," and that he had arrived on the Mountain "not to be in authority," but to spend his life in eremitical seclusion.

The elder upbraided Ioanniky:

All things are good at the right time: it is good to avoid ordination, and good to accept it for the glory of the God, should the Lord so choose. Just as it is evil to seek ordination, so it is evil to resist God's will. That you are weak in health, the Lord knows better than you …. He chose you; He will grant you health. As for what you say of wishing to conquer your passions in eremitical seclusion … one can achieve this [as a hermit], provided that one lives according to God's will. But in the cenobitic life one can both [conquer the passions] and [be one with God], for eremitical seclusion merely deadens the passions, whereas the cenobitic life destroys them entirely, burying them in humble obedience and the cutting off of one's will …. For nowhere can one find true monastic life other than in a cenobium. Further, you desire to save but two souls. Go and save twenty, and in time fifty. You must care for everyone. You must set up the Russian house and through you it will gain glory. Oppose God's will no more.[13]

For two weeks Fr Ioanniky and his disciples gave the chattels stored in his *kellion* away to the poor, who were fed by two cooks working full time. A year's supply of flour, fish, oil, and wine was distributed. Fr Ioanniky's party eventually left for the monastery on twelve mules, taking with them his vestments, clothing, and books.[14] The future spiritual father and leader of the Russian brotherhood had come to the Holy Mountain a wealthy man. This was a far cry from rigorous non-possession of his own spiritual father, Elder Arseny; and unlike his predecessor, the humble Pavel, he would prove to have a strong character and indomitable will.

Fr Ioanniky (Solomentsov) and his disciples were received with joy at St Panteleimon Monastery on October 20, 1840; a month later he was ordained priest, and the following year he was tonsured to the Great Schema with the name of Ieronim. Thus, four years after his arrival on the Holy Mountain, unwillingly but in obedience to his elder, Priest Ieronim of the Great Schema found himself to be the spiritual father and leader of a small but growing Russian brotherhood in the mainly Greek St Panteleimon monastery. There were eleven Russians there in 1840, one hundred in 1859, and five hundred at Fr Ieronim's death in 1885.

Spiritual Father Ieronim

The reluctant leader of the Russian brotherhood was now committed to the crowded life of a busy cenobium. It pained him to be deprived of the peace of eremitical seclusion: "From my youth I was strongly attached to silence … I did not wish to leave my *kellion* for the monastery, for I sought an even more secluded *kaliva* / eremitical dwelling." The monastery fathers came to his rescue, telling him: "You gather the Russian brethren and establish them, and you will occasionally be able to withdraw into eremitical silence."[15] For the next five years Ieronim stayed in secluded *kellia* belonging to the monastery; thereafter, he lived in the monastery itself, occasionally retreating to a *kellion*.

Quietude must have helped Fr Ieronim to bear the heavy cross of ill health. Shortly after his arrival at St Panteleimon's, he saw in a dream that sickness would be granted him as expiation for his sins:

> When his vision ended, he felt as if his [innermost parts] were torn. He awoke to find that he had an enormous hernia. It remained with him permanently and was so great that he always had to carry it around with him in a bag tied to his belt.[16]

He explained years later: "I spend my time struggling with ailments, and for this I thank God, for He cleanses us of our sins, of which I have many."[17] Once Fr Ieronim, while convalescing from periodic paroxysms in a remote *kellion* / hermitage, had to go by mule to meet important visitors.[18] The ride brought on spasms so acute that he and those with him thought he was dying. He took Holy Communion and kissed the miraculous icon of the Kievo-Pecherskaya Mother of God. "Just then he felt relief from the swelling. Little by little with the help of a doctor … the hernia was pushed back into place; Spiritual Father Ieronim experienced complete respite, but owing to his weakness he had to lie on his back for twenty-four hours."[19] It is remarkable that he lived into his eighties, although the agony he suffered on his deathbed from the paroxysms and vomiting was terrible.

Somehow Ieronim was able to lead an intensely busy life. In a letter to his sister, he describes his daily routine thus:

> After the liturgy[20] I receive either guests or pilgrims, or else I inspect our work sites, of which there are many …. This takes about three hours …. Then I eat, and afterwards again receive guests or pilgrims, or the brethren, or the crafts-men, or else I am busy with the stewards. And then, if I feel inclined to sleep, I hasten to lie down for a while, and I sometimes manage to sleep; sometimes I do not, depending on my spasms—in which case I'll either read or sign letters or dictate to my scribes.

The Spiritual Father found time to read voraciously. In the same letter to his sister he explains:

> With God's help I read rather a lot, both day and night, for without reading I am much out of sorts and cannot cope …. If I abandon reading even for a short while, I suffer from evil thoughts. When my mind is idle, I remember

all manner of things and everything worthless that comes to it; but when I am constantly occupied with reading, my mind and memory are clear and at peace.[21]

He saw to it that the Russian brethren read and used the library: they were expected to know the Psalter by heart and be well acquainted with the Holy Fathers. The Englishman, Athelstan Riley, found that the St Panteleimon library was the only monastic library that he visited to be used by the monks.[22]

Fr Ieronim expected of his Russian flock the mental and physical toughness for survival in the strictest of cenobia. Once, during the exhausting first half of Holy Week, some of the brethren came to the Spiritual Father begging to be allowed to have a little tea to give them strength:

But he with a smile answered, "If we in the last week of the Fast cannot with-stand the superfluous demands of the flesh, how can we without shame dare to sing at Easter 'Thou wert buried, o Christ'? .... Let us at least deny our-selves this tea-drinking pleasure, so that we can sing, 'I arise today with you, o risen Christ, who wast crucified yesterday.'"[23]

Archimandrite Porfiry (Uspensky) explained Ieronim's indomitability thus:

Priest-Monk Ieronim, who suffers from a hernia, … is remarkable for his intel-ligence, strength of will, genuine and deep piety, ability to preach, and inner prayer and the experience of its sweetness. He even uses mystic methods dur-ing the hours of prayer in his cell: he holds his breath in his chest, centers the Jesus Prayer on his heart, and lies face down on the floor, his body cruciform and stretched out. I respected him and he warmed to me.[24]

Others were in awe of Fr Ieronim. In the words of Konstantin Leont'ev,[25] he was "firm, unshakable, fearless and enterprising; at once bold and cautious; a pro-found idealist and practical to the core; both physically and spiritually strong."[26] Monk Parfeny (Ageev) found him to be "a learned man, externally and spiritually wise, well read and knowledgeable in the scriptures and Holy Fathers …. He spoke beautifully, firmly and wisely."[27] Svyatogorets observed that although Ieronim had received "no systematic education in any school, [he] was on a par with the best of the contemporary [Athonite] elders … thanks to his spiritual … experience, and subtle understanding of the workings of the heart and mind, along with his vora-ciously eclectic reading."[28] Others were amazed by the elder's intellectual prowess: "Oh, the manifold gifts the Lord has given him! He has a profound understanding of the Holy Scriptures and knowledge of Greek, and experience in spiritual life; and he is acquainted with the external affairs of the monastery, and can accurately assess everything."[29] Although Fr Ieronim had received only four years' formal education in his local school in Stary Oskol, he was "able to develop his powerful native intellect through reading."[30]

All found him redoubtable. One of the brethren observed: "Our spiritual father has the gift of foresight. No sooner does he speak than he looks at you and can see who has transgressed ... And his eyes! He looks at you most kindly, but also piercingly. All those he observes feel that he can see into their very soul."[31] Athelstan Riley, visiting St Panteleimon's toward the end of the spiritual father's life, wrote of "a certain ghostly man (πνευματικός) who lives in great retirement at Russico." Riley heard of Fr Ieronim from Athenians visiting Athos, who feared the Russians and opposed them, and believed that the elder's powers of prophetic foresight were aided by a network of informants working in the St Panteleimon dependencies.[32]

Fr Ieronim's greatest gift was his love, especially for the *pustynniki* / hermits and *siromakhi* / wandering beggar-monks. His devotion to them was perhaps due to his longing for the eremitical life. As soon as the monastery could afford it, he instituted regular alms giving to the hermits and wanderers. In his *Spiritual Testament*, he explains the importance of such charity:

> You are aware of how long the Lord tested our house with poverty and even severe debts .... Our monastery decided with complete selfless dedication to share its last crusts of bread with the hungry beggar-monks, and from that time on we saw abundant alms flowing in to us from every corner of Russia. Thanks [to these alms], our house did not want for its upkeep, but fed a great many others who were in need. Such is God's love of the virtue of sharing and charity.[33]

Fr Ieronim told his spiritual father, Elder Arseny, that the monastery spent 10,000 rubles per year[34] on alms distribution to the poor Athonite monks; by the end of the nineteenth century the sum increased to 40,000 rubles.

Fr Ieronim was personally involved in the charitable distribution. One of the brethren describes the Father-Confessor's generosity thus:

> On Sundays and feast days huge crowds gather at the monastery. The wretched sight of the visitors dressed in tatters, half-naked, exhausted and sick is striking .... Among them you can see Greeks, Bulgarians, Moldavians, and Russians. They are all fed at the second sitting in the refectory, after which

they go to Spiritual Father Ieronim's cell. Here they receive gifts prepared for them in advance, each according to their needs: monastic habits, hats, under garments, etc. Some are given money …. It is good to see the saintly Ieronim distributing alms. Usually the poor gather in his corridor, which is often too small to accommodate all who come. The saintly elder comes out of his cell and is greeted with welcoming reverences. First he goes round all the petitioners and then hands things out …. Each petitioner explains his needs and Fr Ieronim talks with every single one in his native tongue. Furthermore, as he well knows the way of life of each petitioner, they all address him as their father and benefactor, fully confident that he will never refuse anyone anything.[35]

Fr Ieronim Lays the Foundations

When Fr Ieronim arrived at St Panteleimon's in 1840, there was not enough money for charity to the poor, let alone for the monastery's daily needs. His first priority was to enrich it. A recently arrived Russian monk observed that the future of the monastery was bright, but its buildings, especially in the Russian quarters, were badly in need of refurbishment and new cells had to be built. Funds were needed to lighten the "leaden yolk lying on the … monastery worthy in every respect of the compassionate love and empathy of the Orthodox North."[36]

In 1841 the tsar permitted alms-gathering missions to take place in Russia. Ieronim lost no time: he chose as his first alms-gatherer Monk Parfeny (Ageev), who had been tonsured to the Great Schema in the fifth week of Lent that year. By having the Great Schema conferred on him, Parfeny was committing himself to an enclosed life within his own monastery, which he should rarely leave; and his hesychastic rule of cell prayer became extremely strict. As early as Lazarus Saturday[37] Ieronim told him about the proposed mission. Parfeny appealed to his spiritual father, Elder Arseny, but the latter, while predicting that the mission would be fruitless, told him to comply for the sake of obedience. Parfeny left the Holy Mountain the week after Easter in tearful anguish.

He returned in January 1843, relieved to back home, but downcast. While on their way to Russia, his brother monk and companion had left him for Mount Athos, taking with him the alms account register. So Parfeny continued on his own. He first tried to convert his Old-Believing[38] foster parents to Orthodoxy and continued from Moldavia on his two-year trip to Russia, whence he returned to his parents empty-handed. This time, however, after much patient reasoning, he persuaded first his father and then his mother to renounce the Old Faith. As soon as he arrived back at St Panteleimon's, he went to straight Fr Ieronim's cell in tears. The Spiritual Father embraced him tenderly, reassuring him that the lack of alms was immaterial; what mattered was that Parfeny had converted his parents. Abbot Gerasimos also comforted Parfeny. The fathers did not ask anything else of Monk Parfeny, who was free to live as he pleased in "a [deserted] *kellion* / hermitage better than my first one."[39] He was even excused monastic duties for a month. Elder Arseny, however, revealed to him the heavy cross he was to bear: Parfeny did not have the blessing to stay on the Mountain; he was to leave for good, eventually to travel 12,000 *versts* / kilometers to Tomsk in Siberia with just 12 rubles.

Parfeny first set off on pilgrimage to Palestine on May 23, 1845. He returned to Athos on May 19, 1846, hoping to see his beloved spiritual father again and to be absolved of his heavy burden. But it was too late: Elder Arseny had died on the eve of Annunciation 1846. Abbot Gerasimos and Fr Ieronim would not give Parfeny their blessing to live on the Mountain, for nobody could absolve him of the elder's command. Parfeny then left for Constantinople and begged the ecumenical patriarch, but he too was powerless to absolve him. So Parfeny had no choice but to continue with his great trek east.

Monk Parfeny's exile was immensely beneficial for the monastery and to posterity in general, for he was forced to become a writer. Bishop Afanasy of Tomsk, after conversing and reading with him for months, persuaded Parfeny in 1848 to write about his travels. His *Skazanie o stranstvii / Tale of Wanderings* was published in 1855, and its second edition came out a year later. St Filaret (Drozdov), Metropolitan of Moscow,[40] was instrumental in getting the book past the censors and published with minimal alterations, so as to preserve its unique blend of Church Slavonic and spoken Russian. The *Skazanie* had great impact, particularly in Russian intellectual circles. According to the poet Apollon Grigor'ev, it was read by "all the serious reading public of Russia."[41] A whole spectrum of writers—Solovyov, Chernyshevsky, Druzhinin, Turgenev, Saltykov-Schedrin, Leskov, and Tolstoy—praised it. Parfeny's work had the greatest influence on Dostoevsky. In the beginning of *Brat'ya* Karamazovy / *The Brothers Karamazov* Dostoevsky alludes to Parfeny's visit to the patriarch as an example of the power of an elder's command.[42] Dostoevsky borrowed a number of themes, expressions, and incidents from *Skazanie o stranstvii* in the Elder Zosima episodes. The influence of Parfeny's writing is also evident in *Nedorosel' / The Raw Youth* and in *Besy /* The Devils. Dostoyevsky's five-volume novel *Zhitie velikogo greshnika /* The

Life of a Great Sinner, which he planned while in exile but later abandoned, was going to be based on Ageev's *Skazanie*.

Another writer who brought Russian Athos to the attention of the reading public was a priest of the Great Schema Sergy (Vesnin), better known by his nom de plume, Serafim Svyatogorets / The Athonite. He was born in Vyatskaya Guberniya[43] in 1814. Having married and graduated from seminary he was ordained a priest in 1834. His wife having died while giving birth to his only child, whom he left to the care of his brother, he embarked on an extensive pilgrimage over Russia and eventually to St Panteleimon Monastery, where he arrived in October 1843. He became one of the monastery's chief secretaries, translated texts from Greek, and was responsible for conducting a prolific correspondence with Russia on behalf of the monastery.[44] Upon his arrival at St Panteleimon's he kept a diary, which he converted into letters to friends. These, writes his biographer, were "ecstatic, vivid and delightful letters, which later became two brilliantly successful volumes."[45] The first volume was favorably received in Russia; after working on the rest of his letters for two years in Vyatka, Svyatogorets sent them to his St Petersburg publishers in 1848. He was lionized in the literary circles of the capital and Moscow. He returned to St Panteleimon's in March 1851, "having collected substantial contributions for the Russian house and sold his books."[46] The second edition of the two volumes appeared in the same year the first edition was published, 1850. By 1895, eight editions had been printed.

What also brought St Panteleimon Monastery and the Russian Athonite community to prominence was the visit of the eldest son of Nicholas I, Grand-Prince Konstantin Nikolaevich, in 1845. The tsar wished to reward his son for his service as a naval officer in the seas of the north. "You can imagine my delight, for this has always been my dream," enthused the deeply religious Konstantin, who was passionately interested in Byzantium and the Orthodox East. In the words of the modern Russian historian, Kirill Vakh: "In his soul he was conceiving grand plans for the future liberation of the ancient Christian capital [Constantinople] from Ottoman rule."[47]

The Grand-Prince sailed to the Mountain on the *SS Bessarabiya*, which anchored off St Panteleimon's on July 16, 1845. The monastery bells rang out in greeting, the clergy vested themselves, the candelabras of the central church were lit, and the abbot took the cross and processed with banners and lanterns to the quay. Having looked through the telescope the Tsarevich said: "That's our Russians for you: they really know how to greet you." When the ship's tender landed, the awaiting monks were asked: "Are there Russians among you? Can at least someone speak Russian?"[48]

Fr Ieronim, Svyatogorets, and one other were invited to board the ship. After receiving their blessing, Konstantin Nikolaevich came ashore to the ceaseless tolling of bells, attended a doxology, and visited the Russian quarters, including the St Mitrofan Church, which was still being built. He was offered coffee and traditional Athonite sweetmeats in the *arkhondarik* / guest quarters and was regaled with a declamation of a poem Svyatogorets had written for the occasion. He listened to it with tears in his eyes and asked for a copy. Next Archimandrite Prokopios (Dendrinos) asked to say a word of welcome, but the offer was declined as the speech was in Greek.

After three hours the royal party left for Xenophontos, Dochiariou, and thence to Zograf, where they spent the night. The next day he went on to Hilandar. He noted in his account for the tsar that the Bulgarian and Serb monks take services in Slavonic, but chant in the "ghastly Greek manner."[49]

His next stop was Esphigmenou, for whose fathers the royal visit was especially welcome. This monastery published their own two versions of St Anthony Pechersky's time on Athos. According to these, the saint was tonsured in Esphigmenou, not Xylourgou.[50] Furthermore, shortly before the Grand-Prince's arrival, the Esphigmenou cave in which the saint was said to have lived was opened for veneration by pilgrims, thus encouraging donations from Russian visitors.

Next the Tsarevich sailed to Vatopedi, where, to the singing of *It is meet and Right* and *Glory to God in the Highest*, he processed with the vested clergy on a carpet strewn with flowers and laurel leaves to the monastery. He was again moved to tears. In Ageev's words:

> Here there was a mighty gathering of monks from all the nearby sketes and *kellia* … for almost all the Athonite fathers and anchorites left their [dwellings] and caves to come and look at the Right-Believing Tsarevich, Grand-Prince Konstantin Nikolaevich. All shed tears of joy, made the sign of the Cross on their faces, and thanked God, for in the Tsarevich they saw a bright angel of God sent from heaven. They were amazed that he came not with pomp or pride, but with humility and discreetly, for he was surrounded not by guards … but just by monks and a few companions; his clothing was neither rich nor military, but the most simple—he carried in his hand a straw hat.[51]

He made an unscheduled stop at Xylourgou, went on to the Prophet Elijah Skete, and he spent the night there. After the liturgy he made his way to Karyes, where he visited the Protaton Church and was received by the Sacred Community. Having declined many invitations to other monasteries, owing to lack of time, he made his way to Xiropotamou. From there he went by sea to the Great Lavra and finally, on the afternoon of July 18, 1845, set sail for Constantinople.

Kirill Vakh explains the significance of Grand-Prince's visit thus:

> From many Orthodox countries, especially Russia ... both pilgrims and rather substantial, and, above all, regular benefactions flowed in. The appearance on the Mountain of the Russian Emperor's son ... gave a fillip to Russian Athonite monasticism. Russian Athos had now acquired the manifest patronage of the Imperial Russian Household, which believed itself to have inherited the power of the Orthodox Byzantine emperors.[52]

For the tireless Fr Ieronim, however, not yet enough had been achieved to establish the material well-being of St Panteleimon's. This time his choice for alms-gathering fell on Monk Sil'vestr (Trofimov), who had joined the monastery in 1843. In October 1849, Sil'vestr was asked to set off with two others from St Panteleimon's. "This proposal greatly scared me. I did not know what to reply and started to object, but my resistance was fruitless," admitted Sil'vestr.[53] His trip was successful. He returned in December 1850 with 4,000 rubles in silver,[54] and a wonderworking icon in precious cladding. During Lent in 1851 he was tonsured to the Great Schema with the name of Selevky and was given the remote St George *Kellion* / Hermitage to restore and inhabit. His life of quietude lasted barely six years, for in 1857 he was ordered to go on a second mission. "He resisted in desperation, but Spiritual Father Ieronim told him: 'We are created not to live only for ourselves, for we must toil for others as well. You can be useful for many.'"[55] Selevky returned to St Panteleimon's in 1862. The grateful monastery fathers did not ask any more of the schema-monk, who spent the next seventeen years until his death in prayerful seclusion.

Perhaps the most successful of many further alms-gatherers was Priest-Monk Arseny (Minin). Between 1862 and 1867 he took with him to Russia, among other treasures, the remains of St Panteleimon, a portion of the True Cross, a piece of stone from the Holy Sepulcher, and the wonderworking Tikhvin icon of the Mother of God. These attracted enormous crowds who gave generously amidst scenes of religious fervor.[56] Numerous miraculous healings took place. There were enthusiastic reports in the Russian press, notably in the *Moskovskie Vedomosti* and *Syn Otechestva* journals. Even *Severnaya Pochta*, the organ of the Ministry of the Interior, wrote favorably about Arseny's missions: these were signs that at last the Russian Athonites would enjoy official approval from St Petersburg.

Some of Fr Arseny's most successful missions were in the Vitebsk and Mogilev Provinces, part of White Russia. Their inhabitants were a mixture of mainly Orthodox Christians and some Roman Catholics. "Nearly all of the sparse Catholic community of Mogilev Province made fervent pilgrimages to the relics," wrote a reporter of the *Severnaya Pochta*. When word got round people from the neighboring provinces of Smolensk, Chernigov, and Minsk came to venerate the relics. The churches were usually too small to accommodate the crowds, so special services were held in the open. Some twenty thousand people gathered at one of these services in Gomel'. During the forty-day mission in Mogilev Province the Athonites gave away more than a hundred thousand icons, crosses, and booklets.[57]

As well as tour Russia with the relics, Arseny and his followers wrote numerous books, pamphlets, and magazines. The most important periodical was the monthly *Dushepolezny Sobesednik / The Spiritually Edifying Collocutor*. It was very popular and the first of its kind; soon the Trinity–St Sergius Monastery started its own journal on similar lines. Everything Arseny published had a huge readership. Most of it was written simply and colorfully, and was either given away or sold very cheaply, so that it was accessible to and obtainable by virtually any Russian who could read.

Not satisfied with alms-gathering missions, Ieronim sought out influential contacts and assured sources of benefaction. Back in 1851, on November 3, there arrived at St Panteleimon a pilgrim from an old and well-to-do merchant family based in Tula, Mikhail Ivanovich Sushkin. Two months previously, in Odessa, on his way to the Holy Mountain, he had met Svyatogorets, who sent word to St Panteleimon Monastery of the imminent arrival of the distinguished young visitor. Well-bred and a potentially useful benefactor, Sushkin was warmly received. Ieronim exclaimed: "Here is the man for whom we have asked the Lord."[58]

Although Mikhail Sushkin was eager to join the brotherhood, the abbot and Fr Ieronim coldly rebuffed him: "Let him live [here] a bit as our guest, and learn. Let him ask his father's permission to be tonsured .... Then we'll see." Ieronim justified his caution:

> The Sushkins are very wealthy and powerful people, *so we hesitated to tonsure him. His father might have accused us of somehow rushing to tonsure him because we hoped for a rich contribution. We did not wish to have such notoriety in Russia and thereby harm our house.*[59]

Despite his bitter disappointment, Sushkin was determined to join the brotherhood, so he set about obtaining his father's blessing. He was sufficiently close to his mother to ask her not only to persuade his father, but also send gifts for the monastery. We read in his letter to her written on November 9, just six days after his arrival at the monastery:

> I am sure that you are not going to put me off but persuade my father .... At the moment I dare not ask [him], but with time [I should] ask him to give something for the building works here .... Please forgive me for daring thus to write to you of my joy, for I hide nothing from you, and that is why I write to you especially. Mother, give me your blessing. Do not grieve but pray and have a *moleben* / office of praise served to the Bogolyubskaya Mother of God icon, and the Lord will comfort you and me .... Encourage father to give [me] his blessing.[60]

In the event, Mikhail Sushkin did not have to wait for his father's blessing. Having posted the letter, he set off on a tour of the peninsula. While descending from the peak of Mount Athos, he caught a chill and arrived back at St Panteleimon's gravely ill. The fever grew worse; Sushkin's demise was imminent. Fr Ieronim was still unwilling to tonsure him, but on hearing the doctor's prediction that the young man would not survive the night, relented and summoned the abbot. On November 27 Mikhail Ivanovich Sushkin was tonsured to the Great Schema, with the name of Makary.[61] The malady continued until January 1852 when the young schema-monk staged a miraculous recovery. He then set about asking his family for donations. In response the Sushkins sent gifts for the monastery churches and money. On October 11, 1852, Makary's parents paid for the Chapel of the Athonite Saints in the monastery infirmary. Many other gifts came from them, notably an annual covenant of 500 rubles from Makary's father.

On June 3, 1856, Makary was ordained priest and shortly after appointed as deputy spiritual father to the Russians—*vtoroy dukhovnik*. His meteoric rise to prominence is understandable: Fr Ieronim was prey to bouts of sickness and was unable to cope alone with the burden of confessing all the Russian brethren, who now numbered more than eighty. Above all, he and Makary enjoyed a father-son relationship. Both Makary and Ieronim were well connected, came from and understood the Russian merchant *milieu*, and had good financial sense. They made a formidable team: Makary had energy and enthusiasm, and Ieronim was the wise head on young shoulders. Moreover, the burgeoning Russian community needed presentable, well-spoken people at the helm. Good public relations attracted benefaction.

Thanks to the generosity of the wealthy merchants G. Chernov and I. Stahkeev, like Svyatogorets natives of Vyatka, the great Russian Pokrovsky sobor / *Katholikon* / Central Church of the Protecting Veil of the Mother of God was built on the fifth floor of the Russian brotherhood residential block.[62] This was just one of the many major building projects undertaken at St Panteleimon's at the time.

Fr Makary the Apprentice

As Konstantin Leont'ev spent a year in St Panteleimon Monastery, he became intimately acquainted with Spiritual Father Ieronim and his disciple, Makary. Leont'ev greatly liked the latter, whom he found cheerful, kind, charming, and intelligent, and Fr Makary warmed to Leont'ev.[63] Weakened by the long Holy Week services, Leont'ev became unwell during the Easter vigil. Fr Makary was so concerned that he came out of the sanctuary and arranged for a monk to take Leont'ev back to his cell and lay him down on his bed. Other pilgrims criticized Leont'ev on seeing him smoking, but Fr Makary "told them that I was a very good Christian and … that I had nothing but bread and kvass for four days in Holy Week. I was told this and the Lord knows how much just this praise comforted me." Fr Ieronim, on the other hand, to whom Leont'ev was lovingly devoted, "himself exhausted and sick, came [on Holy Thursday] to my cell and almost angrily chased me out to church."[64]

Fr Ieronim's uncompromising strictness extended to his disciple, whom he was wont to reprimand harshly. Once Fr Makary was made to undergo the humiliation of having a punishment he had meted out to an erring monk publicly revoked. On another occasion Makary concelebrated a liturgy in an impoverished chapel outside Athos with a priest from a village neighboring Ierissos. Although the villagers were unfriendly toward Athonites, Makary gave the priest the finely embroidered cloths for the Holy Gifts he had brought with him from St Panteleimon's. Leont'ev, who accompanied him, observed: "Fr Makary told me with that cheerful expression beaming with intelligence and kindness that I so loved: 'I wanted to comfort him as well, the poor man.'" Upon their return Fr Ieronim was harshly disapproving and sent his pupil away with a flea in his ear:

> "Fr Makary!—well, did you see him? He gave away the cloths to a priest! Why on earth give away the monastery's treasures so lavishly—and to none other than to an enemy of an Athonite monastery?" …. Fr Ieronim sighed deeply …
> "I fear that without me he'll spend everything. He's so kind that if you let him have his way he'll give away all the family silver …. The monastery needs its

possessions; Fr Makary has constantly to be restrained and taught discipline. He gets carried away."[65]

Ieronim delivered stinging rebukes to his disciple. Toward the end of the Father-Confessor's life, Makary recalls:

> I wanted a comforting word from *Batyshka*, but he said, What, are you fishing for compliments? Do you imagine that you pleased me when on my name day you brought me the icon of the Holy Trinity with such solemnity—do you think that it was pleasant for me? Had I known, I should not merely have not gone to the *arkhondarik* / guest sitting room but should have locked myself away and refused to receive anyone.

Makary, however, never doubted his teacher's love for him:

> I in my sinfulness asked whether *Batyshka* prayed for me. He answered me with such tender emotion: "How could I pray more for anyone than for you? You have taken the place of my parents, and my brother, and my spiritual friend." I was really happy: for many years I had yearned to hear such words but had never done so.[66]

CHAPTER 5

The Crimean War

Before the surge in numbers of Russian pilgrims on the Holy Mountain in the latter half of the nineteenth century, Russian prestige was high among the Greeks and other Balkan peoples. It was the Russians who encouraged and perhaps inspired the Greeks in their first rebellions against Turkish rule in the eighteenth century. After the Ottoman defeat concluded by the Treaty of Kutchuk Kainardji (1774), Russia was granted the right to build an Orthodox church in Constantinople and to make representations on behalf of those who served it. Many hoped that Grand-Prince Konstantin Nikolaevich would become the City's Christian Orthodox governor, the first since the fall of the Byzantine Empire: hence his rapturous welcome on the Mountain in 1845 (see Chapter 4).

As we have seen in Chapter 2, the Philiki Hetaireia was founded in the newly established city of Odessa[1]; the insurgents Ypsilantis and Capodistrias were important members of Tsar Alexander I's entourage. Russia championed the Greeks more than the other Powers in the Greek War of Independence (1821–1829) and ensured that Greece become an autonomous state in compliance with the conditions laid down by the Powers (Britain, France, and Russia) on Poros in 1828.

Yet Greek disillusionment with Russia had already set in. The expedition of Ypislantis into Moldavia failed; the tsar withdrew his support when he heard of the invasion and did not oppose the Turks sending in their army. Ypsilantis was routed at the Battle of Drăgăşani on June 7, 1821. Shortly afterward the Philiki Hetaireia was dissolved. In the latter half of his reign Alexander I was becoming less willing to help the Greeks against the Turks because he was anxious to preserve the peace and stability of Europe, and for this he felt that the integrity of the Ottoman Empire should be no further eroded; and support for insurgents went against his legitimist principles.

There now seemed to be no unified, effective policy in Russia toward the Greeks. In May and June 1821 Ambassador Count G. A. Stroganov lodged strongly worded

51

protests with the Porte over its treatment of Greek Orthodox Christians. He was outraged by the execution of Patriarch Germanos V. On July 30 official relations between Russia and Turkey ended when the tsarist legation left Constantinople.[2] As if to counterbalance this strong stance, the Russian consuls Pini and Pisani were recalled from Bucharest and Iași respectively for excessive pro-Hellenism. In 1822 Capodistrias resigned from the Russian Foreign Ministry and settled in Vienna in protest against Russian inaction.

Until Alexander I's death in 1825, Russia was to use diplomatic means only to deal with the Turks, anxious not to act without the support of the other Powers. Thus, when Alexander met Francis II of Austria at Czernowitz in 1823, he promised that the Russian diplomatic representative who was to return to Constantinople would do nothing about the Greek question without consulting all of Russia's allies.

Alexander's cautious approach disappointed the Greeks. They disliked Russia's proposal that autonomous Greek principalities be set up like those of Moldavia and Wallachia. The Greeks and the Turks refused to accept it, thus undermining the St Petersburg Conference of June 1824 at which it had been intended to settle the Greek question.

Nevertheless, Russia needed to act. In February 1825 Ibrahim Pasha landed in the Peloponnese. Russia felt that the Powers were deliberately procrastinating, but they too were incapable of making a concerted decision. On August 18 Count K. R. Nesselrode, the Russian Foreign Minister, stated in a circular that Russia would henceforward follow its own views, in its own interests, and without consultation. However, Nicholas I, who succeeded Alexander in December 1825, was unwilling to sacrifice Russia's interests for the sake of a dream of international cooperation.

Two years passed before decisive action was taken and once again Russia did not act on its own. On October 20, 1827, the joint naval forces of Britain, France, and Russia destroyed the Turkish and Egyptian fleets in the Battle of Navarino. Russia eventually declared war by itself on the Turks in April 1828. It was driven to this not on account of the Greeks, but mainly because its passage through the Straits connecting the Black Sea with the Aegean was blocked, in defiance of the Convention of Akkerman signed with the sultan on October 7, 1826. The Treaty of Adrianople signed in September 1829 marked the end of another victory over the Turks. The Russian Empire had expanded into the Caucasus, and gained control of the northern and eastern Black Sea coasts; the Porte now recognized Russian sovereignty over Georgia and parts of Armenia. Yet Russia strove to squeeze more concessions from the Turks. France, Britain, and eventually Austria-Hungary had different ideas. They rallied to the defense of the Ottoman Empire in a bid to curtail Russian expansion and prevent an imbalance of power in the Near East.

In 1843 the French established a consulate in Jerusalem and demanded of the Porte the right to repair the church of the Holy Sepulcher. In 1847 Joseph Valerga was appointed as the first resident Latin patriarch of Jerusalem since the thirteenth century, when the last remnants of the Crusaders were driven from the Holy Land by the Mamluks. Nicholas I saw campaigning for the Holy Places as a means of gaining instant popular support. He was also deeply opposed to the French monarch, Napoleon III (1808–1873), a revolutionary romantic. Conservative by nature, Nicholas was anxious to preserve the status quo in the Holy Land and concede no advantage to the French. The latter resented having Catholicism and national pride being challenged by the Russians.

The Porte seemed to yield to French pressure and make generous concessions to the Latins, but in February 1852 issued a *firman* / decree rendered these concessions invalid. In May the French put further pressure on the Turks by obliging the Sultan to allow the French man-of-war *Charlemagne* to pass through the Straits. The Turks then conceded to one of the main French demands and handed them the keys to the Holy Sepulcher Church. This effectively put an end to the Russian challenge in the Holy Land. At the end of 1852 the position of Basili, the Russian consul in Jerusalem, became untenable and he was recalled.

In July 1853 Russian troops occupied the Danubian Principalities of Moldavia and Wallachia on the Russo-Turkish border. The British fleet was ordered to Constantinople in September; the Turks opened an offensive against the Russians in the Danubian Principalities. At the Battle of Sinope, in November 1853, the Russian Black Sea fleet destroyed a Turkish squadron. The British and French fleets moved to the Black Sea in January 1854 to protect Turkish transports. On February 27, 1854, Britain and France demanded that Russia withdraw; Russia refused. The Crimean War "was virtually underway."[3]

Taking advantage of the Ottoman Empire's weakened position, bands of rebels arrived from the Kingdom of the Hellenes hoping to extend Greek territory into Macedonia. Attacks were carried out on two fronts—south of Thessaloniki and in Halkidiki. Fearing the outbreak of a mass revolt, the Porte sent its representative, Yakoup Aga, to the Mountain with a letter from the Patriarch asking "the monks to desist from all underground, pro-Russian activities."[4]

The St Panteleimon Russians were worried. In 1853, the relatively junior Fr Makary had been unable to reassure them:

> [They] came to me requesting that I ask the elders on their behalf to release all the Russians from the monastery and permit them to go to Russia. I, however, refused to represent them as I did not yet have a voice in the monastic assembly; I was fearful on account of my [junior position] in the monastery that I might upset the elders' peace of mind.[5]

A *synaxis* / council meeting of the senior St Panteleimon fathers was held. Abbot Gerasimos said that all those who had been tonsured in the monastery must stay, but novices and those tonsured elsewhere were free to go. The council "voted unanimously to stay, and if the Turks were to arrive, the brethren should accept it as God's will but not abandon the monastery. But those who were weak and unsure of themselves should be given the opportunity of leaving."[6] Of the eighty Russian brethren in the monastery at the time, ten opted to leave.[7]

One of those wishing to go was Svyatogorets, but the ship which he was to travel on was unable to stop where he was waiting to board, owing to intemperate weather. After two abortive attempts it anchored some distance away, but Svyatogorets had by now fallen severely ill. He wrote a penitent letter to the abbot and Fr Ieronim begging to be received back. He died in the monastery in December 1853.

On April 22, 1854, the Greek insurgents arrived on Athos and Turkish retribution was imminent. One of the monastery's Russian brethren, Priest-Monk Panteleimon (Sapozhnikov), was an eyewitness: "In the recent war of the allied Powers against Russia, the Mother of God showed her wondrous care for the Athonite houses when the massed Turkish forces were on their way and about to set foot on the Holy Mountain to put everything to fire and the sword."[8]

According to Sapozhnikov, a "partisan" named Cham arrived with a detachment of 400 militia. He had chosen Athos because it was excellent mountainous terrain for his guerilla tactics. He was also counting on the support of the Athonite population. The monks, however, were not on his side, for he was "sea pirate" and memories of the bloody events of 1821 were still fresh.[9] Not one of the twenty monasteries offered to help him or even let him in their gates. Cham therefore went to Karyes and stationed his forces at Megali Vigla, on the Athonite border with the mainland, whence his scouts were to report on enemy shipping.

In May 1854, 1,600 Turkish troops commanded by a bey landed at Daphne. Upon catching sight of the ship, the Russians of St Panteleimon's bewailed: "Look, our cutthroats have at last arrived! There is nothing more to wait for: death is facing us."[10] A three-man Turkish delegation was sent to Xiropotamou to find out about Cham's movements. They were assured that Cham was not in any of the Twenty, but at the land border. Twelve of his guerillas, however, were hidden in the bushes on the crags overlooking the Daphne–Xiropotamou path. The Turks then landed at the port. They were fired on from the bushes and beat a hasty retreat to their ship believing that they were being attacked by a substantial force. The ship disappeared from view on its way north and anchored at Krumitsa, a St Panteleimon dependency on the north-west side of the peninsula close to the border. Here the troops set up camp. Two thousand reinforcements arrived, and the bey started marching slowly south to exact revenge for collaboration with Cham and for the hostile fire on the Xiroptamou–Daphne path.

The St Panteleimon brethren particularly feared the bashi-bazouks (irregular soldiers of the Ottoman army), who could "fiercely attack the monasteries … and wipe the Russian Monastery off the face of the earth, both leaving not a single of its inhabitants alive and razing its buildings to the ground."[11] Chaos reigned in the Sacred Community; twenty-hour meetings were held and every member of the assembly shouted to be heard. All over Athos a three-day fast was held with special prayers to the Mother of God.

The Turks continued their slow march south. Cham was fired on and his band dispersed. The bey sent word that "he would spare nobody if they resisted or … stirred up trouble against the sultan. All would be punished, including state insurrectionists and especially the Russians, who were, he suspected, responsible for this rebellion."[12]

At this point a French warship hove to near the Turkish encampment and fired. A French envoy then landed bearing an official order from the sultan, who was perhaps being pressurized by France or another Power: the bey was to fall back and the Twenty Monasteries to be spared. Cham and his band of 400 boarded the ship and were taken to Athens. His 200 collaborators left the Mountain by their own means. Thus a repeat of the disastrous Turkish occupation of the Mountain in 1821 was narrowly avoided. The Athonites thanked the Mother of God for her miraculous intervention.

There is no historically verifiable record of an insurrectionist called Cham other than the emotional account of Monk Panteleimon (Sapezhnikov), cited above. It is well documented, however, that in April 1854 Tsamis Karatasos sailed north from the island of Euboea with a band of 500 irregulars. On the 16 he landed on Sythonia, the middle prong of Halkidiki. On the 22 he launched attacks on an Ottoman encampment at Ormylia, mid-way between Sythonia and Athos. Hasa Aga counterattacked with a force of 300 bashibazouks; the rebels fell back. On April 29 more Turkish troops arrived from Thessaloniki. The massed army of three thousand under the command of Hâjjî Tâhir Bey left Ormylia and marched on the insurgents. In mid-May Tsamis Karatasos and his band fled to Athos. At Krumitsa he gathered all volunteers fit enough to bear weapons, but was defeated on May 28, having lost ninety men. He withdrew to Daphne. Another Ottoman ship arrived from Thessaloniki. The rebels' cause was lost; some boarded small craft and set sail for the Kingdom of the Hellenes. Finally, Tsamis and the rest of his men boarded the French ship *SS Solon* and an Egyptian ship, and sailed to Athens.[13]

For the Russians of St Panteleimon Monastery the Crimean War was critical. Not only were the brethren cut off from the fatherland for the duration of the conflict (1854–1856), but also their once mighty protector, the Russian Empire, was significantly weakened. A new global order was in force. The Vienna System established after the Congress of Vienna (1814–1815) had collapsed; Russia had lost its gains made as a member of the defunct Holy Alliance. After the Treaty of Paris (March 30, 1856) at the conclusion of the war, a new Concert of Europe guaranteeing collective security and the protection of the Ottoman Empire was in force. Should the "sick man of Europe" weaken further, Russia was to be prevented from strengthening its position in the Near East, especially among the Orthodox peoples of the Balkans. The Powers now made their decisions in London and Russia was no longer in a position to negotiate tête-à-tête with the sultan. Russia's defeat in the Crimean War was a humiliation; its prestige among the Balkan peoples, especially among the Greeks, was damaged.

The Russian Steam Navigation and Trade Organization

The terms of the Paris Treaty forbade the naval presence in the Black Sea of any Power, and Russia could not bring in its warships from outside. The southern fringes of the Russian Empire were thus exposed. Without the backup of the Black Sea Fleet, Russian territorial gains could not be consolidated in the Caucasus. Merchant shipping, lines of communication, and the Russian Black Sea Coast were undefended. Now that the Straits were inaccessible, the navy had access to the Mediterranean only via Gibraltar. Once again, the sole route to Mount Athos open to Russian pilgrims, who had previously sailed to Athos via Constantinople, was the inconvenient and perilous one overland.

In April 1856 Grand-Prince Konstantin Nikolaevich, now admiral and in charge of the Imperial Marine Ministry, proposed to the cabinet of ministers the setting up of a private Black Sea merchant fleet. On August 3 Alexander II granted the Russian Steam Navigation and Trade Organization (RSNTO) its royal charter.[14]

The founding of the organization was timely. As a result of the war, the Russian Black Sea coast was in a parlous state: the merchant fleet had been destroyed, the ports were in disrepair, and shipping companies bankrupt. Industry and agriculture in the region, however, were picking up, but there were no railways or other means of transport for export. The government gave the company a long-term loan, yearly credit, and an additional grant to refurbish ships. By the end of 1856 the organization could afford to open eight shipping routes, and in May the following year it started operating with five ships. Although initially hampered by bureaucracy, lack of specialists, and poor infrastructure, it thrived. The RSNTO ships imported railway tracks from Britain. Eventually the ships carried Black Sea grain to Britain on the return journey.[15]

The Grand-Prince understood the potential religious and geopolitical importance of the shipping company as a carrier of pilgrims. He proposed that the issue of foreign passports to them be simplified. As he explained:

> Thanks to our unbroken ties with various parts of the Orthodox East, [our merchant ships] responsible for the transport of large numbers of pilgrims to Palestine and Mount Athos would significantly contribute to bringing us closer with our coreligionists .... Thus Russia would acquire in the East the significant status so vital to it.[16]

Boris Nikolaevich Mansurov, a functionary in the Imperial Marine Ministry, understood the value of the organization as a promotor of foreign policy. Mirroring the words of his ministry's chief, he declared that the organization supported Orthodoxy "by bringing together our [Russian] church with that of the East and by strengthening our ties with our eastern coreligionists."[17]

As many pilgrims as possible had to travel on the RSNTO ships to make the Palestine/Athos routes profitable. Mansurov was charged with writing a guide encouraging Russian pilgrims to undertake the journey. He promised:

> Voyages to the East have long ceased to be difficult undertakings .... The constant journeyings of tourists have already established almost everywhere certain conditions of European comfort which have become essential for all ... [and] at present visiting marvelous destinations presents few problems, for

without significant expenditure Russian transport can deliver people directly
to all points on the Mediterranean coast in comfort.[18]

Mansurov's promises of European standards of comfort and convenience were
mere blandishments, for the voyage by ship in the latter half of the nineteenth century was far from easy. Stephen Graham, an Edwardian gentleman disguised as a Russian peasant, was an RSNTO passenger and graphically describes the danger and
discomfort of his journey across stormy seas:

> About midnight ... the wind at the force of a hurricane leapt upon us out of
> the clouds, and tore along our decks .... In a moment the impoverished can-
> vas shelters, rigged up over the cover of the hold, were ripped up and torn to
> ribbons .... The pilgrims rolled and prayed, and moaned and shrieked. In the
> hold, where many of the peasants raved like maniacs, there was a considerable
> quantity of sea-water. The waters leaped over the funnels, they smashed the
> glass roof of the second-class cabin and washed one of the boats away.[19]

Why did the often destitute pilgrims undergo such hardship to reach the Orthodox East, and to spend their last *kopeks* on a stormy maritime passage? Many had
already covered thousands of kilometers from their homes, usually on foot, simply
to reach Odessa. For them, true pilgrimage meant self-sacrifice; and they had a pio-
neering spirit of adventure coupled with pious determination impelling them to
unknown lands and distant frontiers. Such pilgrims were hardly tourists.

Mansurov himself sailed incognito in December 1856 to Palestine, Lebanon,
Syria, and Greece. Then he openly went to Mount Athos in a distinguished group of
twelve, including the director of RSNTO, Senior Captain (later Admiral) and Imperial Aide-de-Camp Nikolay Andreevich Arkas. Mansurov boarded the SS *Kherson*
on July 4, 1857.[20] They landed at the Great Lavra on July 10. Having reconnoitered
the southern tip of the peninsula for suitably deep landing stages for future RSNTO
ships, they sailed up the north-west coast. On the way, they were greeted by the joyful peal of bells of Aghiou Pavlou, Dionysiou, Grigoriou, and Simonopetra Monasteries. When they arrived at St Panteleimon's, Fr Ieronim had to ride from his *kellion*
on muleback to meet them and nearly died from his aggravated hernia (see the previous chapter).

From the coast the party made their way inland to Karyes. Here they sought the
blessing of the Sacred Community. The Karyes fathers were delighted: the Holy

Mountain "had become accustomed to protection and material help …. The members of the Sacred Community added that the Organization would instill new life into Athos; they were glad that none other than Russia would take it on itself to make life better."²¹ Obtaining this blessing was easy because not long before a Lloyd's Company ship had stopped at the Mountain. The Austrians had asked for payment for regular visits, but failed to agree a deal with the Sacred Community, so they did not return.

From Karyes Mansurov's group went to the Russian St Andrew Skete and then spent the night at the Prophet Elijah Skete. Finally, having visited Xylourgou, they returned to St Panteleimon Monastery. After services of thanksgiving, Fr Makary with some other brethren blessed the *Kherson* with holy water. A farewell meal was served on board. Senior Captain Arkas greeted his guests "on this Russian ship, this small plot of Russian soil." He then said a few words in Greek, to the delight of the Greek monks present, and concluded: "Soon between the Holy Mountain and the land of Russia a permanent link will be established. We should therefore not say farewell to each other but [let us drink to] our next joyful encounter."²²

On the same day, July 11, 1856, the *Kherson* left. This was the first Russian vessel to visit the Mountain since 1853. Despite limited time, the objectives of the mission had been achieved. Firstly, the maiden RSNTO voyage to Athos was successfully completed and landing depths were sounded. Secondly, Konstantin Nikolaevich had personally sanctioned the visit and the party made a point of calling mainly at the Russian Athonite houses. Furthermore, 1,500 *puds* / 54 tons of essential goods were offloaded at St Panteleimon's. Thirdly, the blessing of the Sacred Community was obtained, thus ensuring the future of the RSNTO Athos route. Finally, the first pilgrims from Russia since 1853 arrived on the *Kherson*—fifteen in number, including Schema-Monk Iriney (Deev), who had been sent by Fr Ieronim to gather alms ten years ago and who had been stranded in Russia on account of the war.

The high-profile visit of the *Kherson* did not pass unnoticed. On October 1, 1857, the Austrian envoy, Baron von Prokesch, arrived at Karyes from Constantinople to find out what had been going on. In May of the next year Archimandrite Porfiry (Uspensky) was sent to the Mountain. He wished to ascertain the feasibility of setting up a Russian alms house there and of establishing a Russian consular presence on Athos.²³ Nothing came of the archimandrite's survey, but shortly after his departure, another concerned European Power made its presence felt: Édouard Anthoine de Thouvenal, the French envoy, arrived at Karyes, and like his Austrian counterpart no doubt made inquiries about what the Russians were up to.

The French and the Austrians were right to be worried. The fifteen pilgrims who arrived on the *Kherson* were the first of a great many. Soon Russian pilgrims would be coming in their thousands; the Russian Athonite community was to grow exponentially, and St Panteleimon Monastery was destined to become the largest and wealthiest house on the Holy Mountain.

CHAPTER 6

The Greek and Russian Brotherhoods at Loggerheads

The Beginning of the Rift

During Fr Ieronim's first decade in the monastery the two brotherhoods were in harmony. The Russians knew their place: they were guests and treated the St Panteleimon Greeks as their elders and betters. Svyatogorets observed in 1843:

There has never been any mention anywhere that a Russian has been in charge of [the monastery] .... [We Russians] are better suited ... as dependents; we cannot assume the right of governing a multi-ethnic brotherhood, which is alien to us in its language and nature. We Russians, guests on the Holy Mountain, should thus unpardonably overstep the mark were we to lord it over our hosts, however great the munificence of our Orthodox Russia to the monastery.[1]

Monk Parfeny (Ageev) revered the Greeks. He found that they were more experienced in cenobitic monasticism and that the Russians should learn from their saintly example: "I would look at them and was amazed, and would often be moved to tears, thanking my Lord God the Heavenly King for making me worthy of seeing these angels in the flesh."[2]

In 1859 Archimandrite Antonin (Kapustin), a learned Hellenophile, visited the monastery. He was impressed by what he saw as the unity of the two brotherhoods and by the enlightened leadership of Fr Ieronim. The archimandrite describes the beautiful Greek-Russian concelebration of the services at the patronal feast. The two brotherhoods sang and celebrated in seamless alternation, then the Russians left for their St Mitrofan chapel, before coming back to the St Panteleimon *katholikon* / central church for the conclusion of the service:

Looking at them, I understood how it was possible that, in the face of all the privations, all the cramped conditions, and all the indescribable toils of Athonite life, the [Russian] brotherhood was formed and increased to more than a hundred upon the arrival of one humble outsider—all thanks to this person, luminous, mighty, and fearless, who shone before us from afar with inner beauty.[3]

Archimandrite Antonin seemed unaware that he had arrived at a critical time, when tension was mounting between the Greek and Russian brotherhoods. A. A. Dmitrievsky was biased against the Greeks, yet his assessment of the situation was more accurate:

Although the Russian monks ... entered the monastery upon the urgent entreaties of the Greek monks, the latter had no intention of considering them as equals. The Greeks looked on the Russians as newcomers, their servants, who, in return for their poor accommodation and extremely humble fare, were obliged to undergo every manner of privation and want .... The Russian brethren's paucity, the hopeless state of the monastery's finances and the utter lack of personal means—all this for the time being obliged the Russian brotherhood to accept its humble position in the monastery.[4]

In his *Istoriya Russkogo na Afone svyato-Panteleimonova monastyrya* / *History of the Russian Monastery of St Panteleimon on Athos*, priest of the Great Schema Feodosy (Kharitonov), a one-time monastery library assistant, assessed the Russians' situation similarly. For sixteen years they had been suffering:

Fr Ieronim noticed and put up with the unpleasant escapades directed at him by certain of the senior brethren, for he hoped that the Greeks would get to know the Russians better and would get used to them—especially because the Russians made every possible concession and humiliated themselves in every way.[5]

During this period Fr Ieronim ensured that the money from alms-gathering missions was handed over to the abbot to be shared equally between both brotherhoods, "except when donations were made specifically for Russian chapels or the Russian brotherhood." All vestments and ecclesiastical treasures from Russia were shared. Nevertheless, the Russians were given only junior obediences and all refectory readings were in Greek. Sapozhnikov adds: "It was no mean ascetic feat to share meals with the Greeks and get used to their food."[6]

From 1857, now that the Crimean War had ended and pilgrims started arriving from Russia again, Fr Ieronim at last found himself in a position of strength. The monastery's finances were robust, its buildings restored and added to, and the Russian brethren was 100-strong and increasing.[7]

The Russians requested that the refectory readings on Wednesdays and Fridays be in Slavonic. This was initially refused, but readings alternating between Greek and Slavonic on successive days were eventually agreed on. Some boycotted the refectory and demanded that Greek-only readings be reinstated. They were ignored and alternate readings continued, both on festive and ordinary days.

Sensing that the change to the refectory readings schedule might be the thin end of the wedge, the Greeks asked for a written *typiko* / rule or charter to be drawn up. Drawn up by the Greeks, it stated that the Russians must never exceed in number one-third of the Greek brotherhood; senior obediences should be reserved for the Greeks; and the abbot of the monastery must always be Greek. The Russians refused to ratify the charter.

In 1858 a Turkish quarantine hut was erected at the monastery wharf to deal with the increasing numbers of Russian pilgrims, while visitors from other countries continued to land at Daphne. Some of the Greek brotherhood protested, ostensibly objecting to the sight of the Turkish flag hoisted on St Panteleimon property. Under the cover of night the monastery's mooring buoy was sunk. Abbot Gerasimos threatened to withhold absolution prayers from the Greek brethren, effectively excommunicating them. The culprits, led by *Pnevmatikos* / Spiritual Father Nifon, owned up, but the abbots of Dionysiou, Zograf, and Xenophontos were invited in to arbitrate. Three unsuccessful *synaxes* / meetings of the brotherhoods were held. Next, images of a cutlass and pistol were daubed on the cell doors of the abbot and his helpmeet, Deacon Ilarion, who was friendly with the Russian brethren. The eminent Greek Athonite historian and bitter opponent of the Russians, Priest-Monk Gerasimos Smyrnakis, described Ilarion as "*athlios* / vile."[8] Tension was finally diffused when twenty-six dissenters, including Fr Nifon, left the monastery of their own accord in 1863, having been paid compensation.

There followed a temporary truce and by 1866 the monastery's debts had been liquidated. High-profile guests raised the prestige of the Russian brotherhood. The first of these was the newly appointed ambassador to Constantinople, Count Nikolay Pavlovich Ignat'ev, who arrived in August 1866.[9] The inscription in the book commemorating his visit is pointedly patriotic: "We are especially grateful to His Excellency for his attention .... It comforts us and is a reward for [our elders'] centuries-old, unfailing zeal for the development of the ancient and royal Russian House on the Holy Mountain."[10] In June 1867, twenty-two years after the visit of Konstantin Nikolaevich, Alexander II's son, Aleksey Aleksandrovich, arrived on the *SS Veikaya knyagina Ol'ga*, which anchored off St Panteleimon's. After a *moleben* / thanksgiving service Fr Makary delivered a patriotic address to the Grand-Prince. The Tsarevich then went on to the Serai, as the Russian St Andrew Skete was called, where he laid the foundation stone to its vast *kyriakon* / central church. In June and July of 1868 Bishop Aleksandr of Poltava was the first Russian hierarch to visit the Mountain.[11] He conferred on Fr Makary the rank of archimandrite in the presence of Patriarch Anthimos VI.[12]

The St Panteleimon Russians hoped that the distinguished visits would consolidate their position. Aleksey Aleksandrovich had promised that he would tell his father about the fine reception he received at the monastery. Ieronim and Makary hoped that they would thus be able "to maintain their house at the desired level of inner and outer good order."[13] On March 7, 1868, the Tsarevich and Count Ignat'ev were presented with fine commemorative photographic albums of their visits. Alexander II's son responded by giving bejeweled pectoral crosses to Abbot Gerasimos, Ieronim, and Makary. Although the imperial family's good will toward the monastery was evident, and many further gifts and photographs were exchanged, the Tsarevich was clearly unaware of phyletic differences or was uninterested in them; he spoke instead of the "peaceful coexistence of the Greek and Russian brotherhoods within the walls of one monastery."[14] No more concrete help came from him. The count, on the other hand, fully understood Ieronim and Makary's plight, and was pleased that the Tsarevich had at least poured oil on troubled waters.

The truce was short-lived. In 1870, "without any pressure from the Russians",[15] Abbot Gerasimos appointed Makary as his successor. It was customary on Athos for the abbot to make such an appointment before his death: Savvas had chosen two successors, as we have seen (Chapter 2). His choice caused resentment.

Pressure from outside the Monastery

A series of external events made matters worse. Firstly, the brotherhood of Aghiou Pavlou Monastery, hot-headed Cephalonians,[16] chose a St Panteleimon Greek as their new abbot: they wished to replace the incumbent, who had long been away in Constantinople incurring substantial debts. The ousted abbot appealed to the patriarch; an exarchate (a patriarchal delegation composed of one or more bishops) was sent to the Mountain and proposed one of the Aghiou Pavlou brethren as the new abbot, a choice unanimously approved of by the Aghiou Pavlou brethren. The Athonite community was divided: "a significant section"[17] of the Twenty Monasteries, including

St Panteleimon, Zograf, Vatopedi and Iviron Monasteries were against patriarchal interference. A delegate from each of the Twenty Monasteries met the exarchate. Fr Evgenios, the Greek St Panteleimon representative, spoke out strongly against the exarchate "with the intention of besmirching [his own] monastery."[18] Nevertheless, St Panteleimon's arranged for the impoverished Aghiou Pavlou to carry out alms-gathering missions in Russia. The Cephalonians asked for the collected money to be kept for safekeeping at St Panteleimon's. For two years, the Aghiou Pavlou problem dragged on, increasing tension in St Panteleimon Monastery.[19]

At the same time, the old abbot of Xenophontos died. The election of his successor—another St Panteleimon Greek—ruffled feathers. Of far more consequence, however, was the attention being drawn to the Russian St Andrew Skete, known as the Serai. It started its existence in 1841 when two wealthy Russian merchants bought a *kellion* from Vatopedi; nine years later it gained its skete's charter and rapidly grew into a sizeable cenobium. The presence in 1867 of Grand-Prince Alexei Aleksandrovich, who laid the foundation stone to its grandiose *kyriakon* / central church, caused a stir. Priest-Monk Gerasimos (Smyrnakis), the Athonite historian, described the building as "unparalleled in size and ornate grandeur on the Holy Mountain." The abbot of Vatopedi, his brotherhood, and senior Sacred Community representatives witnessed the ceremony and were "amazed at the deliberate violation of Athonite protocol," but dared not speak up through respect for the royal visitor.[20] A greater breach of protocol followed in 1873 when Patriarch Anthimos VI presented the Serai's prior Feodorit with a pectoral cross and conferred on him the title of archimandrite, although he had already been elevated to this rank by Vatopedi. Anthimos also addressed him as Abbot, a title reserved for the heads of the Twenty, and granted the skete stavropegic status.

The death in 1871 of Paisy II, prior of the Prophet Elijah Skete, gave rise to another unfortunate incident. Russian diplomatic pressure was applied on behalf of the skete on its ruling monastery, Pantokratoros, over the prior's succession. As in the case of Agiou Pavlou, outsiders were attempting to meddle with the internal affairs of a ruling monastery; Russian intervention was especially resented.

In the summer of 1872, another incident cast an unfavorable light on the Russian brethren. Close to the Athonite border with the mainland, next to the village of Revenikia in Halkidiki, there was a church which housed a wonderworking icon of the Dormition.[21] An elderly Russian nun came to live next to the church, and she was soon joined by two other nuns from Russia. According to Leont'ev, the Russian

Consul in Thessaloniki (April–September 1872), the three nuns were supported and fed by the impoverished villagers. Peace was shattered when Panayotakis, a Westernized agitator from the Kingdom of the Hellenes, arrived and objected to the presence of the Russians. The village was divided into two factions: one comprised of Panayotakis and the local headmen, the other of people like the traditionally dressed peasant Sotiris, who was glad that the icon and the church be looked after by the pious foreigners. Leont'ev himself happened to be passing through Revenikia and he was asked to intercede on behalf of Sotiris and the nuns to the consul in Thessaloniki, N. Yakubovsky.

According to the Austrian Consul in Thessaloniki, von Knapitsch, Leont'ev's wife wanted to become a nun and had approached the bishop of Ierissos about this. She and some other pious, influential Russian women intended to found a convent in the area. They built comfortable accommodation in Revenikia and walled off a "spring of wonder-working water." The villagers, however, took matters into their own hands and tore the buildings down. Leont'ev, meanwhile, had been staying on Mount Athos, ostensibly to refresh his soul but in fact to visit his compatriot monks. The most dangerous of these monks, the Austrian complained, was Ieronim (Solomentsov), who through his influence as spiritual father was in charge of "all Russian propaganda" in the area. As a servant of a rival empire and great European power, von Knapitsch was clearly no friend of the Russians. He reported that the Russians were likely to succeed in acquiring the village despite opposition. They were rich and offered to pay off the 3,000 lira debt the Revenikians owed in taxes to the district governor.[22]

Smyrnakis tells the story differently. A devout Russian nun went to the village with nine others, who were very rich. Fr Makary and some of his Russian brethren would regularly arrive by boat directly from St Panteleimon's to visit the nuns, bearing gifts for the villagers and "promises of good things for the future." A trap had been laid: the Russians wanted to build a nunnery and destroy the village, and they were willing to buy the land at a high price. The villagers, perceiving the danger, expelled all nine nuns but let the original one stay. Undeterred, the Russians persuaded Monk Agathangelos of Xiropotamou Monastery to go to the village, ask permission to live next to the wonderworking icon, and look after it. He was a native of Revenikia and gained the villagers' good will. Immediately, Russian monks started visiting him. They brought gold, laid the foundations for new buildings, and generously distributed food to the hungry villagers. The latter were not fooled and complained to Meletios of Ierissos, their local bishop. Agathangelos confessed all and was sent back to the Holy Mountain. Smyrnakis concludes that no further proselytization of the village succeeded and the area was "now free of Slav influence." However, the Serai sent some 9,000 Turkish lira to the village of Aghios Nikolaos in neighboring Sythonia in order to build huge buildings and later convert the area into a Russian "military base."[23] The villagers enlisted the help of bankers and Turkish officials, kept the money and the Russians had to go away empty-handed.

Although both villages were mainly Greek, they were situated in Macedonia, so many of their inhabitants and neighbors would have been Slavs. Smyrnakis, for instance, says that Monk Agathangelos was of Bulgarian parentage. The agitators from the Kingdom of the Hellenes were obviously worried about the loyalties of the people of Halkidiki, hence the appearance of besuited Panayotakis in the remote village of Revenikia, with which he cannot have had much in common.

Von Knapitsch's report to Vienna has to be taken with a pinch of salt. He was a Roman Catholic and probably did not understand Orthodoxy. Neither Smyrnakis nor Leont'ev mentions the miraculous spring of holy water; perhaps the Austrian was confusing it with the icon.[24] Von Knapitsch's real concern was that the Russians were threatening to gain a foothold in disputed Macedonian territory. The account of Smyrnakis is also biased, but the unashamedly anti-Greek. Dmitrievsky makes no mention of the events. Did Dmitrievsky choose to pass over an episode that would have reflected unfavorably on the Russians?

Not all the Russians can have had ulterior motives. The original nun was allowed to stay, and was still there when Smyrnakis was writing, shortly before 1903. She was merely a pious Russian pilgrim. The idea that the Serai monks hoped to convert Aghios Nikolaos into a military base is typical of the alarmist rumors about Russian expansionist aims in Macedonia fueled by the Greek anti-Russian Constantinopolitan newspapers, such as *Le Phare du Bosphore*. To this day certain Greeks still believe that Russian Athonites, particularly those of the Serai, were secretly officers of the Imperial Army, and that the cellars of the Russian houses on Athos concealed stores of weapons.[25]

The Russians undeniably acted tactlessly. As usual, they aroused envy and bitterness among the poor with their money. The people of Aghios Nikolaos, on the other hand, behaved dishonestly and greedily by keeping the 9,000 lira. But what were the Russians trying to do outside Athos? It is most likely that they were simply attempting to acquire dependencies close to the Holy Mountain. Revenikia had been bequeathed to St Panteleimon by Emperor John Paleologos in 1354, but by the latter half of the nineteenth century the monastery was evidently no longer recognized as its rightful owner.[26] The St Andrew Skete particularly needed dependencies because it had no land of its own on Athos itself. St Panteleimon had by the middle of the century a modest dependency in Kalamaria outside Thessaloniki. No doubt, if the Russians had tried to acquire land in Halkidiki before the Crimean War, few would have objected.

Events outside Athos aggravated phyletic tension on the Holy Mountain. At a time when Bulgarian nationalism was asserting itself, the Orthodox *millet* / community in the Ottoman Empire was becoming increasingly Hellenized; Greek bishops were assigned to mainly Bulgarian-speaking dioceses. The sultan, however, allowed the Bulgarians to have their own church in Constantinople, St Stefan's; and in 1870 the Porte issued a *firman* appointing an independent exarch as ecclesiastical head of the Bulgarians. In 1872 the Ecumenical Patriarchate declared the Bulgarian Exarchate schismatic and broke communion with it. The creation of the Bulgarian Exarchate was seen as a challenge to Greek ecclesiastical supremacy.

The patriarch then asked the Russian Holy Synod to sign a letter condemning the schismatics. Although not openly siding with them, the Synod refused to sign.

> There then arose voices in the East clamoring that the Russians were schismatic .… From that time on Eastern society and the press spoke of the complete unity between the Russians and the Bulgarians, and even considered the two nationalities one and the same. Russia was thus accused of *Pan-Slavism*, the essence and meaning of which nobody clearly understands.[27]

Leont'ev did understand its meaning: "'Pan-Slavism' for the Greeks means nothing other than 'the state unification of all Slavs' more-or-less directly under the might of Russia."[28] In his opinion, the Greeks were unaware that neither was Russia a purely Slav power, nor did a freedom-seeking Bulgaria wish to be shackled to another country.

By the latter half of the nineteenth century, even the richest Greek Athonite houses, such as Vatopedi, the Serai's ruling monastery, were feeling the pinch. They once possessed in the Danubian Principalities over sixty dependent houses with extensive lands.[29] These *metochia* were badly managed and soon owed 29 million lei in taxes.[30] Prince A. I. Cuza[31] secularized the dependencies in 1863; their Athonite representatives were sent home and Greek Athos lost major revenues. In March 1873, Alexander II issued an *ukaz* / decree: all dependencies in Bessarabia and the

Caucasus belonging to the monasteries of Athos and the Holy Land were to be administered by Russian civil servants. The Greek archimandrites hitherto in charge of them were censured for mismanagement; income from the confiscated properties was diverted to defray administrative costs, and to create and maintain local schools and hospitals.[32]

Another monastery to suffer material loss from the confiscations was Iviron. From 1801, following the annexation by Russia of the Kingdom of Georgia, the monastery's Greek brethren increased, gradually taking over from the aging Georgian monks. In 1861, Vakhtang Barklai, a Georgian veteran of the Caucasian campaigns, stopped off on the Holy Mountain on his way back from a pilgrimage to the Holy Land. He found in the Prophet Elijah *Kellion* / Hermitage belonging to Iviron four Georgian monks, among the last of the Iberians who used to live in the monastery. They asked him to leave, for the monastery had forbidden them to admit anyone else into their brotherhood. Wanting to stay and help, Barklai sought advice from St Panteleimon's Spiritual Father Ieronim, who told him to go home, be tonsured as a monk and raise money for the Georgian cause on Athos. This Barklai accomplished: newly tonsured as Priest-Monk Venedikt, he returned with 35,000 rubles.

He and three of the Georgians from the Prophet Elijah Hermitage bought from Iviron the Hermitage of St John the Theologian. According to the *omologon* / deed of purchase issued by Iviron, the new brotherhood was to be restricted to Venedikt, appointed the elder, and three other monks. Soon, however, the brotherhood was joined by forty other Georgians. A bitter struggle ensued. The Georgians attempted to convert the *kellion* into a large cenobium; Iviron pulled down parts of the new buildings, and dug up vegetable gardens, paths, and approach roads. The St Panteleimon Russians supplied the Georgians with building materials, which they somehow managed to deliver.

Venedikt Barklai completed the buildings, but his burgeoning community was never recognized as a skete. None of his brotherhood was allowed back into Iviron, which they continued to claim as their heritage. The involvement of the St Panteleimon Russians did nothing to ease tension between the Greek and Russian Athonite communities.[33]

Greek Athonites now believed that they were victims of a Pan-Slavist plot connected with the Bulgarian Exarchate, which was in schism with the Ecumenical Patriarchate. In the opinion of Smyrnakis, reprisals were secretly carried out by "the Russian government ... against the hierarchy of the Eastern Church [to] protect the

Bulgarian ecclesiastical rebellion."³⁴ Dmitrievsky understood why the Greeks made so far-fetched a connection between the schism and loss of dependencies, for they saw themselves as victims of a concerted plot against them:

> Expelled by force from these dependencies, the Athonite representatives led by the well-known wealthy *Epitropos* / Representative of Vatopedi, Ananias, came to the Mountain raging against the Russian government and the Russians in general. They were looking for an opportunity to give vent to their fury on the Russian Athonite monks, who had done nothing wrong to them …. Appearing in their midst, *Epitropos* Ananias with his colleagues openly and passionately [challenged] their displeased compatriots: "Why gawp at the Russians? It's high time to crush them. They've taken the Bulgarians away from the Church and deprived [us] of our dependencies. I'd be the first," continued the merciless Ananias, "to give a million piastres to crush the Russians and, should the opportunity present itself, expel them from Athos."³⁵

The Rift Made Official
The rift between the St Panteleimon Greeks and Russians widened in June 1873 when Abbot Gerasimos, who was now over a hundred years old, fell ill. The Russian brotherhood wanted to send a telegram to Fr Makary, away on monastery business, asking him to hasten home before it was too late. The Greeks opposed this, but Fr Makary returned and the abbot recovered on St Panteleimon's day, July 27. To Ieronim and Makary's embarrassment, Gerasimos appointed Makary as his acting replacement. The reluctant Makary wrote:

> We Russians, especially the Father-Confessor and I, in no way exerted any pressure [for me] to succeed as abbot to Elder Gerasimos. The very people who have opposed this have forced us to accept it. If they are displeased with [his] choice, why did they not make this known at the time? …. I [therefore] take on this burden only out of obedience …. The Greek brotherhood, however, said: "We beg you [to accept]."³⁶

Whether those who urged Makary to accept were representative of the whole Greek brotherhood is uncertain, but the malcontents among them started plotting. Spiritual Father Savvas from Aghiou Dionysiou was invited to a meeting with the Greek brotherhood. Angry voices were raised: "*Aman* / Alas, our monastery has had it! The abbot is a schismatic, Deacon Ilarion is a schismatic and the Russians are schismatics!" Some proposed burning down the monastery, but the Spiritual Father counselled caution, so as not to play into the hands "of the devil and the heretics."[37]

In January 1874 six incidents further divided the two brotherhoods. On the 4th a row broke out over a Greek novice who was working as a carpenter in the Russian quarters. The Greek *Oikonomos* / Steward in charge of the workshops demanded that the novice go back to the Greek quarters. The Russians' request for another carpenter was refused. The Greek *Oikonomos* then warned Deacon Ilarion (the right-hand man of Abbot Gerasimos and also, of course, a Greek) that a delegation of thirty Greeks would demand that the Russians be prevented from asking for another carpenter. The thirty arrived; the Russian *Oikonomos* was summoned, upbraided for "bullying the Greeks," and told to hand back the carpenter he had taken. The Russian *Oikonomos* replied that he would obey Fr Ilarion's instructions. The Greeks then pleaded with Ilarion to support them: they fell "at his feet," for they wanted nothing to do with Ieronim and Makary. Ilarion replied: "As you wish, but I shall do nothing without Fr Ieronim."[38]

The next clash occurred on the eve of Theophany, January 5, 1874. Fr Makary was asked to bless the waters in the Greek quarters. He pointed out that the abbot wanted the service to be taken by the priest on duty, who happened to be the Russian Fr Nafanail. The Greeks refused to sing, so Makary went after all; but then they declared: "The abbot wants Fr Makary and we don't."[39] In the end, Makary blessed the waters, but appeased the Greeks by letting them do the readings and prayers in Greek.

On January 7, Deacon Ilarion decided that the Greek *Oikonomos* be dismissed for causing sedition over the carpenter, but asked Fr Ieronim for authorization. The next day, Ieronim and the abbot dismissed the *Oikonomos*, who appealed for support from his fellow Greeks. An angry rabble gathered outside the cell of the priest on duty, shouting: "Down with Nafanail!"[40] The frightened priest sought the help of Ilarion, and the rabble clamored for the Greek *Oikonomos* to be left alone. Ilarion then upbraided them for their unmonastic behavior, but took refuge with Nafanail upstairs in the Russian quarters. Ilarion's departure caused uproar. There were calls for a rebellion.

On January 9 and 10 the monastery's reservoir was twice sabotaged, the spring feeding it was blocked off and its stream diverted. The Russians now fearing for their lives mounted a permanent watch in their corridors.

The Greeks next demanded that Deacon Ilarion return to their quarters. He refused, and they asked him to hand over the monastery seal. On January 17, without the abbot's blessing, the Greeks ceased commemorating Frs Ieronim, Makary, and Ilarion at litanies. The Greeks then demanded to be put in charge of the *arsanas /* wharf, wheat store, and the St Panteleimon *konaki /* house in Karyes. It was pointed out to them that they had initially refused these obediences owing to lack of manpower.

Fr Ieronim made a last attempt at reconciliation. At a meeting with the Greeks he pleaded that the hatchet be buried, and the status quo under the leadership of the abbot, Ieronim himself, Fr Makary, and Deacon Ilarion be restored. To the cries of "*Ohi! Ohi! /* No! No!", Ieronim asked for the formal division of the two brotherhoods.

Worn out by the squabbles, Abbot Gerasimos issued a written formalization of the division:

> The two separate brotherhoods of different nationalities gathered together by me ... cannot henceforth cohabit peacefully in one and the same monastery, owing to many conflicts .... I [therefore] ... am obliged to give both communities ... my blessing to split from each other under the terms of equal brotherly rights.

The abbot went on to say in the declaration that the Russians had built up the monastery "with their own money and had paid off [its] substantial debts." They could therefore be called "the house's *ktitores /* benefactors and founders, hence their superior rights in this split."[41]

The sixth and final incident happened on January 28. The Greeks appointed three *sympraktores /* consular leaders, Frs Grigorios, Agathon, and Agapitos, to run the monastery in a bid to undermine the authority of the abbot. They came to Fr Ieronim asking to be involved in the monastery's financial transactions, such as buying and selling goods. His patience at an end, Ieronim Father's snapped: "I hold the purse-strings; I'll do as I please."[42]

The squabbles were concluded on January 30, 1874, when Abbot Gerasimos presented the Russians with a deed testifying to the benefits that their brotherhood and its leaders had brought to St Panteleimon's. The document stated that tens of thousands of Turkish lira had been spent by them on the monastery, which was in excellent condition and in which there now lived 200 Greeks and over 300 Russians.

That day was the Feast of the Three Hierarchs. The Greeks came to the abbot for absolution before Communion. He angrily dismissed them: "What absolution [should I give] for those who have no peace? ... Let them be excommunicated." A crowd of some thirty clamored for absolution. The abbot replied: "Spiritual Father

Ieronim was here and I gave him my blessing for the split, for they are deeply offended by your actions."[43] Nevertheless, Gerasimos relented and read the prayer.

The next month the *sympraktores* asked—unsuccessfully—for the monastery seal, keys, and chrysobulla. They also stopped the rebuilding of Mountain Rusik, which was seen as a possible refuge for the Russians should they be expelled. The felling of trees in the area for construction work was forbidden. Fr Arseny (Minin) was sent from the Moscow dependency to the Caucasus to find a site for a new monastery for the Russian brotherhood in case they would have to leave the Mountain.

Meanwhile, slanderous rumors were being spread among the Greek community about Makary's ancestry and milieu, which were said to belong to the heretical Old-Believers. Soon the St Panteleimon feud was being discussed by the whole Athonite community.

On March 15, 1874, Makary went secretly to Constantinople to enlist the help of Count N. P. Ignat'ev. Next, a seven-man Sacred Community commission came to the monastery on March 21, toward the end of Lent. It held three meetings with the brethren. At the third, the Russians presented their written complaints and requests. The next day the commission announced that the case would be adjourned until after Easter.

A new nine-man Sacred Community delegation arrived on April 23, 1874. It drew up a written *kanonizmos* / charter, according to which:

1. St Panteleimon Monastery was and would always be Greek.
2. The abbot was and would always be Greek.
3. The Russians would be permitted to have their own spiritual father exclusively for spiritual matters; he was to be chosen and could be dismissed by the abbot.
4. The Russians must never exceed in numbers two-thirds of the total Greek brotherhood.
5. The monastery treasury, including all the money collected by the Russians, must be communal.
6. Refurbishment of Old Mountain Rusik must be completed, but no new buildings were to be constructed.[44]

The Greeks were delighted with the charter, but the Russians refused to sign it.

In July 1874 Ignat'ev, accompanied by the German and US envoys, visited the monastery to assess matters for himself. Ieronim knew that only money and the count's help would win the day. The spiritual father wrote to Fr Makary in Constantinople:

In our opinion, it is essential to give without delay however much is needed to whomever necessary. We have written to you how much approximately we propose that you spend on this matter, and you must tell our God-fearing patron [Count Ignat'ev] what you are donating on your behalf from the funds entrusted to you by the brethren. You must not spare the money, but Lord help us secure for ourselves the monastery. Now if we cannot achieve this, then it will forever be lost and will cease to be a Russian sanctuary on Athos. All of Russia, not to mention we ourselves and our benefactors, will grieve [if we were to fail]. We urge you to tell all to our God-fearing patron.[45]

Abbot Gerasimos died on May 10, 1875, aged 103. Makary could not return in time for his funeral, but the Greeks again tried to prevent the Russians from visiting the dying man. Ieronim wrote to Makary:

When [the abbot] was in his death throes, from the third to the ninth hour, they did not remember to tell us and were probably not going to do so. But God inspired ... *Epitropos* / Representative Agathon secretly to let our gate-keeper Fr Ananiya know that our Elder was dying.[46]

Meanwhile, Fr Makary appealed to Patriarch Joachim II. At the same time, a delegation from the Greek brotherhood arrived in the capital to petition the patriarch. The Patriarchal Synod met and found in favor of the Russians, confirming Makary as the successor of Gerasimos. The three *Epitropoi* left St Panteleimon Monastery, and peace was restored. A majority of members of both brotherhoods accepted Makary's appointment. Joachim II, however, cautiously delayed giving his final approval, and sent an exarchate comprising Metropolitans Ioachim of Nicaea and Ioannikios of Derkes to oversee the election of the new abbot. Fr Makary was voted in without commotion. Six more dissenters left the monastery. On September 24, 1875, Abbot Makary returned in triumph from Constantinople. Two days later, he was elevated by the exarchs to the rank of archimandrite—for the second time. A patriarchal amnesty was extended to all the St Panteleimon dissenters on November 1, 1875. Thus ended the most turbulent and unhappy period in the history of the monastery, which had at last become Russian in both name and reality.

Conclusion
Neither Greeks nor Russians had acquitted themselves with honor. The Russians used money and influence to get their way, especially once the old abbot was

powerless in his dotage to control his flock. The Greeks were bad losers and resorted to often violent, unmonastic tactics. Unfortunately, the story of the unseemly squabbles, especially from January 1874, is based on Russian sources, some details of which are dubious. Sabel'nikov and Dmitrievsky did not hide their disdain for the Greeks. Their quotations of the enraged Greeks, such as those of Ananias of Vatopedi, are fanciful, for who was present from the Russians at their stormy meetings—given that most of the Russians did not speak Greek?

It is only fair, therefore, to see what Smyrnakis made of events:

On May 22nd 1874, the body of the Russian Consul General at Thessaloniki, Yakubovsky, was brought without warning to St Panteleimon's in an Austrian steamship specially chartered for this purpose. The body was accompanied by the Russian consul of Monastir. However, the abbot strongly objected, saying that all the fathers of the monastery who die in St Panteleimon are buried outside its walls, and that the arrangements, provisions, privileges and traditions of the Church of this land cannot be altered. Therefore, a layman could not be buried within the monastic walls. The Russian consul had the effrontery to reply: "I take my permission from Ieronim and the Russians." The Consul gave orders for a grave to be dug in the north side of the sanctuary of the church of St Mitrofan, and for a guard to be mounted, which was empowered to strike any Greek who might hinder the burial. The abbot then appealed to the Sacred Community and the Turkish *kaymakam* / civil governor. The latter arrived at the monastery with Ilarion, the dean of Zograf; both advised Gerasimos to yield and allow the burial to take place within the monastery. However, the abbot refused. They then went to the Russians and told them of his decision. The Russians replied that they intended to bury the consul in their own land and had no intention of listening to anyone, be they the Sacred Community or the Patriarch. Then the Russians buried the body unimpeded.[47]

Although, like Dmitrievsky and Sabel'nikov, Smyrnakis resorts to the dubious direct speech quotation, and his narrative is somewhat sensational and emotional, he has a strong case against the Russians: they went against the abbot's will, and allowed nationalist, political interests to impinge on the sanctity of monastic regulations. Dmitrievsky says nothing of the burial. He must have known it happened because the tombstone and record of the burial are there for all to see.[48] Perhaps this was too inglorious an episode to write about.

Fr Ieronim, on the other hand, does write about the burial. He was being deprived of confession with Abbot Gerasimos, who was his spiritual father. In a letter to Archimandrite Makary in Constantinople, Ieronim describes the difficulties he encountered to gain access to the abbot:

> On Sunday … I went downstairs [to the *gerondas* / elder / abbot]. I was met by [Fr] Arsenios, the Greek. I told him that I wanted to see the elder. He replied that the elder was asleep. I said this was impossible, to which he replied: "We'll wake him and bring him to the *arkhondarik* / reception room." I agreed and he was brought to me immediately. He greeted me warmly and shook my hand. I then asked [him]: "On account of the burial of Consul N. F. Yakubovsky, there was unrest. As a result you, father, issued your veto, and so the Russians were outraged and refused to come anymore for your … blessing. Now that it has become clear that your veto applied to your Greeks alone, the Russians have wanted to continue receiving your blessing. So I ask you: should the Russians get your blessing as is customary?" The elder was silent; his supervisor Evgeny replied for him: "If you wish to repent, that is good, for by acting as you did you were disobeying the elder." To this I rejoined: "Had I been allowed to see the elder at the time, I'm sure there would have been no scandal." The elder nodded his head in agreement. Evgeny now raised his voice: "Absolutely not, impossible!" …. And to cut short this endless wrangling …. I retorted: "You hold your tongue. I didn't come here to argue with you."[49]

On July 23, 1874, Civil Governor Hussein Husni Effendi and *Protepistatis* / Head of the Sacred Community Ilarion wrote an open letter protesting about Yakubovsky's burial. In it they pointed out:

> (1) no layman has ever been buried in the monastery; (2) this act is contrary to the customs of the holy place because there is a place specially reserved for the burial of the dead [outside the monastery walls]; (3) the monastery itself is not a cemetery.

The Russians had lived up to the accusations leveled against them. They took no notice of the Turkish authorities or of the Sacred Community, claiming that they "did not recognize the Sacred Community (of Athos) because they in their turn had not been recognized by the Sacred Community." It is significant that the governor and *Protepistatis* were powerless to take any further action and had no choice but to let the Russians go ahead.[50] Furthermore, *Protepistatis* Ilarion was from Zograf: the behavior of the Russians had been so disgraceful that for once even a fellow Slav had to protest. Even Count Ignat'ev disapproved of the burial. In a letter to A. N. Murav'ev, the benefactor and founder of the Serai, the ambassador wrote:

> It was the will of the Russian brotherhood that [Yakubovsky] be buried near the St Mitrofan Church, within the monastery precincts. This was in defiance to the opposition the Greeks, who demanded that the consul be buried in the cemetery. I do not approve of the leader of the Russian brethren … especially because the Father Abbot had pronounced something akin to an interdiction—against Fr Ieronim and those officiating in the burial service.[51]

Smyrnakis also quotes other letters Gerasimos wrote at the time. They show that the Russians were deliberately disobeying their abbot. On February 25, 1874, he wrote to the Sacred Community about the Russians' "seizure" of the monastery's chrysobulla and documents, and their refusal to hand them over. He concluded: "I submit to the Holy Koinotis that this withholding [of the documents] is tantamount to the highhanded seizure of my monastery." On August 21 Gerasimos wrote in a far more desperate vein to the patriarch:

> The Russians have exploited the sanctity of the monastery. They have disposed of the monastery's property, taken away its treasures and abused its emblems. They have seized the donations of benefactors for themselves. Such behavior is contrary in every way to righteous conduct and to the monastic life. The Russians have lavished money on themselves, giving naught but insult, abuse and injury to the Greek brethren. In one of our dependent lands they sold 400 sheep without my permission; they also sell flour daily to their friends; indeed, they take all our money and food without our permission. They consider the Greeks as subservient. Every day they accept into the monastery as many Russians as they can without my permission. A few days ago, they started to build new kitchens and a refectory in the upper part of the monastery, in order to be able to eat separately from the Greeks. For this reason, I have said, and I repeat, the Russian brethren have no other design than to break the cenobitic rule and trample on all the institutions of monastic life.[52]

In all the letters Smyrnakis quotes, the Russians are accused of acting against the abbot's will and in a manner unbefitting monks living in a cenobium.

Smyrnakis claims that on May 9, 1875, Gerasimos wrote his last letter to the St Panteleimon Greek brethren in Constantinople. It is unlikely that someone who was probably on his deathbed could have written with such forceful eloquence. The letter concludes:

Our great Mother Church has not yet sent any tribulation to our disobedient Russian children because she has hitherto been expecting their repentance. As she has done nothing so far to make them repent, we entreat her to put our own tribulations to an end. We do not want a Russian abbot to be appointed, for we know only too well how much they love us …. If this matter is postponed, we shall be both spiritually and morally harmed. Thus, with hot tears we beg you, and also the Patriarch, the Synod, and the National Assembly to make haste to solve our problem before my death, for my extreme old age and my body broken by suffering remind me daily that my death is very near.[53]

The letters Smyrnakis quotes have to be judged in their proper context. Perhaps Gerasimos did not write them, but was made merely to sign them. Forcing a very old and infirm man to do this must have been easy. Passions and selfish interests were by now so inflamed in St Panteleimon's that either side might have resorted to dishonest means in order to achieve its ends. Writing to Fr Makary in Constantinople, Fr Ieronim explains:

In his dotage our *geronda* / elder / abbot is in a state of child-like benevolence. He believes anything anyone tells him. Anyway, his memory has grown weak, so he quickly forgets what he's said. Our opponents have taken advantage of this; they surround him and constantly impress on him what is advantageous to them. For this reason we shouldn't ascribe too much importance to his words, which are uttered because of his confusion caused by those who fight with us.[54]

Abbot Gerasimos died, as we have seen, the day after he wrote his final letter of May 9, 1875.

CHAPTER 7

The Reign of Archimandrite Makary

The Foundation of the New Athonite Monastery
of St Simon the Canaanite in the Caucasus

The Russians suffered great anxiety in the run-up to Abbot Makary's enthronement. As we saw in the previous chapter, the three *sympraktores* / consular leaders stopped the rebuilding of Old Mountain Rusik, lest the Russians use it as a refuge. The Greeks hoped that their opponents would be expelled from Athos altogether.

Before Fr Arseny (Minin) was sent to the Caucasus to find a site for his brotherhood, the Russians called an emergency meeting. They considered petitioning Queen Victoria for permission to buy land in Australia for the new monastery, but decided not to do so.[1]

Fr Arseny came to the Caucasian region of Abkhaziya. It bordered the Ottoman Empire and had been annexed to the Russian Empire back in 1810, but its people were still unruly and rebellious subjects. Missionaries were trying to win the hearts and minds of the local, mainly Muslim population, and to remind them of their ancient Christian roots.[2] The Society for the Reestablishment of Orthodox Christianity in the Caucasus[3] was formed to set up schools, churches, and a monastery.

The Tsar's *Namestnik* / Representative in the Caucasus, Grand-Prince Mikhail Nikolaevich, was given permission by his brother, Alexander II, to found a monastery, and an annual grant of 1,200 rubles for its upkeep was earmarked. A small brotherhood from the Trinity-St Sergius Lavra near Moscow arrived to start the new community. The mission failed, owing to the "moldy climate … [causing] fevers of a particularly severe nature," and insufficient supplies and manpower.[4]

On February 8, 1875, Count Ignat'ev wrote to Mikhail Nikolaevich on behalf of the St Panteleimon Russians. Ignat'ev asked him to grant the Athonite brethren "a corner of land for a skete or a monastery which would belong to the Athonite Monastery of St Panteleimon under the same conditions as enjoyed by the Greek Nikolaevsky Monastery in Moscow belonging to the Athonite Monastery of Iviron."

Ignat'ev assured the Grand-Prince that the St Panteleimon fathers would "be useful and zealous spreaders of Orthodoxy .... Wishing for no grants, they ask merely for the land necessary to build a monastery."[5]

The request was granted and Fr Arseny arrived on August 26, 1875. He was accompanied by Monks Ioann, who knew the area well, and Agapy, a veteran of the Caucasus campaigns and former Cossack *Esaul* / captain. They looked for a site near rivers full of fish, "with the most healthy climate," and large enough "for a monastery not for sixty brethren, but six hundred."[6] The spot they chose was at the ruins of the ancient Church of St Simon the Canaanite, situated on the Black Sea Coast, 26 kilometers from Sukhumi by the River Psyrtskhi on the slopes of Mt Anakopy. On September 6, 1875, they settled into the Genoese tower overlooking the ruins, and set to work. On November 23, 1875, a fourth Athonite joined them, Fr Ieron (Nosov).

Four days later, they were granted some 330 hectares of property,[7] plus a further thousand of woodland for construction, and extra land to house the builders. On the insistence of Abbot Makary and Fr Ieronim, the dependency was to be called "the New Athos, a name bearing testimony to the close, indissoluble bond between the two houses, and to the spiritual integration of the whole region with the ancient Orthodox East and Orthodox Rus'."[8]

By October 1, 1876, less than eleven months later, a new *Pokrovsky sobor* / Church of the Protecting Veil had been built, as well as a block of monastic cells and a school for Abkhazian children. The church was consecrated on October 17.

The founding of the New Athonite Monastery could not have come at a more unfortunate time, for the whole of the Near East was preparing for war. Relations between the Russian and Ottoman Empires were strained; the situation in the Caucasian borderlands was becoming volatile.

On November 29, 1876, the New Athonite brotherhood had to move out of their monastery for their own safety. They went to Galatsky Monastery in the Kutaisy Guberniya, taking with them their church treasures. The school was closed, but Fr Ieron and two novices remained and continued taking church services. When it became too dangerous, they left. Four hundred Turkish troops landed opposite the monastery and razed the new buildings on April 28. Sukhumi was bombarded and burnt, and on May 13 the Tsebel'din Fortress where the church treasures had been stored was destroyed. Until the end of the war, February 1878, the New Athonite fathers worked in military lazarets caring for the wounded and victims of typhoid.

St Panteleimon Monastery during the Russo–Turkish War

Since the Russian Athonites were living in what was effectively enemy territory, they were just as much under threat as their brethren in Abkhaziya. At Easter 1877, pilgrims set off as usual from Odessa for the Mountain on an RSNTO ship. It could not complete its journey and they had to return overland to Russia via Trieste. As in the Crimean War, Russian Athos was cut off from the fatherland. On April 3, 1877, Ieronim and Makary received a telegram from St Petersburg urging their community to leave Mount Athos immediately for the Caucasus on a chartered French ship, avoiding Constantinople on the way. They replied via Thessaloniki Consul T. P. Yuzerfovich that they would stay put, for they feared that, should they not be allowed to return, their hard-earned victory at the monastery would count for naught.

Diplomatic relations with Turkey were cut off on the 11; the interests of the Russian Athonites were entrusted to Mallet, the French Consul at Thessaloniki. War was declared on Turkey on April 12, 1877, and Russian troops invaded Ottoman territory.[9]

Concerns were raised in the Turkish parliament about the "ten thousand" Russians on Mount Athos. This sparked off an anti-Russian press campaign led by the Constantinopolitan *I Thraki*. The Mountain, claimed the newspaper, was being Russified:

> Whence have they come? What do they seek in this Hellenic abode? Can there be so few steppes in Russia wherein to save their souls from the devil as monks? …. The Imperial Ottoman government … must surely rid the Holy Mountain of the hordes of Russian monks … and hand over to their previous owners those houses and their real estate which they, the Russians, have seized.[10]

As reported in *The London Times*, The British ambassador to the Porte, A. H. Layard,[11] wrote in a Blue Book dispatch to the Foreign Office:

> I am informed on trustworthy authority that Russian agents are at this moment actively engaged in promoting a rising of Greeks and Bulgarians, and that the intrigues and money for this object come chiefly from the Greek convents of Mount Athos. The principal person employed in the matter by the Russians is a certain Makarios [Abbot Makary], a man, I am assured, of a princely family, and who, by expenditure of a good deal of money, has had himself elected head (*Hegumen*) of the monastery of Pantelimon [*sic*].

The special correspondent of *The Times* commented: "Since this letter was written the Russian monks have been suspected of even purchasing arms and ammunition, and secreting them in the mountain."[12]

Patriarch Joachim II, meanwhile, assured the Porte that the Russian Athonites posed no threat. He was not believed and was asked to expel the Russians from Athos to the Monastery of Panagia Soumela near Trebizond, on the Black Sea.[13] The offended patriarch tendered his resignation, but the grand vizier favored caution. He and his ministers decided to leave the Russian Athonites in peace, but to send to the Mountain his representative, commissioner and keeper of the archives, Ziver Bey, who was to assess the situation. Joachim sent his exarchs to help with the Ottoman survey.

The St Panteleimon fathers in the monastery's Thessaloniki dependency were treated less civilly. On August 29, 1877, the dependency was raided in what one Russian commentator dramatically calls a "fearful pogrom,"[14] as a result of which Frs Aleksey, Adam, and Glikery were imprisoned. On the morning of September 8 a Turkish warship hove to off St Panteleimon's bearing Ziver Bey. From September 8 to 26, he and the exarchs "instituted a minute investigation, searching the monasteries and making out lists of the monks, with their nationality, age, and term of residence." The Greek monasteries were uncooperative.

The commissioners visited the Russian Monastery on three occasions. Here they found:

> no other arms than missals and beads, and no ammunition more dangerous than the beans, cabbages, gourds, and olives, which form the monks' winter stores. The chief *Hegumen* [Abbot Makary] received the Commissioners in true monastic fashion and found irresistible arguments to convince them that the charges against him and his brethren were unfounded. The Commissioners have come back charmed by the hearty welcome and generous hospitality found on the Holy Mountain. It is not the first time that the chief *Hegumen* has proved more than a match for even the Holy Synod of Constantinople.[15]

The New Athonite Monastery of St Simon the Canaanite in the Caucasus after the War

In the autumn of 1878, most of the New Athonite brethren had settled in the Genoese tower overlooking their monastery. The new buildings were reduced to a "heap of ashes"[16] and the Turks had taken away the metal roof from the tower. In December 1879 the monastery received its full legal rights and imperial sanction. Its official charter was published on June 3, 1880; the Exarch of Georgia[17] urged the fathers: "Value this charter: nobody will ever be granted such great rights and privileges."[18]

Grand-Prince Mikhail Nikolaevich signed the charter. It decreed:

1. The New Athonite Monastery, like that of St Panteleimon on Athos, is to be a cenobium.

2. The New Athonite Monastery is to be governed by the same conditions as the Greek Nikolaevsky Monastery in Moscow, belonging to Iviron; as the Ekaterininsky Monastery in Kev, and the Niamets Monastery in Bessarabia. Whereas the behavior of the brethren is to be monitored by the local bishop and the Holy Synod, the internal governance of the New Athonite Monastery is to be under the control of the Old Athonite Monastery of St Panteleimon.

3. The first abbot is to be chosen by the fathers of St Panteleimon Monastery; subsequent abbots are to be elected by the New Athonite brethren, with the approval of those of St Panteleimon, from among either the New Athonite Monastery brethren or those of St Panteleimon Monastery.

4. Initially, the New Athonite brotherhood is to total fifty; thereafter any number is permitted for the efficient execution of missionary and educational work.

5. The brotherhood of the New Athonite Monastery is to be exclusively Russian. All novices are to be trained and tonsured at the Old Athonite Monastery of St Panteleimon.

6. All passports and other documents for travel between the New Athonite Monastery, Constantinople, and Athos are to be sanctioned and expedited, so as to avoid red tape.

7. Punitive measures against disobedient monks are to be meted out either by the local bishop or by the abbot in consultation with the St Panteleimon fathers. Nobody being punished by the local diocesan authorities or guilty of civil misconduct is to be admitted to the New Athonite Monastery.

8. All the property of the New Athonite Monastery belongs to it exclusively, not to the Old Athonite Monastery of St Panteleimon.

9. Should the situation in the Near East become unstable, thus rendering the continued presence on Athos of the St Panteleimon brethren impossible, the St Panteleimon brethren are to move to the New Athonite Monastery in the Caucasus. In this case, the abbot of St Panteleimon is to become head of the New Athonite Monastery, and the present abbot of the New Athonite Monastery his second in command.

10. Alms-gathering missions may not be carried out on behalf of the New Athonite Monastery, which may not ask for money from the public treasury.

The first abbot of the New Athonite Monastery was Fr Arseny (Minin). He worked tirelessly despite failing health and was touchingly devoted to Frs Ieronim and Makary. Before he came to the Caucasus he oversaw the opening of the St Panteleimon Chapel in Moscow (1873), which was to become part of the Old Athonite monastery's dependency there. Exhausted and with failing eyesight, he longed to go back to Athos, but went to Abkhaziya without demur. In the 1877–1878 war, he played a leading role in the Red Cross.[19] He was again sent to Russia, in 1879. As a result of a fall he badly injured his leg in St Petersburg and died in Moscow of pneumonia on November 15, 1879, aged fifty-five.

The next abbot was Fr Ieron (Nosov). Born in 1829 in a peasant family from the Kostromskaya Guberniya, he spent his youth in St Petersburg working as a shop assistant. He was an avid reader and quick to learn new skills. He joined the St Panteleimon brotherhood in 1862, where he eventually became deputy treasurer.[20] After the 1877–1878 war he was the first to return to the Genoese tower. Just four months later, at the beginning of 1879, the church was rebuilt and the refurbished school admitted fifty pupils.

The driving force behind the restoration was Fr Ieron, who, despite his complete lack of training, turned out to be a brilliant engineer. He drained the stagnant pools of water to rid the area of malaria. A massive dam was built to harness the River Psyrtskhi for irrigation, water mills, and saw mills, and to supply freshwater to deep ponds stocked with trout, carp, and mullet. Professional engineers estimated the cost of the dam at tens of thousands of rubles, but Ieron's project cost just 8,000. He also had built under the river's cascades storage rooms for the refrigeration of perishable goods.

Fr Ieron ascribed the success of his projects to the Mother of God: "Perhaps with me it won't work, but with the Mother of God it will. In fact everything has worked beautifully; we haven't needed to adjust anything. Now would the Queen of Heaven ever deceive you?" His brethren were inspired by his faith. Answering the visitors who were astonished at the fertility of the gardens and orchards where bananas grew along with plants from the north such as silver birches, the monks would say: "Our place is good. We pray, we plant, and tend the land with prayer. God blesses, and everything grows, flowers, and gives fruit."[21]

No less miraculous was the building of the upper monastery. The abbot realized that the brethren needed to be housed away from the crowds of pilgrims and other laity by the seashore. Higher up it was peaceful; the climate was cooler and healthier. The lower monastery would accommodate the guest quarters and other buildings for the day-to-day running of the community.

Work on the upper monastery begun in 1884. In that year Ivan Stakheev, the Vyatka merchant who had funded the building of *Pokrovsky sobor* / Protecting Veil Central Church of St Panteleimon's, gave the monastery 1,000 rubles; a further 200 had been accumulated from collections: that was all Abbot Ieron had at his disposal for the new buildings. He appealed to Ieronim and Makary for more money, but was told: "This sum is, of course, inadequate for such an undertaking. Do not despair at having insufficient money to build the monastery. You will get everything, and in abundance. Just make sure that you live like true monks."[22]

Work started immediately. Twelve Greek stonemasons from Trebizond were employed. When the money ran out, only four remained, but they continued working virtually unpaid. Then unexpectedly, first 14,000 rubles came from St Panteleimon's, followed by another 100,000. Alexander III laid the foundation stone for the new central church when he visited with the Imperial family in 1888. The upper monastery was completed in 1911, after twenty-seven years' construction and housed 730 monks.

The Abbacy of Archimandrite Makary

On November 14, 1885, Fr Ieronim died. The scene as described by the compiler of *SRA 9/1* is a characteristically emotionally charged hagiography:

> Our spiritual father, leader and director, Priest-Monk of the Great Schema Ieronim, lay in the arms of the weeping and sobbing abbot. And all the brethren present gave way to inconsolable weeping and sobbing over their spiritual father and director. At that moment some of the brethren saw a sign from God: a heavenly fire and the stars fell like rain from the firmament; the wind hitherto blowing with fearful strength suddenly abated and a deathly silence fell ….
>
> In the sixth hour [9 a.m.] the monastic funeral preparations began. The abbot himself washed the elder's body with a sponge and warm water. Without a doubt he washed it not with water but with his own tears.[23]

Makary was devastated by his loss: "From this time, those who were close to him saw that he became noticeably drawn and haggard, and that he aged physically. Nonetheless, his spirit was fresh and luminous, and he did not cease to show love to everyone he was in contact with."[24]

The abbot worked as unstintingly as his teacher. Not being burdened by a crippling illness, however, Makary was able to toil physically as well:

> Despite being first in church and constantly busy with administrative business ... the abbot was the first to carry out [general] obediences. When a ship arrived with grain ... Fr Makary would take off his [outer] *rason* / habit, descend into the ship's hold and shovel the grain into sacks, and the brethren, encouraged by their abbot's example, would quickly heave the sacks into the monastery's roomy warehouses. He would spend a good half of the day in the sweltering heat and burning sun. The brethren often saw their abbot carrying sacks ... on his back. He was the first to go to harvest the grapes, and his loving spiritual children would follow him.[25]

Like Fr Ieronim, the abbot hardly slept: "In his last years Fr Makary developed the habit of sleeping 'superficially' in his easy chair. No sooner therefore did the door creak than he was immediately wide awake again. But then he would quickly fall asleep the moment his visitor left."[26]

If anything, Makary was busier than Ieronim had been: the spiritual father was no longer answerable for the running of the monastery and spent more of his time in seclusion, owing to his infirmity. The abbot now looked after the house, its burgeoning brotherhood, and its hordes of visitors and petitioners; he it was whose blessing had to be sought for every matter, for he was the ultimate arbiter of disputes, and problem solver. According to A. Smirnov, Ambassadorial Secretary to the Constantinople Embassy, "He needed no small measure of subtle discernment, tact, humility, and skill to control his brethren, and to get on well with the Sacred Community and with all the [other] authorities. Holding the abbot's stave was no easy matter."[27]

Despite the abbot's punishing schedule, he was unfailingly courteous and welcoming, as we have seen with his reception of Ziver Bey. He extended every hospitality to the Englishmen Athelstan Riley and his companion, the recently ordained Revd. A. E. B. Owen. These callow, recently graduated Oxonians in their twenties were treated like dignitaries, perhaps because they were subjects of a Great Power. They were ushered into the *arkhondarik* / guest reception room where:

the abbot Macarius … was sitting at the top of a long narrow room with chairs all round it, on this occasion occupied by guests and monks. [He] is a fine-looking, middle-aged man, with a long beard just beginning to grow grey, not unlike a Western abbot in his manners. The expression of his countenance is shrewd, his presence dignified, and his air commanding; altogether the sort of man one would expect to find at the head of the 1,600 Russian monks of the Holy Mountain …. He rose to receive us and shook us warmly by the hand, saying he was much pleased to see us. Glyko and "tchai" / sweetmeats and tea / were served, and we conversed, through two interpreters, about the Anglican and Oriental Churches, the monastery, and other kindred topics. However, he could not stay long with us, as the monks required his presence in the refectory; so courteously wishing us good-bye he took his departure.[28]

Riley and his companion again visited the abbot. The frivolity of the Englishman's account shows that he was blithely unaware of how busy Makary was:

We paid a state visit to Abbot Makarius, who lived in a little cell, barely furnished, but with a splendid view of the gulf. Of course we partook of the usual refreshments, but, as we consisted of Russians, Greeks, and Englishmen, owing to the difficulties of language, conversation flagged somewhat …. After a long silence, O[wen]—, feeling that he ought to say something, remarked, "Hot day."

This was translated, and also the abbot's reply, "Not so hot as yesterday."

Five minute having elapsed, I tried my hand. "Polycala" [Greek for *very good*], said I, pointing out of the window at the view. "Polycala," replied the abbot; and after this we gave up all attempts, took our departure, and went to vespers.[29]

Archimandrite Makary proved to be an able administrator. In the words of Smirnov, the consular secretary: "Thanks to the personality of Fr Makary, St Panteleimon Monastery has become as it were an intermediary between the embassy and Thessaloniki consulate on the one hand, and the whole of Russian Athos on the other."[30]

St Panteleimon Monastery was not the only Russian community to be expanding on the Mountain. By the 1880s there were upwards of 500 brethren in the St Andrew Skete. The Prophet Elijah Skete was engaged with its ruling monastery Pantokratoros in a long dispute, in which Makary tried to intervene; yet, the skete's brotherhood numbered around two hundred and was increasing. Furthermore, by the 1880s some twenty formerly empty or impoverished *kellia* with churches had been bought by Russians from Hilandar, Iviron, the Great Lavra, Stavronikita, Simonopetra, and other monasteries; these *kellia* soon became flourishing cenobia with brotherhoods of between thirty and two-hundred-and-fifty monks. Makary fulfilled his role as representative and intermediary so well that he was to become irreplaceable.[31]

During his reign, the Greeks had good cause to fear that the Mountain was in danger of becoming Russified. The Thessaloniki Consul, I. S. Yasterbov, observed: "There are some Greek monasteries, which seem to be empty and by the power of God's providence must be acquired by the Russians."[32] In the 1880s Stavronikita was so impoverished that Fr Nafanail, the St Panteleimon representative at the Sacred Community, proposed a plan to buy it, and install in it a new abbot and brotherhood taken from the Prophet Elijah Skete—notwithstanding the unresolved dispute between the skete and its Ruling Monastery, Pantokratoros. The representative died, however, and his plan came to naught. The Russians had designs on other Greek houses as well. Simonopetra, Xenophontos, Dohiariou, and Konstamonitou were poor and in danger of being taken over; and there were plans to acquire one of the St Anne Sketes.[33]

In the summer of 1883, Professors N. Damalas and P. Pavlidis were sent from Athens to the Holy Mountain to assess the situation and suggest ways of strengthening Greek Athos. They proposed, among other things:

1. To improve the education of Greek Athonites, so that they be intellectually equipped to defend themselves;
2. that a Greek Macedonian consul should visit the Mountain at least once a year;
3. to set up a Greek shipping company to rival RSNTO and to bring Greek pilgrims to Athos, now that some four thousand pilgrims were arriving annually from Russia;
4. that Greek monks seek British citizenship, like those from Cyprus, who enjoyed the protection of the British Empire.

In 1887, the Hellenic consul in Thessaloniki, T. Dokos visited the Mountain. He wrote to his foreign minister, S. Dragoumis, about the need to forbid the Russians from acquiring property in Karyes, which was in danger of becoming secularized. Dokos also suggested that the Athoniada school in Karyes, with its scant twenty-three pupils, be reorganized as a university to combat the threat of Russian intellectual superiority. "By working systematically from one center we can neutralize the actions of the Russians, who are supported by powerful protectors, for they work single-mindedly, are organized with military discipline, and are subject to political organizations abroad," suggested Dokos.[34] He also proposed to install an Hellenic representative in Karyes, as well as one in each monastery. Furthermore, the Great Lavra, Vatopedi, Iviron, and Koutloumousiou should give an interest-free loan to Stavronikita; the Russians should be forbidden from joining Greek monasteries, and from buying Athonite *kellia*; the Greeks should be stopped from going on alms-gathering missions to Russia; and the rivalry between Phanariot Greeks and Greeks from the Morea[35] should be stopped, as should giving bribes to the Turkish *kaimakam* / civil governor.

The reports of the professors and Dokos had little effect. The Russians continued to buy Athonite *kellia*, but Stavronikita, the poorer Greek monasteries, and the St Anne Skete were untouched.

In St Panteleimon Monastery, meanwhile, life under Archimandrite Makary was peaceful. The pre-1875 phyletic tensions had evaporated, and the two brotherhoods coexisted harmoniously. The dissatisfied *sympraktores* and their supporters who had left were only a handful; now the rest of the St Panteleimon Greeks were able to get on with their orderly, cenobitic lives.

The abbot saw to the development of the monastery's property outside its walls. He arranged for the cultivation of Krumitsa, an Athonite St Panteleimon dependency.[36] He told the writer and publicist I. F. Kraskovsky: "How sad I was … when I saw the extensive lands belonging to the monastery completely neglected and uncultivated. When I first arrived at Krumitsa [1853], I was simply thrilled by the beautiful view that unfurled in front of me." Kraskovsky concludes:

> Now Krumitsa boasts a fine church [consecrated in 1882], which has been built at the personal expense of Fr Makary. The land once covered by an impenetrable thicket now yields every year from its extensive vineyards and groves 18,000 *vyodra*[37] of excellent wine and almost the same amount of olive oil. More than a hundred strong young monks work there with their pruning hooks and knives for the grape harvest.[38]

Kraskovsky accompanied Fr Makary on a visit to Krumitsa. Affectionately known as *Igumenskoe Mesto* / The Abbot's Place, it was especially dear to the Makary. The trip there enabled him to recharge his batteries:

No sooner had he freed himself of his various monastic responsibilities, than he stepped on board his steamer, and blessed the monastery. As the speeding vessel noisily parted the waves, a good-natured smile lit up the father abbot's face, the furrows on his brow disappeared, and he breathed deeply. Now he could rest; he cheerfully took his seat on the small, carpet-covered platform in the middle of the deck and sank back into his leather cushion .... He chatted cheerfully with those around him, readily answering their questions and reminiscing, and all the while his head would sink ever more deeply into the cushion. The conversation would somehow die of its own accord, all would fall silent, people would tiptoe past, and the father abbot, who never was able to enjoy untroubled sleep in the monastery, would fall into a deep slumber cradled by the rocking boat.[39]

Ten kilometers closer to St Panteleimon's along the southern Athonite coast is another of its dependencies, Novaya Fivaida. Its development was commissioned by Elder Ieronim for the *siromakhi* / the wandering beggar-monks who received weekly charitable donations at the monastery and worked on the Mountain as hired laborers. Abbot Makary and a small group of brethren came to assess the site in 1879 and the next year Priest of the Great Schema Uriil started building *kellia* there. Construction continued for seven years and Novaya Fivaida became a skete. Its *kyriakon* / central church was consecrated in 1881. In 1888, 120 hermits lived in huts around the skete, which housed a further 100 brethren. The monastery spent 20,000 rubles on Novaya Fivaida annually.

Disasters struck at the end of Makary's abbacy. In August 1888 the monastery's *Pokrovsky sobor* / central Church of the Protecting Veil was all but reduced to rubble by a conflagration incurring 100,000 rubles[40] of damage. According to an eyewitness:

Amidst the general confusion and jostling we could clearly see the stocky figure of our abbot of blessed memory. He was dressed in a drab little habit highlighting his long grey beard. The elder stood motionless, as if rooted to the ground, holding aloft in his thin, trembling hands the Jerusalem icon of the Mother of God.[41] His tear-filled eyes were turned to heaven. It was thence [he] sought salvation for his beloved monastery now wreathed in bright flames.[42]

Miraculously, the Holy Table was virtually untouched, and the wooden iconostasis was unharmed. On August 29 that year, Makary's beloved Krumitsa was devastated by a fire which took four days to extinguish. Five hundred hectares of forest were destroyed. On the 30th, the abbot addressed those gathered in the *arkhond-arik* / guest reception room. Having expressed his loyal wishes for the emperor, whose name day it was, he turned his tear-filled eyes to the windows from which the conflagration's billowing smoke could be seen. His voice quavering with emotion, he exhorted the brethren to "love one another and accept the misfortune that has befallen us by submitting to God's will."[43]

Later in 1888 another fire destroyed one of the monastery's blocks of cells. Next, several vessels and one of the monastery steamships were sunk by a storm on October 1; and finally, the monastery's cargo ship *Pokrov* laden with essential supplies sank in the Bosporus.

There was a limit to what Archimandrite Makary could bear. Before Easter of 1889, sensing that his end was near, he arranged for his successor to be chosen by apostolic ballot.[44] Among the candidates for election was Archimandrite Ieron, but he asked to be excused, owing to his responsibilities in the Caucasus. Before the lot was drawn, the brethren underwent a three-day fast. "On the third day, after the liturgy, in the presence of the entire monastery, Priest-Monk Avel', having received the abbot's blessing, withdrew the name of brotherhood's spiritual father, Fr Andrey (Veryovkin)." The future abbot tearfully begged for another to be chosen, but Makary told him not to refuse: "It is not we who have not chosen you, but the Lord God Himself."[45]

During one of the Pentecost services Archimandrite Makary suffered a mild stroke. He died on June 19, 1889, just three years and seven months since the passing of his beloved teacher.

Makary's greatest legacy was his humility and love. To his last breath he remained a faithful disciple of Fr Ieronim. Together they wrote the *Ustav* / *Rule* of the monastery.[46] It is an all-embracing, yet concise document based on, among others, Saints Basil the Great, John Chrysostom, Theodore the Studite, and Isidore of Pelusium. Until Elder Ieronim died, however, "there was no need for a written *Ustav*, for he himself was as it were a living monastic rule and example for the brethren of adherence to the cenobitic way."[47] The same was true of Fr Makary, whose deathbed testament is a distillation of the *Rule*.

Makary's testament can be summarized in the following four points:

1. The brethren must scrupulously fulfil their sacred duty to commemorate the names of the monastery's benefactors;
2. the brethren must love one another selflessly;

3. the strictest cenobitic order must be scrupulously adhered to, and can be ensured only if all the brethren reveal their innermost selves to the abbot or their spiritual fathers;

4. "May the gates of our house never be shut on the mendicant and poor, and needy."[48]

Abbot Makary's wake was a fitting tribute to the generosity and spirit of non-possession so important to the once-wealthy merchants Ieronim and his pupil:

> The great monastery refectory did not close its hospitable doors for the whole of that day, for the intention was to feed all the *siromakhi* / wandering beggar-monks, and hermits, and anchorites who had come to pay their last respects to the deceased. At the monastery gates they gave these people bread, rusks, and money in memory of Fr Makary's soul.
>
> That day, a tearful and deeply moved Fr Ioann, his devoted cell orderly, fulfilled the abbot's dying wish: he gave away at the gates to the beggar-monks the abbot's threadbare habits, his little old monk's hat, his worn-out shoes, and some of his undergarments. These were the only personal possessions the deceased could bequeath. Those lucky enough to receive the precious bequest of "the kind *batyushka* / father" did so with tears of joy.[49]

CHAPTER 8

Makary's Successors:
Abbots Andrey and Nifont 1889–1905

Archimandrite Makary was a hard act to follow. On August 4, 1889, a meeting was convened in the cell of newly elected Abbot Andrey (Veryovkin), and it was decided to promulgate the *Ustav / Rule* of the monastery, which had been written in 1881 by Ieronim and Makary. Of course, the *Ustav* was no substitute for the abbot's authority; much would depend on the personality of Fr Andrey. The brethren, all of Athos, diplomats, and secular leaders had been used to the natural authority and wisdom of the charismatic Makary.

St Panteleimon's, the largest and wealthiest Athonite house, was growing so rapidly that with weak leadership its brotherhood risked becoming unruly. By the end of the century, numbers had reached two thousand monks: over 1,500 lived in the monastery itself, the rest in dependencies and *kellia / hermitages*. The monastery's lay population, made up of workers, pilgrims, and other visitors, totaled up to another three thousand souls. St Panteleimon's had become a metropolis. As Athelstan Riley observed: "The whole place is more like a small town than a monastery …. All around it and down to the water's edge are workshops, and storehouses, and dwelling houses; and still the monks are building more, so that the great monastery is increasing in extent every year."[1]

The monastery housed over 130 different artisanal workshops. Each was manned by crews of monks, not by laymen, and was headed by a master craftsman holding the honorary title of *Starets / Elder*. All novices possessing specialist training, skills, or aptitude were assigned to the appropriate Elder. Over a third of the brotherhood was employed for: the wharves of St Panteleimon's and Krumitsa; the Tsar's, the general and the Greek *arkhondariky / reception rooms*; the library as librarians, editors, bookbinders, and copyists; the hospitals as doctors, nurses, and orderlies; the monastery's three main vessels; the three *kantselyarii / offices*—the *Synodic* Office, in which the names of benefactors were entered on lists for commemoration at services, the Great Office, and the Abbot's Office; the icon-painting studio; the vineyards and olive groves; the cooperage; the two main kitchens; the monastery's overseas dependencies in Constantinople, Odessa, Moscow, and Taganrog; the Old and the New mills; the monastery's farmsteads in Kalamaria (next to Thessaloniki), Kassandra (the neighboring Halkidiki peninsula), and Krumitsa; the Great vegetable garden and orchard, and the gardens of Old Mountain Rusik and of ten of the monastery's *kellia* / hermitages. The other specialist obediences were those of plumbers, decorators, roofers, blacksmiths, bakers, gilders, carvers, fire crew, tailors, tanners, boot-makers, candle-makers, joiners, carpenters, laundrymen, welders, clockmakers, foundry workers, pharmacists, telephone technicians, salt mill workers, furriers, and even umbrella repairers. There was a dental surgery complete with mechanical drills. The monastery's photographic studio was one of the best equipped and most advanced in the world. One of its pictures is claimed to be that of Priest of the Great Schema Pavel (see Chapter 3), who died in 1840; it has not been authenticated, but if it were, it would be one of the earliest in the world.[2]

All able-bodied monks performed general obediences, helping with harvests, handling cargo (see the previous chapter), emergency repair work, dowsing fires, and building. There were also the traditional monastic obediences: singers, servers, and *ekkleziarkhi* / church service supervisors; bell-ringers, salesmen in the monastery's shops, gatekeepers, bakers of liturgical loaves, cellarers, and vestment makers.[3]

Was Abbot Andrey a strong enough leader for the vast house he inherited from Archimandrite Makary? His principal biographer, Fr Makary (Makienko), gives little away.[4] Aleksey Veryovkin was born in the Khar'koskaya Guberniya in 1834, to a peasant family living and working on state-owned land.[5] In 1846, he trained as a field hospital medic in the Voronezhkaya Guberniya, and venerated the relics of St Mitrofan of Voronezh. In 1863, he set off with his parents' blessing for the Mountain (Athos) via Kiev. He was tonsured Monk Andrey at St Panteleimon Monastery, in March the next year. In July 1868, he was ordained priest and tonsured to the Great Schema in 1871. He lived in Krumitsa until 1873. He was then sent to the monastery's chapel in Moscow. Having worked there for three years, he asked to return to St Panteleimon's, where he was made *Bratsky Dukhovnik* / Spiritual Father to the Brethren. Such were the unremarkable events of his life thus far.

Fr Makary (Makienko) emphasizes the positive aspects of the new abbot: he was an exceptionally gifted church reader[6]; Joachim III awarded him an unusual pectoral icon of the Crucifixion as a mark of appreciation. Makienko observes: "Fr

Andrey was by nature peace-loving … and trusting, for he wished constantly to do everything for everyone."[7] Did this denote "strong" leadership or a desire to pacify and avoid confrontation? Spiritual Father Agafodor (Budanov) was unambiguous: "The governance [of the monastery] after the death of Fr Makary became noticeably weaker. Abbot Andrey did not possess firmness of character and agreed to anything that was asked of him."[8] Makienko, however, is ever anxious to eschew criticism and emphasizes the abbot's extraordinary generosity. Makienko quotes another part of Father Agafodor diary:

> [Abbot Andrey] never had anything to do with the material running of the monastery, for he was a spiritual man, one who was "not of this world." He was as simple as a child and trusting. He had not the slightest notion of meanness, and seemed not to believe in wickedness. He considered all to be angels on earth, and would give generously left right, and center.[9]

Not all were keen on Archimandrite Andrey's charity: "His generosity and love of the poor was not to everyone's taste, especially to those running the monastery's finances. They were troubled by the largesse of their superior, whom they considered extravagant."[10]

Such discontent threatened the distribution of alms to the *siromakhi* / wandering beggar monks insisted on by Ieronim and Makary. In the summer of 1903, the Sacred Community, annoyed by the great crowds of ragged petitioners gathering at the St Panteleimon gates on Sundays, asked the monastery to stop the practice. Unable to decide how to proceed, the abbot convened a meeting with the monastery's senior fathers. Opinion was divided. The majority were in favor of continuing as before. The abbot, however, insisted that first prayers be said to the Mother of God, the Abbess of the Holy Mountain. On August 21, the third Sunday since the Sacred Community's interdiction, a photograph was taken of what was to be one of the last distributions of alms. The photographer captured a female figure unperceived by those present; it was seen as a visitation by the Mother of God, a clear sign that the almsgiving must continue. The Sacred Community agreed.[11]

According to Makienko, "like his great predecessors, [Abbot Andrey] considered that at the very core of the spiritual life was the unquestioning obedience to one's spiritual superior." Unfortunately, the abbot could not command such obedience.

Although not openly critical of Archimandrite Andrey, *SRA 5* alludes to his weak leadership. In the space of two pages the abbot's predilection for the spiritual is repeated three times: "Fr Andrey paid more attention to spiritual matters and delegated the running of the house to the *ekonom* / steward."[12] On the third occasion we read: "During the abbacy of Fr Andrey, despite his predilection in the main for spiritual matters, the expansion of the monastery proceeded rather successfully thanks to the active part played by the steward, Fr Pavel (Durnev)."[13]

The steward was therefore running the monastery. Priest of the Great Schema Pavel (Durnev)'s name had been one of those put forward for the election by apostolic ballot of Makary's successor in the spring of 1889. Spiritual Father Agafodor (Budanov) assesses Durnev's importance thus: "He had been the principal helper of Frs Ieronim and Makary in running the monastery .... After [their] death he was the *de facto* master and, one might say, abbot: nothing was done without him and all deferred to him."[14]

An outsider would have noticed nothing extraordinary happening in the monastery during reign of Abbot Andrey. In September 1890 Admiral V. G. Basargin arrived on the gunboat SS *Zaporozhets*. He announced that the heir to the Imperial throne, Nikolay Aleksandrovich (the future Nicholas II) and his brother Grand-Prince Georgy, who were on a world cruise, planned to visit Athos. An official invitation was issued by the monastery in Athens, but the royal visitors never came. In the same year, the monastery's new sea-faring vessel was launched and its on-board chapel was consecrated. The great Preobrazhensky Korpus was completed in 1894.[15]

On May 23, 1894, the great bell for the new belfry arrived on board a Turkish steamer. The bell is the largest on the Mountain; it was so huge that it had to be hauled up the hill to the main gates on specially constructed rails. For three days the ground was excavated, boulders were removed, and part of the monastery walls was knocked down in order to allow the bell to enter the main courtyard. The bell was hoisted on May 31 and finally ready for use in the belfry on June 1.

The brotherhood was now growing too rapidly. All who wished to join, including undesirable characters, were being admitted. Perhaps unable or unwilling to address the brethren directly, the abbot wrote the following address to his brethren:

> I have long noticed that certain among you are uncontrollably consuming strong spirituous liquors, yielding to the destructive passion of intoxication and paying heed neither to my advice nor my admonitions nor my interdictions. Rather, they heedlessly descend the path to their destruction and to that of others.[16]

A strong leader would have expelled the drunkards. Instead, the abbot forbade drinking on monastery grounds and in its dependencies on pain of excommunication. Pharmacies, where doctors and pharmacists could assume the responsibility of administering alcohol, were exempt. The ban gave rise to murmurs of discontent against Spiritual Father Agafodor (Budanov), who was thought to have influenced the abbot.

Then one of the brethren became so drunk that he was in a delirium for twelve days. During this period he had a vision in which St Anthony Pechersky thrice instructed the abbot to forbid the consumption of *raki* in the monastery. The inebriate monk reported to the abbot that according to the saint, "on account of *raki*, 7,000 monks have perished." Fr Andrey immediately forbade the consumption of this liquor in the monastery. That the crazed vision of a delirious monk prompted the abbot to issue a second interdiction cannot have inspired confidence.

In April 1895, the abbot gave his blessing for a habit and vestments to be sewed for one Monk Paisy, but the steward considered this unnecessary and overruled Fr Andrey. His authority embarrassingly undermined, Fr Andrey wrote to Fr Pavel that he no longer felt worthy to continue holding the office of abbot. The steward had become too powerful: "His influence extended not merely to the material running of the monastery, for in fact not a single decision was now taken without him. Fr Andrey was often sick: one can easily imagine how significant Fr Pavel had become for the monastery."[17] On December 5, 1895, the steward suddenly died. "Patriarch Joachim III himself elected to come to his funeral, as did all the abbots of the [Athonite] cenobia. All honors were accorded to [Fr Pavel] as if he had been the actual superior of the monastery."[18]

How did Abbot Andrey cope without Fr Pavel? A *synaxis* / meeting of the monastery elders and abbot was held. It was decided to reaffirm adherence to the *Ustav* / *Rule* of the monastery. Was it thus recognized that under Durnev's influence the monastery had become too secular, and that Ieronim and Makary's values had been forgotten? Perhaps even the stewardship of the monastery had been mismanaged. Some of the St Panteleimon buildings were hastily reassigned and the monastery's daily affairs improved: "Such a rapid rearrangement of the house's domestic management showed that the entire running of the monastery had been in Fr Pavel's hands: and not all were happy with this situation .... Certain aspects of the monastery's material life after Steward Pavel's death improved."[19] In January 1896, it was decided to build a new monastery hospital and church with the 85,000 rubles[20] collected by the superior of the Moscow dependency, St Aristokly (Amvrosiev).

Priest-Monk Nifont (Chetverikov) was chosen by apostolic ballot as Abbot Andrey's successor on February 11, 1896.[21] The abbot died on October 30, 1903, after a prolonged illness.[22] Fr Nifont was enthroned abbot on November 3 the same year and made archimandrite on 8.

In 1905, Fr Nifont fell ill. On May 26, no doubt because the abbot felt that his death was imminent, an apostolic ballot was held: Priest-Monk Misail (Sapegin) was chosen as his successor. While taking a service on October 24, 1905, Abbot Nifont declared: "Something's not right in my stomach."[23] He died the same day. Owing to the brevity of his tenure, "he had no time to do anything of note."[24]

CHAPTER 9

Archimandrite Misail

The Abbot

Mikhail Grigor'evich Sapegin was born into a peasant family in the village of Izhevskoe, of the Ryazan' Guberniya, in 1852. His entire education amounted to just two years at the local school. His brothers worked in the family fish factory in Astrakhan',[1] but at the age of twenty-two, instead of joining them, Mikhail received his parents' blessing to become a monk. He arrived at St Panteleimon's in 1874 and was sent as novice to work at the monastery's fish factory near Taganrog on the Azov Sea. Five years later, he went back to the monastery where he was tonsured with the name of Misail. Elder Ieronim and Abbot Makary saw the potential of the uneducated young monk: they put him to serve as secretary for ten years in the monastery office, an obedience usually reserved for more literate brethren. In 1885, he was ordained Priest-Monk. Upon the death of Archimandrite Makary, in 1889, he was sent to Constantinople, where he was head of the monastery's dependency. This was a post of great responsibility: the Constantinople dependency was the second most important one belonging to the monastery; it was situated at the first port of call on the trade and pilgrim route between Russia and the Mediterranean, and it was close to the Phanar, the seat of the ecumenical patriarch. Fr Misail was then transferred to the principal St Panteleimon dependency, in Odessa, of which he was in charge until he became abbot of the monastery.[2]

His illustrious predecessors, Frs Ieronim and Makary, were educated men of gentle birth. Archimandrite Nifont's parents were merchants; they would have seen to it that their son had at least a sound basic, and probably private schooling. Archimandrite Andrey, Makary's immediate successor, was of peasant stock, but had received a school education for seven years,[3] and he was then taught to sing and read Church Slavonic by his father. Fr Misail's two-year schooling seems modest by comparison. Even his monastic status seems inferior. To this day, all the monastery's abbots since Makary have been tonsured to the Great Schema, except Misail and Evlogy, the present-day incumbent.[4]

99

What he lacked in status, education, and background he made up for in character and inner qualities. Those who met him, particularly visitors from outside Athos in the 1920s and 1930s, were struck by his strength of spirit, for by that time he and his charges had endured wars, revolutions, natural disasters, and a major internal rebellion. In November 1935, he suffered a stroke, which paralyzed his right side and confined him to a chair; yet he continued to run the monastery until his death five years later. What impressed his visitors most was not so much his stoicism. As Russian émigrés, they saw in him the embodiment of the holy motherland, which they idealized and to which they would never be able to return. The writer Vladeslav Mayevsky, a Ukrainian living in Serbia, wrote rapturously:

> When I ... left Archimandrite Misail, I was enveloped in the spell of this extraordinary and great elder .... In his demeanor there was something patriarchal, something of the ideal monk from the good old times .... He seemed to be ... the true allegorical representation of the benevolent and mighty spirit of Holy Rus'.[5]

For Russian émigrés the monastery itself was a nostalgic reminder of the unattainable past: "it was nothing less than a museum of great old Russia's spiritual beauty."[6]

Hardly surprisingly, given their emotional state, these visitors tended to describe the abbot in exaggerated, hagiographic terms:

> Merely a glance at this holy elder inspired a strong filial love for him. Who could not be warmed or calmed and encouraged by his cheerful, luminous smile? "An angel in the flesh" is what his spiritual children call him. And to nobody on Athos is this description more suited than to *Batyushka* Fr Misail. I have never seen a more perfect embodiment of innocence and Christ-like love.[7]

It is clear that Abbot Misail had "presence." In the monastery's *Monahologion* his laconic description reads, "Medium build, auburn hair, and grey eyes."[8] To visitors, however, he seemed physically imposing. According to Mayevsky, he was "tall in stature, with broad shoulders and strongly built ... even when [he] sat in his deep armchair, to which his grave malady confined him."[9]

Through the haze of reverential awe, certain individualistic and believable characteristics are common in the accounts of many of those who knew the abbot. He lived in sparse quarters. I. A. Gardner, another émigré living in Serbia, describes his cell as "clean and furnished really rather modestly."[10] Its doors were open from morning to night for those who wished to see him. He rarely left the monastery and made a point of attending all services, even when infirm. He spoke and chanted in church in a pleasant baritone.[11] In his last years, he was mentally alert despite his paralysis.

There are other recurring features, which stand out from the hagiographical tropes. Meekness and humility are frequently mentioned, as are his tact and economy of words. True to his humble origins, he was down-to-earth. The writer Boris Zaytsev, who came to Athos from France in the 1920s, observes:

Fr Misail bears himself with thoroughly Russian simplicity and firmness, [so] typical of the ordinary people, to whom any kind of show is alien. With equal assurance and firmness, he both serves in church, and reads the Six Psalms in his rich baritone, and gives his hand to be kissed, and [with everyone else] makes prostrations, and listens to *Eis Polla Eti, Despota* being sung to him.[12]

The recently canonized (2019) Sophrony of Essex, who joined the St Panteleimon brethren in 1925,[13] portrayed his abbot as very much one of the people:

When [Fr] Misail became abbot, he used to like drinking. Every evening a monk would come to his cell to prevent him from drinking. He got out of the habit. He then forbade [all the brethren] from drinking within the monastery walls, [so] some would drink with their heads outside the window—some; not all.[14]

On the other hand, St Sophrony was in no doubt about his abbot's spiritual authority: "If anyone offered the slightest resistance to an order or command of Abbot Misail's, the mighty ascetic, ignoring his own position of authority, would usually reply, 'Oh well, do as you wish;' and he would not raise the matter again."[15] Instances of disobedience or questioning his authority were rare, for most of the 600 brethren alive in St Sophrony's day held their abbot in awe bordering on fear.[16]

This unquestioning respect was due to Fr Misail's unusual spiritual gifts. St Sophrony observes:

He was a strange man …. When he said something, it happened …. Everything the abbot foretold happened. He would be asked how he knew. He knew nothing. People would speak to him. He would reply jokingly. And it happened …. He had the gift of foresight. Someone asked him, "Have you got the gift of foresight?" He replied, "I don't know, but sometimes what I say happens."[17]

Above all, the abbot was able unerringly to predict when the brethren were to die. St Silouan the Athonite declared in 1938 that he was to die that year: Archimandrite Misail had foretold it.[18] And in September that year the monastery's greatest saint did indeed die.

Perhaps the abbot's most notable gift was his generosity. At its material apogee, the monastery received from the Russian government and the Holy Synod an annual grant of 100,000 gold rubles.[19] This sum supplemented the considerable income from the St Panteleimon dependencies, regular alms-gathering missions in Russia and numerous donations from benefactors. When, in the years between the World Wars, St Panteleimon's was becoming poor and even basic food was lacking, Fr Misail insisted on continuing in the tradition of Elders Ieronim and Makary, and of Abbot Andrey, to give to the needy, in a true spirit of non-possession. S. Verin visited at Easter in 1923 with fellow Russian students of the Belgrade Theological Academy. They marveled at the patristic books on sale in the monastery shop, but could not afford to buy any of them. The abbot saw to it that they could have the books for a 75% discount. "We thus acquired many fine patristic books more-or-less free of charge. This, of course, is but a grain of sand in this wondrous elder's sea of generosity," enthused Verin.[20]

Circumstances combined with Archimandrite Misail's humble spirit of non-possession helped to convert St Panteleimon's into a paragon of generosity in poverty. When he acceded to the abbot's throne, the monastery was at the zenith of its material might.[21] The brethren numbered 1,700.[22] By 1913 the monastery seemed to be expanding inexorably. A vast new central cathedral, dedicated to the Holy Trinity, was to be built. Emperor Nicholas II was to lay its foundation stone and would have been the first Russian monarch to visit Athos. The patriotic fervor of the monastery's planned loyal greeting to the tsar was full of self-assurance and confidence in a prosperous future: "In the conjunction of Your Majesty's successful arrival here with the growing necessity of building a more spacious central cathedral we see most clearly the hand of God and the desire of the Queen of Heaven."[23]

At Abbot Misail's death in 1940, there were fewer than 300, mostly elderly and infirm monks.[24] Many of the once-imposing buildings were in ruins; money and food were scarce: the monastery was becoming as impoverished as it was when the Greeks begged the Russians to reinhabit it a century before.

Liberation from Turkish Rule

The decline in the fortunes of St Panteleimon's was brought about by revolution and war. The first great change happened on November 6, 1911, when, by a majority of eighteen voices to twenty, the Sacred Community accepted a new set of canons to replace those of 1877. Both sets were drawn up by Patriarchs Joachim II and III, who intended radically to restrict the number of *kelliots* per *kellion*. As just under a quarter of the Athonite population was of Russians *kelliots*, St Panteleimon's was opposed to this measure.[25] Objections were also raised about a planned alteration of the status of a coenobitic monastery's abbot: his autocratic powers were to be weakened by the institution of short-term elected *epitropoi* / senior elders, like those running idiorrhythmic houses. It was proposed that an abbot's election be no longer solely decided internally, but that it would have to be ratified by the ecumenical patriarch. On October 31, 1912, there was another vote in the Sacred Community on the new canons, as well as on a patriarchal charter restricting the number of *kelliots* per *kellion* to six. Only fourteen out of the Twenty Ruling Monasteries voted for the new measures; the representatives of the three Slav monasteries and those of three Greek houses abstained. A month later, however, only St Panteleimon's, supported by Zograf, was in opposition. Throughout Abbot Misail's reign, the unwavering opposition of St Panteleimon's to the new Athonite regulations was to prove detrimental to the well-being of the monastery.

Armed struggle came close to Mount Athos as a result of the disintegration of Ottoman rule in Europe. The First Balkan War with Turkey started on September 25, 1912. Greece made sweeping gains in Macedonia and Thrace. The Bulgarians had similar designs and raced toward Thessaloniki, but the Greeks beat them to it by a matter of hours. Having sent an advance company of Cretan militia to secure the city, the Greeks obtained its surrender from the Turkish governor on St Demetrius' Day, October 26, 1912.

Greek Athos enthusiastically supported its fellow countrymen. Greek Athonites set off for the Balkan front and the Sacred Community gave orders that daily doxologies be served for the war effort. The Greek monasteries also offered help and hospitality to their compatriot soldiers.

The stage was now set for one of the greatest changes in the history of Athos. After almost 500 years under Turkish suzerainty, the Holy Mountain was liberated by Greek forces. The Greek flag was hoisted on Athonite territory on Friday, November 1, 1912. The liberation occasioned an emotional outpouring of national pride on Athos. At noon the next day the Greek Destroyer *Thyella* anchored off Daphne. Sixty-seven marines and officers landed and hoisted the Greek flag. One-and-a-half hours later two other destroyers, the *Ierax* and the *Panthir*, and the Battleship *Averof* appeared. Vice-Admiral P. Koundouriotis,

> who was moved by the occasion and wore on his breast his Cross of Jerusalem, with which he never parted, immediately telephoned the Sacred Community in Karyes to demand that the Turks and Civil Governor, Ali Talaat Bey Mounalazde, lay down their weapons.[26]

The Admiral then commanded Lieutenant T. Kourmoulis, Chief Officer of the *Thyella*, to assume temporary governorship of the Holy Mountain.

Meanwhile, the civil governor and his small group of Ottoman officials took shelter in St Panteleimon's. One of the Greek warships anchored in sight of the monastery and twenty Greek troops disembarked. On the advice of Abbot Misail, the Turks surrendered peacefully and were taken away on the warship.

The liberating forces entered Karyes in triumph at ten in the evening. Every belfry rang; the road was strewn with laurel branches and was lined by hundreds of rejoicing Athonites. The liberators, crowned with laurel wreaths, were met by the Sacred Community headed by Priest-Monk Grigentios of Iviron. Lieutenant Kourmoulis read out the Admiral's declaration that Mount Athos had been conquered from the Turks in the name of King George. There followed wild rejoicing. Guns were fired all night, civilians threw down their fezzes, and people hailed each other with the Paschal greeting—*Christ is risen! He is risen indeed!* The next day, 800 Greek artillery, cavalry, and infantry landed at Daphne.[27]

On November 7 a detachment led by Demosthenes Xanthopoulos was solemnly met at the gates of St Panteleimon's. The troops were put up in the monastery, which did as the other monasteries in offering hospitality to the Greek liberators. Three days later, St Panteleimon's received with honor three senior officers, who were visiting the Slav houses.

A potentially tricky situation arose the next month when a detachment of sixty Bulgarian troops, commanded by Lt G. Tsvetanov, arrived at St Panteleimon's, which once again rolled out the red carpet. The following day, the Bulgarians attended the liturgy and the lieutenant made a speech in praise of Russia's help in liberating the Slavs from the Turkish yoke. On December 6, the troops left on the monastery's ship for Zograf, where they were to be garrisoned for its safety. Overall, seventy Bulgarian troops were stationed at Zograf, Hilandar, and Xilourgou. The following summer Greece was to fight against Bulgaria in the Second Balkan War; hostility was increasing between the representatives of the two rival nations on Athos. Fortunately, the Bulgarian troops withdrew, so "the occupation of Mount Athos by the Greek armed forces was completed, as befitted this quiet corner of the globe … without any bloodshed, in the most peaceful and indeed successful manner."[28]

Although the bells of the Russian St Andrew Skete rang jubilantly with the rest, and the Paschal greeting was also heard in Slavonic, the mood of the Russians was far from joyful. At the two synaxes held in the Sacred Community on November 3 and 5, fervently patriotic statements were drafted:

> On November 3rd, the antiprospoi / representatives of all the monasteries except for St Panteleimon's met and appended to the minutes of their meeting their signatures testifying to the dissolution of Turkish rule. A formal act [to this effect] was passed on November 5th 1912.[29]

According to A. A. Dmitrievsky, the liberation of the Holy Mountain "cast gloom over the Slav monks."[30] This was a characteristically anti-Greek exaggeration of his; the Bulgarians and Serbs were probably not as depressed as the Russians. The Zograf representative was a member of the Sacred Community delegation which went to Athens in October 1913 on a visit to the king, Prime Minister Venizelos, and Metropolitan Theoklitos, head of the Church of Greece. The delegation, headed by *Protepistatis* / Senior Representative Klimis of Hilandar, handed their three distinguished hosts copies of the patriotic letters, minutes of the recent synaxes held in Karyes, and the Vote of Loyalty to Greece and her king taken by the Sacred Community earlier that month. According to Lora Gerd, the Russian historian of the Near East, "the Bulgarian and Serbian representatives [i.e., of Zograf and Hilandar], who had already been intimidated by the Greeks, could not bring themselves to refuse to put their signatures on this document."[31] The signature of the St Panteleimon's representative was, however, absent.

That Zograf took part in so patriotic a delegation might seem surprising, in view of the second Balkan War. Before that, throughout most of the second half of the nineteenth century, the Bulgarians had vied with the Turks and Greeks for supremacy in

Macedonia. Not only did they try to annex territory there and capture Thessaloniki, but they even challenged Hellenism itself: scholars such as Velenin, Rakowski, and Verkovich had put forward far-fetched theories about the Slav nature of Alexander the Great, Olympic Zeus, and Demosthenes.[32] The Greeks saw the Bulgarian Exarchate as another challenge. As we saw in Chapter 6, the new Bulgarian Church had been formed in 1870 without the blessing of the patriarch; Zograf remained patriarchist, although the Exarchate's metropolitans received hospitality there. Greek Athos could not forgive the Bulgarians for the schism.[33]

The Greeks blamed Russians for helping and promoting the Bulgarians. They would not forget Count N. P. Ignat'ev's role in the Treaty of San Stefano (March 1878). Although nothing came of his proposal to create Greater Bulgaria, and he had to retire having been politically isolated and opposed in St Petersburg, the Greeks believed that he typified the Russian-backed Pan-Slavism that was spreading like a disease into Macedonia.[34] Even the calamitous defeat the Greeks suffered at the hands of the Turks in 1897 was attributed by some partly to the Russians, who had been mistakenly relied on as one of the three Powers thought to be guaranteeing Greece's security.[35]

After 1897, Athens was in a turmoil of confusion and doubt. Expansion into Macedonia seemed out of the question. The Greek Macedonian guerrillas, the *Makedonomachoi*, however, continued their heroic struggle in the north. Their ardor was voiced by the publicist Ion Dragoumis.[36] He made passionate appeals for concrete action: there was no point in the Greek state's cautiously appointing diplomats to avoid problems rather than pursuing a proper foreign policy. Greece ought to harness the "boundless forces" at its disposal in Macedonia and Thrace; for "even if there were not a single Greek in Macedonia, Macedonia would have to be Greek."[37] It was not until 1910, when E. Venizelos became prime minister, that concerted action was taken.

The patriotic ardor sweeping over the Holy Mountain in 1912 led to a dangerous increase in the antagonism between Greek and Russian Athonites. Their rivalry was turning into enmity. The gloom that Professor Dmitrievsky described particularly affected the old-style Pan-Slavists, of whom he was one. He not only admired the "mighty, ... ever-memorable benefactor and defender of Slav monks," Count Ignat'ev,[38] but also complained about:

> How difficult Slavs and especially Russians find life on the Holy Mountain. The Greeks ... have until the most recent times been united here by both tribal bonds and a mistrust of the Slavs in general, and especially of the Russians.

"Pan-Slavism" is a special kind of nightmare, which has crushed and befuddled the conscience of the Greeks, preventing them from seeing straight.[39]

Even the most moderate Russian Athonites felt that they were not fairly represented in the Sacred Community. Although just over half the population of Athos was Russian, the Slavs had only three votes out of twenty in Karyes: those of St Panteleimon's, Hilandar, and Zograf. Ignat'ev had tried through the Treaty of San Stefano to increase the Slav vote to five by promoting the two Russian sketes (the St Andrew and Prophet Elijah Sketes) to full monastic status, but this provision was omitted in the Treaty of Berlin, which superseded San Stefano.[40] The Russian sketes lobbied for promotion at the London Conference of Ambassadors held after the conclusion of the Balkan Wars in 1912–13. Athos was mentioned at the conference, but the sketes' petition ignored. Thus, concluded Dmitrievsky, the Russian sketes were left "in the same abased, disenfranchised position [as before], rendering them wholly dependent on their ruling monasteries."[41]

Overall, the Russian Athonite community pressed for more fundamental changes. St Panteleimon's wished to be promoted to the rank of lavra along with the Great Lavra, Vatopedi, and Hilandar; and the largest Russian *kellia* felt that they should be granted skete status. The 1877 canons and those of 1911, however, emphasized that the whole territory of the Holy Mountain was divided exclusively among the Twenty Ruling Monasteries, whose number and rank were *ametavlitoi* / immutable, as was the number of sketes.

Understandably, Greek Athos dug in its heels. If more Russian monasteries and sketes had been added to the Athonite community, the Russians' threatened takeover of the Holy Mountain might have become a reality. As it turned out, the status quo was maintained: St Panteleimon's remained nineteenth out of twenty in seniority; there were only three Slav votes in the Sacred Community, and the two sketes continued to be subservient to their Ruling Monasteries.

It is as well that the Russians did not bully their way into a position of unassailable strength on Athos. They scorned the Greeks, whom they considered spiritually and socially inferior. The Russian Foreign Ministry opposed the integration of the Holy Mountain into Greece, for such a move "could in some way be justified only if Greek Athos possessed genuine moral virtue. Unfortunately, the time when the spirituality of Greek monasticism was in the ascendency has long passed."[42]

The Russians could get their way only through external pressure. Russian diplomats adopted a three-pronged attack: income from the Greek monasteries'

Bessarabian dependencies was blocked; donations from Russia were frozen, and alms-gathering missions were stopped. The Greek monasteries particularly affected by these restrictions were quick to make concessions to their dependent sketes and *kellia*,

> and a golden shower poured copiously from the embassy and consulate into the pockets of the cupidinous [Greek] brethren. Soon, however, new misunderstandings would arise on Athos and once again our government would resort to its tried and tested methods, and so the process continued endlessly.[43]

Urgent action had to be taken during the Second Balkan War. In January 1913, the king of the Hellenes decreed that Greek soldiers be billeted in all twenty monasteries. The Russian Athonites appealed to the Great Powers, but in the summer, Greek troops once again occupied St Panteleimon's. Russian diplomats and the Foreign Ministry strongly objected; the troops left the monastery, and, on August 17, all Greek forces left the Holy Mountain.

Another way Russian Athos could get its way was by ensuring that the Holy Mountain remain under the aegis of the ecumenical patriarch. In this the Russians were successful, despite the wish of some Greek Athonites to submit to the metropolitan of Athens, the head of the Church of Greece.[44]

Both Russian diplomats and Russian Athonites were keen that the Holy Mountain become not a part of Greece, but an international, independent protectorate of the six Orthodox nations in the Near East. Russia would be the senior of these. The protecting nations would be responsible for the policing and civil administration of the Holy Mountain, as the Turkish civil governor had been. Naturally, the liberated Greeks opposed the planned protectorate. For them, becoming part of the kingdom of Greece was the fulfillment of a patriotic dream and realization of liberty.

The Sacred Community wrote in its *Réfutation* of the Russians' Memorandum for the London Conference of Ambassadors that the international neutrality of the Holy Mountain was unthinkable. Athos, which had been conquered by, and therefore rightly belonged to, the king of the Hellenes, was going to have to be shared with the Slav barbarians. "Liberty," proclaims the *Réfutation*,

> is an Hellenic creation and, together with Greek learning, has powerfully contributed to civilization and the appeasement of the whole of Humanity. If, therefore, in this period, savage and barbaric peoples should enjoy this boon under the Hellenic flag, are we, the monks of Mount Athos, to be subjugated

under the scepter of a less liberal, less progressive and less civilizing race? Never!![45]

Once again, St Panteleimon's was the fly in the ointment. It opposed the union with Greece, just as it had taken no part in November 1912 synaxes or in the delegation to Athens, and had withheld its signature from the loyal declaration. The Russian monastery, however, needed more support in the Sacred Community; it wanted to alter the structure of Athonite governance and opposed the new canons. An international protectorate would have been very beneficial to St Panteleimon's.

CHAPTER 10

The Name of God Dispute

Just when Greek and Russian positions were becoming ever more polarized, and wars and the overthrow of centuries of Turkish rule were making the situation on the Holy Mountain increasingly volatile, a major internal upheaval posed an even greater threat to the Russian community. For some five years until 1913, St Panteleimon's and the St Andrew Skete were in the throes of what became known as the *Afonskaya smuta* / Athonite Troubles.

As an historical phenomenon, the Troubles were in keeping with the upheavals affecting the whole of Russian society at the beginning of the twentieth century. The revolutions leading up to the abdication of Tsar Nicholas II and the Bolshevik takeover are well documented. Less well known, yet in keeping with the troubled spirit of the times, were the monastic rebellions inside Russia.

Life in three major monastic centers in Russia was seriously disrupted at the same time as it was in the Russian Athonite community. After the war with Japan (1904–1905), a number of those serving in the army and navy entered the Solovetsky Monastery, on the White Sea. The Holy Russian Synod allowed them to take their monastic vows more rapidly than usual. By 1913, they had fomented a rebellion against the abbot, who was deposed in August 1917. In 1908, there was a rebellion in the Glinskaya Pustyn' (Sumskaya Oblast', close to the north-western border of today's Ukraine), a year before the beginning of the Athonite Troubles. In 1910, there were upheavals in Optina Pustyn' (Kozel'sk, south of Moscow).[1] Priest-Monk Simeon (Kulagin) of Optina Pustyn' observes:

> These ... monastic rebellions simultaneously seized hold of several of the largest Russian monastic houses .... It is hardly necessary to speak of some external coordination of these upheavals, although such a theory will doubtless have its proponents. These events were a direct result of the changes Russian society was undergoing. The events ... were the result of rebellions by a part of the brethren against ecclesiastical authority—in all four cases [i.e., the

110

Name of God Dispute and the three rebellions in Russia] against the head of the house—as well as against the elders. [Furthermore], the events, despite certain individual characteristics in each case, such as geographical location, chronology, specific reasons for the rebellions and the numbers involved, were the undoubted result of revolutionary movements in Russian society at the beginning of the twentieth century. During the first Russian revolution of 1905–7, the underground revolutionary activity and mass discontent simmering beneath the surface ... erupted into every corner of society .... It goes without saying that the revolutionary and rebellious spirit could not fail to penetrate the Church and especially the monasteries .... Ancient canonical traditions, especially those of obedience to the abbot and elders, were brought into question by some monks. A secular revolutionary idea of "fairness" had entered the monastic confines.[2]

The Athonite Troubles were sparked off by the appearance in 1907 of Schema-Monk Ilarion (Domrachov)'s *Na Gorakh Kavkaza / On the Mountains of the Caucasus,* which describes the life of hermits in the Caucasus.[3] His principal thesis, based on his personal experience and examination of the Jesus Prayer,[4] states that "in the very name and the very words Jesus Christ the Godhead is present"; hence "the name Jesus is God Himself."[5]

The well-known Moscow theologian, Fr Pavel Florensky, wrote the book's foreword. *On the Mountains of the Caucasus* was passed by the Church censors and initially caused little reaction in Russia. Soon, however:

> The Grand-Duchess Elizabeth Fyodorovna (Tsar Nicholas's sister-in-law) saw no reason not to finance [it] through her convent of Sts Martha and Mary; ... and a remarkably large amount of the Russian public saw no reason not to buy it. Within three years its popularity even called forth a second edition .... By 1912, subsidies were no longer needed, and the Kievo-Pecherskaya Lavra reportedly paid Ilarion a large sum for the right to issue the third edition that year.[6]

On the Holy Mountain, however, the book gained fame almost by mistake. The St Panteleimon spiritual father and Karyes *antiprosopos* / representative, Fr Agafodor (Budanov—see Chapter 8), "became the unwilling initiator of the Athonite disputes over the Name of God."[7] In 1908 Fr Ilarion sent him his book. For his part, Fr Agafodor sent a copy to Prior Ieronim (Silin) of the St Andrew Skete, describing the book as "very harmful" and asking whether the prior could find an educated monk who could "pick holes in it."[8] The prior asked Priest Schema-Monk Antony (Bulatovich) to cast his eye over it. Initially, Fr Antony was unimpressed, but he gradually warmed to the book and soon became an active supporter of the Name-Glorifiers.

Fr Agafodor commented on Fr Ilarion's letter to him accompanying the book:

> Fr Ilarion asked me to find out from the ascetics here who practice the Jesus Prayer what they think of his book. He also asked me to find out what Fr Khrisanf of the Prophet Elijah Skete thinks. This ascetic responded to Fr Ilarion with a whole review of his book. On the request of Fr Khrisanf, I sent this review to Fr Ilarion because Fr Khrisanf, who did not know the address, sent [the review] to me for forwarding with the proviso that the review be written solely for Fr Ilarion personally, and not for publication.[9]

Khrisanf's review was sharply critical; it incensed Fr Ilarion, who started corresponding particularly with the monks of the St Panteleimon Novaya Fivaida Skete. He exhorted them to stand up for the name of Jesus, in return for which they would gain the crowns of confessors. Fr Ilarion also asked Fr Agafodor to justify himself.

The book soon caused a stir in the Russian Athonite community. It was read with interest in St Panteleimon, Novaya Fivaida, and the St Andrew Skete, and divided its readership into two camps. The majority were taken with the book; they were for the most part simple, uneducated monks, who were versed in the ascetic life and practiced the Jesus Prayer. As one of the St Panteleimon brethren observed:

> Anyone ... who dislikes this book has a bad time of it .... There are, especially in our St Panteleimon Monastery, no dogmatists, but the simple-minded monks consider the book to be unimpeachable .... The well-read monks, who understand the Russian language, call this book with its dogmatic mistakes nothing short of heretical and say that it should be burnt.[10]

One of the book's principal opponents was Priest-Schema-Monk Aleksey (Kireevsky), a senior and influential monk of St Panteleimon's.[11] He was of gentle birth and had received a university and seminary education.

Typed copies of the review were circulated among the Russian community. Archimandrite Misail commented:

> Schema-Monk Ilarion's book ... was not initially widely circulated among our brethren. When Priest Schema-Monk Aleksey ... openly declared himself to be against it and he was supported by many of the brethren, and when ... the

review of Monk Khrisanf of the Prophet Elijah Skete appeared, only then ... a certain movement began, not so much in favor of ... Ilarion's book as against ... Aleksey and Khrisanf.[12]

By 1912, the opponents and supporters of Ilarion's book had become irreconcilably entrenched in their respective camps. In February that year, Fr Aleksey sent Fr Khrisanf's review to Archbishop Anthony (Khrapovitsky) of Volyn', an influential member of the Russian Holy Synod. The review appeared in the archbishop's ecclesiastical journal, *Russky Inok*, thus affecting "the course of the controversy and [giving] it a new lease of life."[13] Those who subscribed to the divinity of the Name of Jesus referred to themselves as *Imyaslavstsy* / Name-Glorifiers—or *Ispovedniki* / Confessors; they called their opponents Name-Fighters / *Imyabortsy*. In the opposing camp, the Name-Fighters disparagingly called them *Imyabozhniki* / The Name of God People.[14]

Archimandrite Misail noticed an ominous change in the demeanor of the St Panteleimon Name-Glorifiers:

They all ... immediately displayed a spirit of impatience, enmity, anger, hostility and ... aggression towards those of the brethren not agreeing with their religious delusions ... Everyone in our monastery noticed that as soon as anyone started to incline towards Ilarion's delusion ... he became gloomy, choleric and tetchy, despite his formerly exceptionally humble and docile nature.[15]

In the autumn of 1911 Archimandrite Misail went to Novaya Fivaida, which was by now a stronghold of the Name-Glorifiers. A *sobor* / meeting of its monks was convened and a statement was drawn up to be signed by all attending: "I believe and I confess that in the Name of Jesus Christ He Himself is present."[16] The archimandrite wished to placate the Name-Glorifiers and was ready to sign, but was prevented from doing so by Fr Aleksey. At Easter next year Fr Misail issued a strong warning to the Fivaida Name-Glorifiers. If they did not desist from involvement in or spreading of their contentious doctrine, they faced excommunication. It was too late; the Name-Glorifiers would not be swayed.

Meanwhile, *On the Mountains of the* Caucasus inspired Fr Antony (Bulatovich) of St Andrew Skete to write. With the blessing of his prior, he sent his first article, *O poklonenii Imeni Bozhii / On the Veneration of the Name of God*, to Odessa, where it was published in the skete's journal in April 1912. In Lent that year Fr Antony published a brochure entitled *O Iisusovoy molitve / On the Jesus Prayer*. In May, he addressed a letter to Archbishop Anthony (Khrapovitsky). It was signed by "Athonite Monks" and refuted Fr Khrisanf's criticisms of *On the Mountains of the Caucasus*. The archbishop replied by urging the Fivaida fathers to be obedient to Archimandrite Misail; he also wrote an excoriating commentary on Fr Ilarion's book in the May issue of *Russky Inok*. Meanwhile, the Pochaevskaya Lavra[17] published Fr Khrisanf's refutation of Fr Antony's *On the Veneration of the Name of God*.

Fr Antony (Bulatovich) did not stop writing. The culmination of his work in 1912 took two months of ceaseless toil: a team of brethren read Patristic literature about the Name of God and supplied him with excerpts, which he conflated in *Apologiya very v Bozhestvennost' i imyon Bozhiikh i imeni Iisus / An Apology for the Belief in the Godhead of the Names of God and the Name of Jesus*. On July 23, seventy-five typescript copies were distributed among the Russian Athonite community.

Until the summer, Archimandrite Ieronim (Silin) had been on good terms with Fr Antony (Bulatovich). On July 19, however, the prior was visited by Fr Aleksey (Kireevsky), who handed him a letter from Father-Confessor Agafodor. The spiritual father wrote that Archbishop Anthony was furious both with the prior for permitting such goings on in his skete and with Fr Antony (Bulatovich). Fr Aleksey insisted that Fr Antony be stopped from writing a word more about the Name of God and from receiving the Fivaida hermits.

The prior wrote back promising to do as he was asked. When Fr Antony presented him with the *Apology*, the prior coldly upbraided him for "daring to oppose Archbishop Anthony, a Doctor of Theology and senior Russian hierarch."[18] On July 25, 1912, the prior ordered Fr Antony to burn the *Apology*. The latter refused, so the prior excommunicated him. Accusing the prior of heresy, Fr Antony left the skete for the *Kellion* of the Annunciation belonging to Elder Parfeny, a fellow Name-Glorifier. There Fr Antony continued his writing unabated. His *Apology* was published in Moscow the next year and two further major works of his promoting the Name-Glorifiers' cause came out in Petrograd.

On August 13, 1912, Fr Antony wrote to Patriarch Joachim III requesting him to defend the Name-Glorifiers. At the same time, Fr Aleksey (Kireevsky) came to petition the patriarch in support of the Name-Fighters. Greek Athonites had also warned the patriarch about what they called a new heresy being professed by the Russians. Although Joachim did not receive Fr Aleksey, he took the side of the Name-Fighters. He commissioned the Halki Seminary to examine the new doctrine. On August

27, the seminary declared it to be heretical. On September 12, Joachim III issued an encyclical condemning the "new false doctrine" and forbidding the reading on Athos of Ilarion's book because "it contains much which is erroneous, and leads to delusion and heresy."[19]

The patriarchal missive was read aloud to the senior St Panteleimon monks. It was an unimpressive document. Couched in the most general terms, the text made it clear that its author was unfamiliar with Ilarion's book. Indeed, it was possible that nobody in the Halki Seminary knew Russian well enough to understand it, let alone read it in the short time the patriarch allowed for its perusal.[20]

Archimandrite Misail felt he had to act. On August 20 he and the monastery's Council of Elders drew up the *Akt o nedostopokloyaemosti imeni Iisus / Directive Against the Veneration of the Name of Jesus.* Just as in the Fivaida Skete the previous autumn, the statement was read publicly and all those present had to sign it to show their agreement. Unfortunately, the abbot's move proved to be more divisive than decisive. Many of the brethren refused to accept the directive; seditious meetings were held in the monastery to decide how to combat the Name-Fighters.

On December 2, more than a hundred brethren gathered in Novaya Fivaida Skete to discuss *On the Mountains of the Caucasus* and Fr Khrisanf's review. The meeting concluded with the statement:

Based on Scripture and the writings of the Holy Fathers, we confess that the Name of God is God Himself. The Name of Jesus Christ is the Lord Jesus Christ Himself and is to be glorified equally with the other Names of God. But as the review of Monk Khrisanf is contrary to Holy Scripture, we deem it to be heretical. We therefore cast it aside and, as a mark of the steadfastness of our confession, we kiss the Cross and the Gospel Book.[21]

In the St Andrew Skete, Fr Antony (Bulatovich) staged a coup. His prior returned to the skete on January 8, 1913, after an absence of more than two months in Macedonia. Four days later, Archimandrite Ieronim and eighteen senior brethren were expelled, followed shortly by thirty others. His place was taken by Archimandrite David (Mukhranov), a prominent Name-Glorifier.[22] On January 13, Bulatovich led Fr David into the central church and solemnly handed him the prior's staff in front of the gathered brethren. Vatopedi, the governing monastery, was taken by surprise; it refused to accept the new appointment, on the grounds that no ballot had been held. The next day the skete presented a petition to the monastery with 307 signatures requesting ratification of the new prior's appointment. Vatopedi agreed to confirm the appointment on January 19, but on the day before gave way to pressure from the Russian Embassy in Constantinople and postponed the new prior's enthronement for a few days. Prior Ieronim had been complaining to Ambassador M. N. Giers, for whom the Rebellion of the Name was a threat to the prestige and privileges enjoyed by Russia on the Holy Mountain.

The Sacred Community was now under considerable pressure to act. Vice-Consul V. S. Scherbina demanded that Fr Ieronim be reinstated: Russia did not recognize the new prior and would treat the Name-Glorifiers as rebels. At a series of synaxes held in Karyes between January 18 and 29, 1913, Fr Antony (Bulatovich) was declared to be a heresiarch, who had forced the skete fathers to take on the "new dogma on the divinity of Jesus." Finally, "the wrong-believing Priest-Monk Antony Bulatovich, Archimandrite David, as well as all their fellow dogmatists" were excommunicated pending trial by the patriarch. The declaration concluded: "The Ecumenical Patriarch and the Athonite Sacred Community ... while safeguarding the purity of Orthodoxy, find that those who do not recognize the authority [of the Patriarch and Sacred Community] must not reside on the Holy Mountain."[23] Once again, no doubt fearing the dangerous ambiguity of the wording, the cautious St Panteleimon representative was the only one belonging to the Twenty not to append his signature.

Ambassador Giers applied further pressure on the St Andrew Skete. For five months all outgoing and incoming mail was blocked; no money could be transferred to the skete and supplies arriving by ship were stopped. The Name-Glorifiers responded by becoming more active. In St Panteleimon's, a dynamic and vociferous group led by Schema-Monk Iriney (Tsurikov) opposed the established order.

They staged a mini-coup in St Panteleimon's. On January 14, 1913, Archimandrite Misail read to the brethren assembled in the Pokrov Central Church the Patriarch's letter condemning the Name-Glorifiers. At a meeting held on January 21, in the presence of Vice-Consul Scherbina, the Name-Glorifiers for the first time publicly declared their beliefs. Two days later, without the blessing of the abbot, they rang the great bell to summon the brotherhood. Fr Misail believed that he had no choice but to sign the rebels' *Ispovedanie Imeni Bozhiya / Confession of the Name of God* and to destroy his own *Directive Against the Veneration of the Name of Jesus* of August 20, 1912. The Name-Glorifiers then read out a condemnation of the monastery's senior fathers, who were accused of Name-Hating heresy and of spreading Fr Khrisanf's "sacrilegious" review. Eight elders were singled out; as "the principal disseminators of the heresy," they were to be expelled from the monastery. The abbot, Dean Varlaam, and Treasurer Averky signed the condemnation.

Was Archimandrite Misail's capitulation to the Name-Glorifiers the act of a helpless, weak man, or did he save the monastery from the fate which had befallen the St Andrew Skete? Father-Confessor Agafodor, one of the eight to be expelled, justified his abbot's actions:

> Although [he] signed the condemnation, he did so against his conviction and will, while recognizing that Orthodox people had been wrongfully accused as disseminators of heresy .... Had [he] not signed, he would have instantly been expelled from the monastery, as happened in the St Andrew Skete.[24]

For his part, Archimandrite Misail later wrote that he had complied in order to safeguard the monastery's treasury and prevent the outbreak of complete anarchy.

A constitutional regime was instituted in the monastery, which was to be governed by a council of elders elected every three years; the abbot was to become a mere figurehead. Thus one of the main reasons why St Panteleimon's had opposed the new canons drawn up by Joachim III and proposed by the Sacred Community was becoming a reality. No ballot was held for the election of the twelve; their names were read out to tumultuous applause. There followed the same rejoicing as when Athos was liberated by the Greeks. The brethren hailed each other with the Paschal greeting of "Christ is risen!" and wept with joy.

On January 25, 1913, the expelled fathers left the monastery. The newly appointed council soon acquired the keys to the treasury from the abbot. As Archimandrite Misail and the minority of brethren still supporting him stayed on, however, the Name-Glorifiers' victory was not complete. The latter made a further five unsuccessful attempts to seize complete control of the monastery. On March 15, agitation was caused by rumors circulating to the effect that a new abbot was about to be chosen and all the Name-Haters were to be expelled. On March 19 a meeting was held at which demands were made to restrict the abbot's powers. The crisis was averted because a small detachment of Greek soldiers arrived, and calm was restored.

Meanwhile, Fr Antony (Bulatovich), hoping to petition the Holy Synod and other authorities on behalf of his cause, had left the Holy Mountain for Russia on February 12, 1913, never to return. On February 15 Patriarch Germanos V[25] summoned Frs Antony (Bulatovich) and David (Mukhranov) to Constantinople to explain themselves.

On March 7 the Russian Foreign Ministry sent State Councilor and Senator P. B. Mansurov to St Panteleimon's and the St Andrew Skete to pour oil on troubled waters. His mission ended in failure. As he explained in a report addressed to the foreign minister, S. D. Sazonov, and the procurator to the Holy Synod, V. K. Sabler: "Religious activity during my stay on Athos became extremely turbulent. People were walking about as if in a haze, constantly arguing about the Name of God."[26]

Sabler warned that the situation was difficult to handle because the views of the Name-Glorifiers were similar to those of Fr John of Kronstadt, who had become very popular in Russia.[27] Indeed, as Antony (Bulatovich) himself had pointed out in his letter to Archbishop Anthony (Khrapovitsky) the previous year:

> These [words] belong not to us or to Fr Ilarion [Domrachov], but to the Russian Pastor John of Kronstadt of most blessed and gracious memory: "When you say to yourself in your heart or pronounce [out loud] the Name of God, the Lord or the Most Holy Trinity, or the Lord of Sabaoth, or of the Lord Jesus Christ, then you have in that Name the entire essence of the Lord .... His name is He himself."[28]

Bulatovich greatly admired John of Kronstadt, whom he had met and conversed with. Bulatovich entitled one of his main works in defense of the Name-Glorifying dogma *Moya mysl' vo Khriste / My Thought in Christ*. This title is strikingly similar to the title St John's memoirs, *Moya zhizn' vo Khriste / My Life in Christ*.[29]

Sabler's report written in April 1913 to Foreign Minister Sazonov was presented to Emperor Nicholas II, who underlined the following sentence: "If the State in its power were to clash with these two whose names are dear to the people [i.e., those of John of Kronstadt and the Holy Mountain], it would be treading on very dangerous grounds."[30]

Fr Iriney (Tsurikov) of St Panteleimon's now became the leader of the Name-Glorifiers. At the beginning of April 1913, Igumen Arseny, a former synodic missionary, arrived at St Panteleimon's.[31] According to Archimandrite Misail, he played a critical part in the monastery rebellion. In his commentary on the "Events in St Panteleimon Monastery During the Religious Ferment of 1913," the abbot wrote:

> The arrival on the Holy Mountain of ... Igumen Arseny (who has now died outside communion with the Holy Church and who had initially denounced Schema-Monk Ilarion, author of *On the Mountains of the Caucasus*, and its apologist, Priest Schema-Monk Antony Bulatovich, but then became a

zealous defender of the above-mentioned people) once and for all convinced the majority of our monastery's brethren to take the side of Ilarion's folly.[32]

The abbot wrote that Igumen Arseny used his authority as a synodic missionary both to "inspire those who were losing their way" and to sway a few who had hitherto remained "faithful to the teachings of the Holy Church." Furthermore, the Union of "Confessors" established by him [the Archangel Michael Union of the Confessors of the Name of God, April 11] and the distribution of his proclamations succeeded in stirring up the brethren against the "lawful authorities of the monastery, which, despite all temptations, continued to be loyal to the doctrine of our Mother, the Holy Church."[33]

Although the Name-Glorifiers outnumbered their opponents on Athos, opposition to them strengthened from the Russian Holy Synod, the Patriarch, and the Russian Foreign Ministry and diplomatic circles. Archbishop Nikon (Rozhdestvensky),[34] a Synod member, wrote to St Panteleimon's a letter conciliatory in tone. In it he urged the brethren not to read *On the Mountains of the Caucasus* because it brought about conflict,[35] and he warned that the Russians risked losing their houses if they did not heed the Patriarch.

On April 5, 1913, Patriarch Germanos V sent an encyclical condemning the doctrine of the Name-Glorifiers as pantheistic, "newly appeared and unfounded," and based on "sacrilegious scandal and heresy."[36] That same day, Fr David (Mukhranov) appeared before the patriarchal court. Having promised that he would not lay any claims to becoming prior of St Andrew's Skete, he was allowed to return to the Holy Mountain.[37]

In the sixth week of Lent, the six fathers expelled from St Panteleimon's read out in Karyes a statement of recent events in their monastery. The Sacred Community responded by sending Archimandrite Misail a letter explaining that should the expelled fathers not be allowed back, the monastery would be declared heretical. At first, the Name-Glorifiers chose not to respond, but then replied that they would do as they were told and awaited a visit from the Sacred Community. Nothing more happened from Holy Week to a fortnight after Easter.

On April 29, 1913, the Name-Glorifiers sprang into action. They cut the telegraph wires linking St Panteleimon's with Daphne and Karyes. Once again, an attempt was made to oust the abbot and seize the treasury. As on March 15, a detachment of Greek soldiers arrived in response to a call for help from Archimandrite Misail and calm was restored.

On May 1 there was another Name-Glorifiers' meeting conducted by Fr Iriney (Tsurikov). He read out a confession of the Name-Glorifying faith and invited all present to show their support by signing it, and then take an oath of allegiance by kissing the Gospel Book and Cross. Deacon Ignaty (Mitryutin) then urged everyone to join the Archangel Michael Union of the Confessors of the Name of God, which had been founded on April 11 by Igumen Arseny. About a third of the monastery's brethren, 554 monks, did so.

On the abbot's invitation, an eighteen-strong delegation from the Sacred Community arrived at St Panteleimon's on May 3. In front of the assembled brethren in the Pokrov Central Church, a Sacred Community representative read out the patriarch's encyclical condemning the Name-Glorifiers' dogma as sacrilegious heresy. The brethren were invited to sign the letter to show that they were renouncing their folly. The meeting threatened to descend into chaos. Writing in "Events in St Panteleimon Monastery During the Religious Ferment of 1913," Archimandrite Misail observed:

> Monk Iriney and the other ringleaders caused a commotion in the church, urging the brethren not to sign the patriarchal letter. A scandal was averted only by the exit of the abbot and the Sacred Community [delegation]. Furthermore, as the patriarchal letter was being read, many of the rebels were addressing curses to the Sacred Community, and were calling the patriarch, the Sacred Community, the abbot and his successor, and the rest of the brethren who disagreed [with the Name-Glorifiers] heretics and yids.[38]

Another meeting took place the next day. Fr Iriney asked for the patriarchal letter to be read out again. When Deacon Ignaty reached the patriarch's explanation that the dogma had been examined and found to be false by the Halki seminary, "Iriney stopped the reader and poured scorn on the Holy Church and the patriarchal encyclical: 'Do you hear that, brethren! In Halki—we don't know any Halki; but show us the Holy Fathers: we don't recognize Halki.'"[39]

At this point one of the monastery's guests, a Moscow Theological Academy lecturer, Priest-Monk Panteleimon (Uspensky), tried to reason with the Name-Glorifiers, but he was shouted down and called a madman: "When he started to explain that a mere name could not possibly be called God, a loud commotion was raised in the throng and he had hastily to retreat because he risked being beaten up (if not killed)."[40] The Sacred Community delegates held one more meeting, which also ended in failure. They returned to Karyes on May 8, 1913.

Abbot Misail's position was becoming increasingly uncertain. On May 15 Fr Iriney and some of his followers went to the Novaya Fivaida and the Krumitsa Sketes. They deposed the Fivaida head, Priest-Monk Seraphim, and replaced him with a fellow Name-Glorifier, Priest-Monk Flavy. On May 26 the Greek soldiers left the monastery; Fr Misail no longer felt safe enough to appear in church or the refectory, confining himself instead to his own quarters. In desperation, he telegraphed the emperor: "Your Majesty, save our monastery from revolution."[41]

It was decided that concrete measures had to be taken against the Name-Glorifiers. The Holy Synod through Procurator Sabler authorized Archbishop Nikon to stop the schism in the name of the emperor. According to Sabler:

> The danger was that all Orthodox Russian monks could be expelled from the Holy Mountain by the Name of God People, and then, at the orders of the patriarch and the Sacred Community, the Name of God People themselves would be expelled by the Greek armed forces occupying the Holy Mountain. It goes without saying that the Russian government authorities could permit neither the expulsion of Orthodox Christians by heretics nor allow the subjection of thousands of Russian subjects or of the Russian houses' property, worth many millions, to the disposal of another state. For after the patriarch had given every chance to the Russian ecclesiastical authorities to appease the Russian houses, even the ecclesiastical authorities could not allow [things to continue thus].[42]

On May 23, 1913, Archbishop Nikon (Rozhdestvensky) set off for Mount Athos accompanied by V. S. Scherbina representing the Foreign Ministry, and Professor S. V. Troitsky, a theologian and expert in canon law. On June 5 Abbot Misail learnt that the Name-Glorifiers intended imminently to apprehend him in his quarters, by any means of force necessary. Fortunately for him, the Russian naval vessel, the SS *Donets*, with the archbishop's party anchored off St Panteleimon's the same day.

Archbishop Nikon, Troitsky, and Scherbina, accompanied by the Constantinople consul-general Shebunin, the secretary to the Russian Embassy in Constantinople, B. S. Serafimov, the ship's captain, and his armed crew landed at St Panteleimon's. The abbot greeted them amidst a throng of monks who eyed the visitors with unfriendly curiosity. The archbishop addressed the brethren in the central church. He began innocuously by recounting some childhood memories but went on to say that he had learnt of a great temptation, which had caught the whole Orthodox world unawares, about the Name of God. His audience uttered not a word. After taking coffee in the *arkhondarik* / guest hall, he shut himself away in the *Donets* for a week, while Troit-sky, Shebunin, Serafimov, and Scherbina, escorted by officers and crew, frequently visited the monastery to try and win over the rebels. Meanwhile, all those who had been expelled by the Name-Glorifiers were allowed back to St Panteleimon's.

The archbishop's party with its armed escort was an imposing sight. Many of the brethren must have thought of changing their allegiance. Fr Iriney's group continued to show their vigorous opposition, however. On June 7, Shebunin's meeting with the monastery's senior fathers was loudly heckled and the rebels tried to lock the gates. Professor Troitsky arranged to meet in the library any of the brethren who wished to discuss the theology of the Name with him, but his opponents either stayed away or came in groups and vociferously upbraided him.

On June 8, 1913, the dispute threatened to descend into a brawl. Serafimov and Scherbina with armed officers and soldiers came to the cell of Fr Iriney, whom they wanted to arrest. The incident is described colorfully by the Name-Glorifiers:

> Serafimov started stamping and yelling, "Hand over Iriney!" Meanwhile, Scherbina hammered at the door with all his might …. Finally, Fr Iriney appeared, greeted them and asked, "What do you want, gentlemen?" Serafi-mov said, "Come along to the guest hall and see His Excellency the Consul." "Fine, let's go." On the staircase, for no reason at all, Serafimov barged into [Fr] Savvaty, who said, "Don't shove me." Serafimov said loud and clear, "I'm not just going to shove you; we've been ordered to beat you." Then Iriney turned to Serafimov, laid bare his chest and said, "Come on, beat me." At this Serafimov said nothing and made to lead Iriney on by the arm, but Iriney said, "I'm not a prisoner; I can walk on my own."

When word got around that their leader was being taken away, the alarm was rung and Fr Iriney's followers surrounded him crying, "Don't leave us, father, we're ready to die with you."[43]

The next day after the liturgy, the abbot read out to the whole brotherhood and the consul the letter from the Holy Synod condemning the Name-Glorifying doc-trine. When he had finished, Fr Iriney asked the abbot: "The <u>name</u> of our Lord Jesus Christ—the most sweet Name *Jesus*—is it God or not?" Fr Misail replied: "The name *Jesus* is not God."[44] The Name-Glorifiers now knew for certain that their abbot opposed their doctrine, despite his signed statement to the contrary in January.

On June 11, the archbishop once again ventured ashore. Closely surrounded by a protective cordon of crew, he confronted a hostile congregation of the brethren from the ambo of the Pokrov central church. He spoke unhindered, then touched on theology: Bulatovich was wrong in saying that the Name of God was God himself, for there are many words to designate God, none of which are the Godhead. At this point the archbishop was shouted down: "Heretic! His teaching is that Christ is not God, that there is no God." Troitsky hastily explained that the Archbishop's words meant that "only the name Jesus is not God; Christ Himself is our God." The hecklers shouted louder, calling the archbishop a "crocodile, a seven-headed serpent, a wolf in sheep's clothing."[45] At this, Archbishop Nikon lost patience. Banging his episcopal staff against the floor he raised his voice, "Don't anyone dare to contradict me!"[46] He then beat a hasty retreat through the sanctuary.

Next the archbishop demanded that the Name-Glorifiers give their written compliance with the patriarchal encyclical and the letter from the Holy Synod. The request was refused. The rebels again seized the keys to the treasury, as well as those to the vestry, larders, and other strategic points. They now threatened to start a fire.

Negotiations were at an end. As Archbishop Anthony (Khrapovitsky) had long been urging, the only solution was force. That same evening, June 11, 1913, the steamship *Tsar'* arrived bearing five officers and 118 soldiers of the 6th Platoon of the 50th Belostoksky Regiment. The brethren were told that they had arrived to protect the monastery from the threat of arson. The platoon had arrived without the permission of the Greek civil governor, who protested. On June 13 Archbishop Nikon told the Sacred Community that the "heretics" should certainly have to leave the Holy Mountain lest they be expelled by the Greeks. On the same day, the platoon manned the key positions of the monastery: its six gates, the treasury, the vestry, the chapels and churches, and the watermill.

For the next few days the archbishop and the professor were in the library vainly attempting to talk to the brethren. They visited Old Mountain Rusik and Novaya Fivaida, but with just as little success. Everywhere they were accused of being heretics and freemasons. The archbishop also distributed leaflets about the folly of the new doctrine.

From June 14 to 19, the archbishop carried out a census in the monastery to find out how many of the brethren declared themselves obedient to the patriarchal encyclical and synodic letters, and how many opposed them. Some 700 declared themselves obedient to the church authorities and a thousand dissented.[47] Finally, the archbishop declared that he intended to officiate at the services of the Feast of Saints Peter and Paul. At two in the morning, during the feast's vigil, June 29, he was awakened from his slumbers in the episcopal guest quarters by a messenger bearing an urgent letter from the Consul Shebunin, who advised him not to take the liturgy but leave the monastery immediately: the Name-Glorifiers were intent on causing a scandalous commotion in the church. Once again, the archbishop took refuge on board the SS *Donets*.

Despite the stubborn resistance and humiliating retreats, the archbishop had been persisting for nearly a month in trying to reason with the Name-Glorifiers. At last, fearing the imminent seizure of the Russian houses by the Greeks, Shebunin decided that force was the only way to quell the rebellion. On July 2 the SS *Kherson*,[48] on which the Name-Glorifiers were to be deported, anchored next to the *Donets*. The consul gave them twenty-four hours to decide between a harmonious life in the monastery with the rest of the brethren or voluntary deportation to Russia. If they refused, they would be expelled by force.

The Name-Glorifiers demanded compensation: half the monastery's capital assets and shelter in Novaya Fivaida or a monastery and dependency in Russia. This was refused, so they barricaded themselves in the corridors of one of the monastery's buildings.

On July 3, 1913, the military attacked.

> Finally, the trumpet rang out with the command to "shoot" and the calm of the Holy Mountain was rent by the roar … not of firearms, but of fire hoses. After an hour-long "cold shower" dampened the monks' spirits, the sailors rushed the building and began to drag recalcitrant devotees of the contemplative life out of the corridors.[49]

The event was variously reported as a minor scuffle and as a scene of brutal violence. Archbishop Nikon blamed the "Judaizing" press for dramatic exaggeration. According to him, "those who tried to defend themselves from the strong jets of water with boards or icons did not escape without grazes …. There were twenty-five 'wounded,' i.e. grazed monks."[50]

Fr Antony (Bulatovich), who was, of course, not present, claimed that some of the victims were knocked unconscious and four were killed.[51] In a witness statement given upon his arrival in Odessa, one of the victims of the attack reported:

> The order was given and intense jets of water were directed from two fire hoses: one point-blank into the corridor and the other from above. [This went on] for an hour and five minutes, but the monks, defending their faces

with holy icons and crosses, did not budge, although they shuddered all over with cold while calling out ... "Lord Jesus Christ, Son of God, have mercy on us!" .... The soldiers took iron boathooks ... pokers and other implements and started to smash the holy icons, crosses and portraits of the tsars, which they wrenched out of the hands of the confessors and trampled underfoot. With the same implements they then grabbed the monks by the head, neck, legs and clothes, and heaved them into the ... dirty water, then dragged them to the ship .... The soldiers were ordered by Staff Captain Munzov to use bayonets and rifle butts as well.[52]

The wounded Name-Glorifiers submitted to the ship's doctor a written statement of the injuries they received.[53] They listed injuries to forty brethren in total: five pierced by bayonets, nine receiving cuts and gashes, and fifteen bruised by rifle butts.

The next day some 400 St Panteleimon Name-Glorifiers had been delivered on board. From July 6–7, 183 brethren of the St Andrew's Skete were installed on the *Kherson* peacefully and without resistance. On July 9 the *Kherson* left for Odessa carrying 621 Name-Glorifiers. The SS *Chikhachev* took a further group of rebels. By July 17, 1913, over a thousand Name-Glorifiers had been deported.[54]

When they arrived in Odessa most were shorn, made to wear civilian clothes, and stripped of their monastic and sacerdotal status. Nearly all were forbidden to join a monastery and were excommunicated. Many found themselves in prison and penniless. They had been inveigled into signing away their rights and possessions, and accepting a miserly financial compensation.

Inevitably, the brutal treatment meted out on the rebels was condemned. According to Russian press reports in the latter half of July 1913, Patriarch Germanos V protested that the lack of respect for Athonite tonsure shown by the Russian authorities diminished the prestige and authority of Eastern Orthodoxy, and was disrespectful toward the Patriarchate.[55] The patriarchs of Alexandria and Jerusalem joined in the protest. Emperor Nicholas II and his consort, Alexandra Fyodorovna, granted a three-man deputation of Name-Glorifiers a private, lengthy audience at Tsarskoe Selo on February 13, 1914. At Easter that year, Procurator Sabler delivered to the Holy Synod a note from His Imperial Majesty:

> In this Feast of Feasts, when the hearts of believers are directed towards Godly love and the love of their neighbors, my soul mourns for the Athonite monks who have been deprived of Communion of the Holy Mysteries and the comfort of being in church. Let us forget the division; it is not for us to judge about

the greatest of holies, the Name of God, and thus bring down the wrath of the Lord on our motherland. The case against all the monks should be dropped; all of them should be housed in monasteries, their monastic rank should be restored, and they should be allowed to serve in church.[56]

Conclusions

Did the rebels, who were engaged essentially in a passionate theological dispute, deserve physical violence, imprisonment, defrocking, and deprivation of fundamental civil liberties? How right were the Russian Holy Synod and the ecumenical patriarch in condemning the doctrine of the Name-Glorifiers? To this day the theological debate continues about the Name of God. In Russia and in the post-1917 emigration, eminent theologians have supported the Name-Glorifiers. Among the most notable of the supporters was Fr Pavel Florensky, who, as we have seen, wrote the foreword to *On the Mountains of the Caucasus*. Among others who shared his views were the Slavophile, M. A. Novosyolov, and the theologians, Fr Sergy Bulgakov and A. F. Losev. Gradually, the Name-Glorifiers gained support within the Russian Church hierarchy and even the Holy Synod. One of the main items on the agenda of the 1917 *Pomestny sobor Rossiyskoy Pravoslavnoy Tserkvi* / Local Council of the Orthodox Church of Russia chaired by Patriarch Tikhon was the Name of God Question. Perhaps the Name-Glorifiers might have been rehabilitated, but by September 1918 the Bolsheviks had forced the Council to close.

Writing in the 1960s, the émigré historian I. K. Smolitsch observes:

> We cannot ... consider the question to be canonically or theologically resolved .... All this story about the Athonite troubles nonetheless shows that the Russian monks of the Holy Mountain were engaged in spiritual problems. Was the doctrine of the Name Glorifiers true or false? That is another question, but the mere fact that it was formulated shows that despite the wholly excessive wealth of the Russian houses on Athos, a genuinely ascetic life was being developed in them.[57]

The Athonite Troubles caused by the dispute over the Name of God remain an unsolved and highly controversial question in the Russian Orthodox Church. The theological debate continues; as for the events, few Russian historians have been able to describe them impartially and clearly.

Most accounts of the dispute are either on the side of the Name-Glorifiers or against them. Igumen Pyotr (Pigol'—see Chapters 7 and 13), is resolutely opposed to them. The title of his monograph makes this clear: *Afonskaya tragediya: gordost' i sataninskie zamysly / The Athonite Tragedy: Pride and Satanic Schemes.*[58] The American author, Tom Dykstra, supports the Name-Glorifiers. Little is given away by the title of his treatise, *Hallowed Be Thy Name: The Name-Glorifying Dispute in the Russian Orthodox Church and on Mt. Athos, 1912–1914.* The front cover of the book, however, is startling: it features an icon of Antony Bulatovich with the inscription "St Antony Bulatovich the Athonite Confessor"; in his hand he holds a scroll with the words "An Apology for the Belief in the Name of God and the Name of Jesus."[59]

Bishop Ilarion (Alfeev), author of *Svyaschennaya tayna tserkvi: vvedenie v istoriyu i problematiku imyaslavskikh sporov / The Sacred Mystery of the Church: An Introduction to the History and Problems of the Name-Glorifying Quarrels*, which is the most detailed of all published accounts of the Troubles, and deals with both the theology and events, found impartiality and clarity difficult to achieve.[60] The title is cautious, but "Name-Glorifying" suggests that the author is sympathetic to the rebels.

In his last chapter the bishop arrives separately at his theological and historical conclusions. In the latter, he points out that many of the Name-Glorifiers' supporters, such as Metropolitan Makary (Nevsky), Emperor Nicholas II and Empress Alexandra Fyodorovna, his consort, Grand-Duchess Elizabeth Fyodorovna, St Kuksha the New, and St Varsonofy of Optina, have been canonized by the Russian Orthodox Church. Bishop Ilarion also reminds us that "The Name of God is God Himself" was first uttered by St John of Kronstadt. Nevertheless, Ilarion hopes that the definitive and final judgment will be made by an official Russian Orthodox Church commission. He cautiously concludes that, when this happens:

> be it considerably late in the day, justice in the case of the Name-Glorifiers will be restored and a church doctrine will be put together about the veneration of the Name of God. "The Sacred Mystery of the Church" will at last be comprehensible—insofar as it is altogether possible to comprehend the mysteries, which extend far beyond the limits of human consciousness.[61]

Bishop Ilarion wrote both as a scholar and theologian, and as a representative of the Moscow Patriarchate.[62] For all its circumspection, his conclusion is quite bold, for the Name of God dispute continues to cause division and is generally avoided by the cautious. In preparation for a conference held in the Kievo-Pecherskaya Lavra May 21–23, 2015, on "Athos and the Slavonic World," I asked to deliver a paper on the dispute. The request was turned down by the Organizing Committee:

St Panteleimon Monastery ask that we [decline the request to speak about] Name-Glorifying. [The monastery] finds the topic painful and fears its revival, especially because recently in Russia there have been moves to resurrect Name-Glorifying. It is a very complex question.[63]

The Organizing Committee promised that the dispute would be amply dealt with at the conference, but the topic was not mentioned.

St Silouan the Athonite was one of the brethren at the Monastery when the dispute took place. As a renowned hesychast and practitioner of the Jesus Prayer, he would have been particularly concerned by the rebellion. His biographer, St Sophrony, however, emphatically stated that St Silouan was in no way involved:

Bearing constantly in his heart the most sweet Name of Jesus, for the Jesus Prayer did not cease to work within him, [Fr Silouan] nonetheless kept himself away from any dispute about the nature of this Name. He knew that through the Jesus prayer the Grace of the Holy Spirit enters one's heart, that calling the Divine Name of Jesus illumines the entire man and burns up his passions. But he avoided dogmatically interpreting what he was experiencing, lest he "fall into the error of intellectual reasoning."[64]

St Silouan was one of the hundreds of the Russian Monastery's brethren who silently put up with the upheavals and got on with their ascetic life. Taking sides would have been contrary to their vows of humility and obedience.

Were the Name-Glorifiers therefore guilty of unmonastic, disruptive behavior? They certainly shattered the prayerful calm of Athonite cenobia. Indeed, the manner in which Fr Antony (Bulatovich) and his followers deposed their prior was as shockingly violent as the Name-Glorifiers' deportation in July 1913. When Bulatovich initiated the coup, he jumped onto a table shouting "Hurrah!" and the assembled monks started to brawl. Fists flew, hair and beards were pulled; the supporters of the prior had first to pass along a corridor being kicked and punched by rows of their opponents, and then were thrown downstairs. A couple of Name-Fighters were defenestrated; some took refuge in the coal cellar.

Archbishop Anthony (Khrapovitsky) was furious with the Name-Glorifiers. Although he did not read *On the Mountains of the Caucasus*,[65] he poured scorn on their doctrine. What really angered the archbishop, however, was their disregard of ecclesiastic authority. He accused Fr Antony (Bulatovich) of "violent agitation ... inciting the brethren of several houses ... and uncouth disobedience of all the authority of that holy and spiritual man Ecumenical Patriarch Joachim III of blessed memory."[66]

In drawing conclusions from the sorry events of the Athonite Troubles, we must ask whether Fr Antony (Bulatovich) and the other Name-Glorifiers were right to propagate with such passion the teaching about the Name of God expounded in *On the Mountains of the Caucasus* by Fr Ilarion (Domrachov). It is not our place to pronounce on the teachings themselves; that is for theologians. We can see no reason why *On the Mountains of the Caucasus* should not have been read, discussed, and made known. That the book should have been destroyed and its reading forbidden, as the Patriarch and the Russian Holy Synod ordered, seems excessive. Such censorship was to become all too common in the Soviet Union and other totalitarian states. Furthermore, many new teachings and revivals of old teachings in the Orthodox Church have caused upheavals and met with resistance—for instance the Hesychast controversy and the Palamas-Barlaam dispute in the fourteenth century, or the Kollyvades question in the eighteenth century. Why should not the Name-Glorifiers therefore bring their teaching to public attention and discuss it?

We believe that they were entitled to, but that they were wrong in their methods. Violence, bullying, and rank disobedience are out of place in the monastic life. There is evidence that Fr Ilarion (Domrachov) was a willful and disobedient monk. It is not known why he left St Panteleimon's for the New Athonite Monastery of St Simon the Canaanite in Abkhazia, but once he was there he would frequently leave for the mountainous wilderness without permission of his abbot. In the view of Igumen Pyotr (Pigol'):

> Abbot Ieron of the New Athonite Monastery was a great spiritual elder and a disciple of the Elders Ieronim and Makary. He knew the author of the book, Fr Ilarion ... to be a disobedient and self-assured monk, who lived according to his own whims and left the monastery to [be] a hermit without the abbot's blessing. Naturally, Fr Ieron could foresee that these passions—pride, disobedience and willfulness—would bear their evil fruit, and that is what eventually happened on Mount Athos.[67]

Tom Dykstra accused the ecclesiastic authorities of using their authority in a "mind-boggling" way to perpetrate "shocking cruelties on those with whom they disagreed." He fails to mention the cruelty and sedition caused by Bulatovich and his followers. On the other hand, Dykstra is right to say that in

> Orthodoxy varying opinions can and do peacefully coexist; however, this is not because mutually contradictory beliefs are considered as acceptable; rather, it is because of a recognition that people, including hierarchs, are

fallible, and their making mistakes does not necessarily make them "heretics." However, when disagreements are perceived to be about essential truths of the faith, and especially when at least one side wants to force its view on the other, it becomes necessary to seek a definitive resolution to the question.[68]

Bishop Ilarion (Alfeev) deplores the significant loss of numbers of Russian Athonites due to the deportation of the Name-Glorifiers. He considers that the Russian Foreign Ministry and diplomatic corps were short-sighted in fearing that all of the Russian Athonite community risked expulsion at the hands of the Greeks: deporting almost one-and-a-half thousand rebels seriously weakened the Russian community; the operation was tantamount to cutting off the nose to spite the face.[69] The events in the first decades of the twentieth century prove the bishop wrong. Owing to the First World War and the Bolshevik Revolution, the Russian Athonite community was doomed to wither away almost to the point of extinction, regardless of its original size. Perhaps having to feed and look after fewer brethren in the hard times following 1914 was, statistically at least, a blessing: less food and fewer resources were needed to cater for fewer brethren.

The Aftermath

The close of the Athonite Troubles was somewhat anticlimactic. Fr Antony (Bulatovich) served for a while as an army chaplain in the war. He returned to his estate near Petrograd almost blind from an eye infection and was killed one night by armed robbers.[70] Schema-Monk Ilarion (Domrachov) died at the age of seventy in 1916, in Tyomnye Buki, a remote area of the Caucasus. Several of the Name-Glorifiers made their way to the Caucasus. In 1924, the New Athonite Monastery of St Simon the Canaanite in Abkhazia was closed; its brethren were arrested, deported, or shot, and a similar fate awaited hermits living elsewhere in the Caucasus. Prior Ieronim of the St Andrew's Skete was unable to get over the rebellion in his house; he died of a heart attack in 1920, aged fifty-four. Igumen Arseny, the synodic missionary and staunch supporter of the Name-Glorifiers, suffered paralysis, and died in August 1913.

Now that the rebels had left Athos, Fr Misail was once again the undisputed head of his monastery. The Patriarch awarded him a gold pectoral cross and an *epigonation*[71] for his part in suppressing the rebellion. Peace was restored to Novaya Fivaida and the St Andrew Skete. As we have seen, the Troubles did not affect the Prophet Elijah Skete. This was partly because it was a Little Russian house, whereas the

Name-Glorifiers were in the main Great Russians. Nevertheless, the Great and Little Russians seemed constantly to be squabbling. As the historian Lora Gerd observes, Ambassador Giers "was inclined to consider the Athonite events from a purely political point of view, believing them to 'be caused by the long-standing tendency of the Little Russians to seize power in the St Andrew Skete and St Panteleimon Monastery.'"[72]

What is harder to understand is why the Name-Glorifying dispute seemed not to touch the Russian *kelliot* community, which formed a substantial part of Russian Athos. Gerd explains that the Russian *kelliots* were a law unto themselves. Enterprising peasants mainly from southern Russia flocked to the Mountain from the second half of the nineteenth century, and bought from the Ruling Monasteries *kellia* which they rapidly converted into populous cenobia, having raised considerable sums from successful alms-gathering missions at home. These *kelliots* were more interested in setting up their houses than in theological disputes, ethnic quarrels or challenging ecclesiastical authority.[73]

It was as well that order was restored to St Panteleimon Monastery. Archimandrite Misail was about to face renewed opposition from the Greeks, and he was to learn to fight his own corner without the help and backing of his country.

The future of the monastery's material welfare looked grim, yet it was a time of great spiritual strength. Not only were the brethren led by a humble and stoic abbot with a gift of foresight, but also some of the monks were remarkable ascetics. St Silouan and many of his fellow brethren came to the monastery with little education, like Archimandrite Misail, yet they soon became well versed in Patristics. A Roman Catholic theologian visiting in 1932 spoke with one Fr V. about the astonishing depth of the monks' reading:

> "Do your monks read these books? …. Only our professors read them." Father V. told Fr Silouan of this conversation. The Elder remarked: "You could have told the doctor that our monks do not merely read these books, but could themselves write similar ones. For there are already many fine books and they benefit from them; but if these books were for some reason to be lost, the monks would write new ones."[74]

Many of St Silouan's fellow brethren were saintly. Writing just before the saint's canonization (1987), Archbishop Vasily (Krivoshein) of Brussels, a contemporary of St Sophrony's at the monastery, commented: "If Elder Silouan is to be canonized, every one of the monks living at the time of Elder Silouan should be canonized—all of them, not just one .... I ... consider him a saint, but we cannot slight the others—all of them led highly spiritual lives, even more so than he."[75] Eleven of St Silouan's contemporaries at the monastery were martyred in the USSR in 1937–1938, and have been added to the list of New Martyrs and Confessors of the Russian Orthodox Church.

St Silouan himself became a member of the St Panteleimon brotherhood in 1893. Three years later another future saint joined, St Kuksha the Confessor of Odessa. He was wrongly implicated in the Name of God dispute and deported in 1913. Following arrest in 1933, he survived prison camps and exile in Siberia until 1947, but was persecuted by the NKVD until 1960. He had many spiritual children in Kiev, Pochaev and Odessa, and died four years later.[76]

CHAPTER 11

From 1913 to Abbot Misail's Death in 1940

Until the 1917 Bolshevik Revolution, the Russian Athonite community could rely on the support of the Russian diplomatic corps in Constantinople, Thessaloniki, and Athens. The diplomats liaised with the Russian Foreign Ministry and the Holy Russian Synod. Abbot Makary (Sushkin) of St Panteleimon's had been the unofficial spokesman for all of Russian Athos and acted as the main channel of communication with the Russian Embassies and Consulates.[1] After his death in 1889, the monastery remained the principal point of contact between Athos and Russian official channels.

As A. A. Dmitrievsky pointed out, the Greek Athonite monasteries invariably responded by becoming more cooperative with Russian Athonites when the income from their Bessarabian dependencies was frozen and Russian donations or alms-gathering missions in Russia were stopped. However, by the first decade of the twentieth century, the punitive measures of Russian officialdom were losing their effectiveness. The Russian Athonite community unsuccessfully lobbied the London Peace Conference and London Conference of Ambassadors in 1912 in the hopes of securing improved status for their houses.[2] Their requests were ignored; the official Russian representatives at the two conferences had little say.

Russian diplomats also tried exerting pressure on the Constantinople patriarch, Joachim II, as we have seen, had been amenable to Russian requests. It was in great measure thanks to him that Archimandrite Makary became the first Russian abbot in modern times of St Panteleimon's, which henceforward became Russian—*Rossikon*—de facto as well as in name. To this day some Greeks believe that the patriarch was bribed by Count N. P. Ignat'ev.[3] Although some believed Patriarch Joachim III, his successor, also to be a friend of the Russians, his were the canons St Panteleimon's objected to. Basing them on the ones written in 1877, he ensured that the status of the Twenty Ruling Monasteries remained immutable and that the two Russian sketes would never succeed in gaining monastic status. Subsequent ecumenical patriarchs, especially Meletios IV,[4] were, if anything, hostile to the Russians.

The First World War further weakened Russian Athos. Russia was undergoing a series of crises: war with Japan was followed by the 1905 revolution and growing civil unrest. From August 1914 there was a general call to arms; Russian Athonite novices and junior monks went to the front, mostly to serve in the Red Cross or ambulance corps, or as military chaplains. Some 700 Russian monks were mobilized; 100 of these were from St Panteleimon's: a mere 10 percent of all who had left were to return from the front.

In 1917, the situation on the Holy Mountain became more precarious. The Russian Athonites felt beleaguered: after the February Revolution, the emperor abdicated and the provisional government was sworn in. The new republic was greeted with dismay: "The monks were greatly upset .... Orthodoxy is so securely bound with autocracy and so close are the moral ties of the tsar with the people that the vast majority of monks does not want anything to do with the republic as Russia is now called."[5] Nevertheless, litanies were altered so as to commemorate the provisional government, special prayers (*molebny* and vigils) were said and fasts were observed for its victory in the war.

The First World War divided Greece: the Venizelos government sided with the Entente (France, Great Britain, and Russia), whereas King Constantine I, while remaining nominally neutral, favored the Germans. The Russians, Serbs, and some of the Greeks on Athos supported the Entente. The Bulgarians and a large part of the Greek Athonites were royalist and pro-German. They set up a telegraph station for the Germans and beacons in two monasteries to communicate with U-boats. Disputes arose between Russian and Bulgarian monks. In 1916 the monks of Zograf had tried to seize Hilandar, whose brethren were a mixture of Serbs and Bulgarians.

Order was restored on January 4, 1917, when a Franco-Russian detachment was sent from the Thessaloniki front to Mount Athos. One hundred Russian troops, led by Corporal Ditsch, and fifty French soldiers were billeted mainly in St Panteleimon's, Zograf, and Vatopedi. On February 15 another fifty Russian and twenty French troops arrived. A blackout was imposed throughout the Holy Mountain and no vessel was allowed to venture further than 500 meters from the shore without military permission.

The first aim of the detachment was to secure allied shipping from U-boat attacks. A number of collaborators supplying the German vessels with fuel and provisions were arrested. Monks mainly from the Great Lavra, Vatopedi, Iviron, and Zograf were arrested, and deported to the Island of Mytilene. Next the soldiers seized arms caches in the Protaton building in Karyes. In all, some 400 rifles, 150,000 rounds of ammunition, and a large number of daggers were removed for temporary storage in St Panteleimon's before being taken away to Thessaloniki. Many of the weapons had been in the building since the Balkan wars (1912–1913). Several senior Karyes monks and representatives of the Twenty were arrested and deported. After their departure, the now-republican Sacred Community sent a letter to Venizelos expressing support for his government and for the Entente.

Naturally, the Russian community greatly benefited from the presence of their armed protectors. For the first time since the 1870s, the brethren of Iviron had no choice but to accede to some important demands from its Georgian Kellion of St John the Theologian. In July, Vatopedi at last begrudgingly granted the St Andrew Skete permission to build its own *arsanas* / jetty, thus allowing the skete to load and unload its own vessels, and avoid having to pay import duties. The Prophet Elijah Skete also needed to have its own jetty, on the Pantokratoros shore, but did not avail itself of the opportunity of asking for one. However, the skete did manage to transfer to Thessaloniki through Corporal Ditsch of the Franco-Russian detachment 8,000 drachmas[6] for the purchase of provisions. He also secured from Pantokrator permission for the skete to fish from its own vessel.

Respite for the Russians was all too brief. On June 29, 1917, the Franco-Russian detachment received orders to leave. On the morrow the Russian troops bade a warm farewell in St Panteleimon's; the last of the French left Daphne on July 2. Once again, the Russian monks were vulnerable. In a fit of pique, the Great Lavra denied privileges to the Russian *kelliots* and hermits living on its land; the *Kellion* of St John the Theologian had its newly acquired privileges revoked by Iviron, and the St Andrew Skete lost its jetty. On August 16, a shipment of 2½ tons of wheat from St Panteleimon's dependency in Kalamaria was stopped by a U-boat. The Germans seized the cargo and blew up the monastery's vessel.

After the Bolshevik Revolution of 1917, Russian Athos continued to appeal for the support of Russian diplomats. Their mainstay was Elim Pavlovich Demidov, imperial plenipotentiary in Athens since 1912. He and his wife[7] aided the community of the Church of the Holy Trinity attached to the Russian Diplomatic Mission in Athens, offering succor to some of the three thousand-odd wounded Russian soldiers in Greece. At the end of the First World War, Elim Pavlovich was engaged in negotiations for the return of the Russian Athonite dependencies in Constantinople, and he later directed his attention to restoring requisitioned property of

St Panteleimon's and confiscated Russian Athonite lands in mainland Greece. After the official recognition of the USSR by Greece on March 4, 1924, the Demidovs could no longer help.[8]

There was a deceptive glimmer of hope on September 17, 1918. News came to Athos through the Russian Diplomatic Mission in Athens that two anti-Bolshevik governments had been set up, in Archangel and Omsk. In May 1919 the Russian Athonites petitioned Admiral Kolchak's Siberian government for a loan of 700,000 drachmas, of which 220,000 was to be for St Panteleimon's. Two months later, Demidov announced that the Admiral had to decline the request, owing to a lack of resources. By 1920, Denikin's forces in the south and the anti-Bolshevik governments in the north and east had capitulated; Soviet rule was established: no more support could come from the once all-powerful motherland and defender of the Orthodox.

King Alexander I Karagiorgievič of the Serbs, Croats, and Slovenes (from 1930, of Yugoslavia), and the Serbian patriarchs now became the chief protectors of Russian Athos. In 1924, an impassioned appeal was made on behalf of the whole Russian monastic community to the king:

> An emboldened hand has cut down the precious life of our Emperor Nicholas II, and to this day the might of Russia is in the thrall of [its] bitter enemies. Now that we have lost support from Russia, we have had to sell our entire inheritance in order to survive, and have thus incurred insurmountable debts. We therefore have no hopes for the future.[9]

Since the liberation of Athos in 1912, the Greek civil authorities had become increasingly unfriendly toward the Russians. Athonite customs officials were rude and aggressive.[10] The post office, once run by the helpful Papayannis brothers, who were Russified Greeks, was taken over by the far from friendly Mr. Stamatis. Russian Athonites missed Turkish officials, who had been polite and impartial by comparison. In the monastic community, too, there was growing hostility toward the Russians, as exemplified by the guest master of Aghiou Pavlou Monastery flying into a fit of rage and striking a *kelliot* elder, Fr Nikolay, in the face.[11] Naturally, the Russians had become more unpopular than ever by the summer of 1917, after the departure of the Franco-Russian detachment. There were scores to be settled.

In the autumn of 1915 A. A. Pavlovsky had come to the Holy Mountain as permanent diplomatic representative and liaison officer between the Russian Consulate in Thessaloniki and the Russian Athonites. Based in the St Andrew's Skete, he worked tirelessly to organize and unite the community. He set up the United Brotherhood of Russian Kelliots and, when the war made food and resources scarce, the Provisions Commission, which helped to stave off starvation and extreme need throughout the community. On August 10, 1919, Pavlovsky and Archimandrite Sergy (Dibich) from the Diplomatic Mission Holy Trinity Church in Athens were conducting a survey of the Russian sketes and *kellia* to plan for effective aid. The authorities decided to put an end to their activities and arrested them. They were deported from Daphne, never to return to the Holy Mountain.

St Panteleimon's nevertheless continued to defy pressure from the Greeks. Every time a demand came from the ecumenical patriarch or the Sacred Community to accept or sign the new canons, the monastery refused. On May 10, 1924, a five-man commission of the Extraordinary Double Synaxis of the Sacred Community incorporated the new canons into the Constitutional Charter of the Holy Mountain.[12] The Russian Monastery did not accept the Charter, objecting mainly to what it perceived as interference with its internal affairs; it did not wish the abbot's autocratic authority to be compromised by subjection to a council of elders, as happened in 1912 during the attempted coup of the Name-Glorifiers. Fr Misail believed that St Panteleimon's was being forced "to accept legislation which is detrimental to us. [We ask to be allowed] to live peacefully according to our ancient rule, as we have done hitherto."[13]

The monastery also disagreed with the excessive powers the Charter invested in the civil governor, who could intervene in the internal affairs of a house on behalf of the Greek state. St Panteleimon's continued to oppose the immutable division of the Holy Mountain into the territories belonging exclusively to the Twenty Ruling Monasteries, of which St Panteleimon's remained nineteenth in rank. Even after the establishment of Soviet power and the loss of the motherland, Russian Athonites objected to becoming Greek citizens: according to the Charter, anyone entering the Holy Mountain as a novice or monk automatically becomes a Greek subject.

Another major sticking point for St Panteleimon's was the declaration in the Charter that Mount Athos, while spiritually under the direct jurisdiction of the ecumenical patriarch, is a self-administering part of the Greek state, which has sovereignty over it. The Russians continued to hope that Mount Athos might become an international protectorate, but after the Treaties of Sèvres (1920) and Lausanne (1923), and the official recognition by Greece of the USSR (March 4, 1924), this was unrealistic.[14]

Although St Panteleimon's doggedly refused to append its signature to the Charter, it periodically agreed to certain of its stipulations in order to avoid detrimental conflict with the Sacred Community and the patriarchate. In reply to the demand of Patriarch Photios II (1929–1935), July 8, 1931, that the monastery accept the Charter, Abbot Misail wrote:

> As for ... the New Constitutional Charter ... our holy house is always trying to comply with it and apply its statutes. For example, we present [for inspection] a list of our monks and our internal rule, we contribute financially to the upkeep of the Athoniada School, we correspond with the Ecumenical Patriarch through the Sacred Community and we meet other obligations, which are stipulated in the Charter and which had not been in force before the Charter's existence.[15]

In 1926, the Greek government accepted the Constitutional Charter of the Holy Mountain, which was enshrined in the Hellenic Constitution in 1927. The authorities saw to it that from 1928 there would be no more Slav visitors from outside Athos to the Russian Athonite community. The brotherhood of St Panteleimon's seemed thus condemned to die out of old age: no more Slav pilgrims would be allowed to visit it, and no further novices or monks would be able to join. From 1922 to 1928, twenty-two monks managed to join from Carpathian Czechoslovakia; they were the last people allowed to enter St Panteleimon's.

Restrictions were imposed on visiting senior Russian clergy as well. Metropolitan (formerly Archbishop) Anthony (Khrapovitsky) was refused entry to the Holy Mountain and permission to serve there on several occasions. He was hoping to relinquish headship of the Russian Orthodox Church Outside Russia (ROCOR) based in Sremski Karlovćy[16] and then retire to Mount Athos. On the eve of his departure for Greece in 1923, however, news came from Fr Misail that Metropolitan Anthony had been denied an entry visa. In 1924, the archbishop was in St Panteleimon's for Easter, but did not have permission from the patriarch to take services. Bishop Ioann (Bulin), formerly of Pechersk, came to Athos in 1934. He was not allowed to ordain and was initially forbidden to take services. In 1936, Archbishop Feofan (Gavrilov) came to St Panteleimon's from Serbia with the wonderworking Korennaya Icon of the Mother of God. Although he could take services, he did not have permission to ordain.

In the two decades following the First World War, there were several attempts both by the civil authorities and the Sacred Community to control St Panteleimon's. In 1922, the Sacred Community sent Fr Misail a letter asking, without preamble or explanation:

Why does your monastery not accept Greek monks or have its Greek brethren ordained for services in Greek?

Why are [the Greek brethren] not given monastic duties but are considered as outsiders with no rights?

Why are they completely deprived of fatherly care, not properly looked after by the monastery or given suitable clothing?

Why are Greek singers no longer being hired to sing at vigils?[17]

The abbot replied on September 12, 1922, that four Greek brethren joined the monastery that year, and that others had joined in previous years. Furthermore, the Greek brethren were given lighter duties than the Russian monks, and were even allowed to have oil and wine at meals during fast days.

After the defeats in Asia Minor at the hands of Turkey in 1919–1922, and the exchange of populations in 1923, Greece was impoverished and its armed forces were weakened. One-and-a-half million homeless refugees arrived in Greece from Asia Minor. Land was urgently needed to accommodate them, so many Athonite dependencies in Greece were appropriated by the state. At the beginning of 1924, St Panteleimon's lost its lands in Kalamaria, Sikia, and Kassandra. In 1928–1929, the League of Nations made Greece pay for the loss of Athonite dependencies. St Panteleimon's, like the other houses, received a small sum of money paid into its account with the National Bank of Greece. The amount was calculated according to the land's worth, which was deliberately undervalued. Only the interest earned by the deposited amount could be withdrawn.

The Sacred Community itself was in financial difficulties. On June 18, 1925, an extraordinary meeting of the Double Synaxis was held to deal with the Sacred Community's debt of 99,000 drachmas.[18] It was decided to ask the Twenty to raise the money. As St Panteleimon's still had the largest brotherhood, it had to pay 18,750 drachmas, which was almost a fifth of the total. Abbot Misail protested and suggested that the debt be equally divided between the Twenty Monasteries. The Sacred Community took steps to ensure that the Russian Monastery pay the full amount. On August 27 St Panteleimon's representative, Priest-Monk Pinufry (Erofeev), was expelled from the Sacred Community. All ties were temporarily cut between the Sacred Community and the Russian Monastery, which now had in addition to pay interest on the sum owed. Eventually, St Panteleimon's had no choice but to pay up, but Fr Pinufry was not reinstated and had to be replaced.

The army had its eye on the great buildings of St Panteleimon's and, in 1923, requisitioned the Preobrazhensky Korpus.[19] The monastery had to move out twenty-six elderly monks who had been taken into care, the hospital, icon studios, shop, and the refectory and kitchen for workers. One thousand two hundred wounded Greek troops were installed in April, along with medical staff. They stayed until September, to the distress of the brethren, who complained not only of the loss of one of their principal buildings, but of the noise and disruption: well into the night, the soldiers listened to loud music, played games, and even watched films on a makeshift outdoor screen erected in front of the main gates. After the departure of the military, the building stood empty, under armed guard. The monastery appealed to the Kingdom of the Serbs, Croats, and Slovenes to intervene. At last, eighteen months later, the Preobrazhensky Korpus was fully restored to its rightful owners.

In 1929, two senior St Panteleimon's representatives,[20] who were in Serbia, appealed for political support from King Alexander I:

> The Greek government has broken the promise it made in August 1920 to the Allied Powers in Sèvres and subsequently confirmed in the Lausanne [Treaty]: to keep secure from interference the rights and privileges of non-Greek monastic houses of the Holy Mountain …. We therefore need temporary political protection from [Serbia], as represented by its King, His Majesty Alexander, the ruling monarch and defender of God's Church. May the Royal Government, under the Most August Patronage of His Majesty, permit us to seek aid in time of need from the diplomatic representatives of the King of the Serbs in Greece and generally in other countries.[21]

The main help the king, his patriarch, and government were able to give was financial rather than political. They gave permission for the monastery to carry out a number of alms-gathering missions. Between 1926 and 1934 seven missions took place and collections were made by the Serbian Church. In total 1¼ million dinars[22] were gathered, a substantial amount of which went to the Russian monastery. This money was particularly welcome because it staved off starvation. For instance, in 1926 the Russian community was able to buy substantial provisions. On November 6, Patriarch Dimitrije of Serbia (1920–1930) suggested in a telegram to Abbot Misail that of the 120 tons of wheat and 10 tons of beans bought after the first alms-gathering mission, 40 tons of wheat and 4 tons of beans should go to St Panteleimon's, whose brotherhood at the time numbered 580.[23]

Financial help also came from wealthy philanthropists. In May 1922 Charles R. Crane, a noted American Arabist and industrialist, arranged for a shipment of 400 sacks of flour, 2 loads of fabric, and 10 meters of leather, worth a total of 95,000 drachmas, to be delivered to St Panteleimon's. A further three such shipments arrived between 1923 and 1926.

In 1925, just before material aid came from the Serbian and American benefactors, the monastery had enough to survive in the short term. Writing in May to V. N. Shtadtmann, the former Russian ambassador in Belgrade, Abbot Misail said that his 500-strong brotherhood had enough to feed itself from the monastery's land for five months, now that its Greek dependencies had been confiscated. Extra provisions could be bought only by selling ecclesiastical and domestic goods, and timber. Although most of the brethren were themselves aged or infirm, the monastery continued to offer shelter for forty mendicant hermits and run its hospital.

In the 1920s and 1930s, there were several fires, earthquakes, floods, and shipwrecks. The most damaging fire lasted for six days in the summer of 1927, destroying a large part of the Krumitsa and Novaya Fivaida forest, and five Russian *kellia*, at the cost to the monastery of some three million drachmas. The monastery had to contend with disease as well as with natural disasters. The Spanish flu claimed a number of lives from 1919.

The physical survival of St Panteleimon's was rendered more challenging by the unrelenting hostility of the Greeks. On June 14, 1931, the abbot had to call an emergency meeting of the council of elders to discuss the difficult case of the 29-year-old novice, Paisios Ypsilantis, who had been in the monastery for just nine months. A fellow Greek monk, Fr Gerasimos (Tsanarakis), announced that he felt obliged to leave the brethren because he had been constantly bullied and insulted by Paisios. Another Greek monk, Fr Grigorios (Grigorakis), had already left St Panteleimon's for the same reason. Furthermore, St Sophrony (Sakharov) complained of Paisios's improper behavior in church. It was decided to expel the novice.

The Sacred Community immediately accused the monastery of oppressing its Greek brethren. On June 19, Fr Misail had to write a detailed justification of the expulsion of Ypsilantis. Both the civil authorities and the Sacred Community then decided to intervene. On June 30, on the orders of the civil governor, Major Tsanakakis, armed gendarmes,[24] and Senior Sacred Community Representative Nikodimos of Koutloumousiou Monastery appeared at the monastery's gates with the expelled novice. The major demanded that Ypsilantis be immediately reinstated; if not, the abbot and council of elders would be arrested and sent to Thessaloniki where they would face trial.[25]

A few days later, Patriarch Photios II wrote to Fr Misail about the suppression of Greek monks in St Panteleimon's. Once again, the abbot had to write a detailed letter of justification. Unsatisfied by this, the patriarch sent him another letter about "contraventions in the Russian Monastery" and the intention to expel all Greeks from it. "We also demand on account of this," concluded Photios, "that your Holy Monastery recognize without fail and accept the New Constitutional Charter … blessed by the Church and confirmed by the state as legally binding."[26] Shortly afterward, Ypsilantis left the monastery of his own accord. He was later arrested and convicted in Athens for drug dealing.

Throughout Abbot Misail's reign, no matter what crisis had to be dealt with, the monastery fed and looked after the wandering beggar-monks with unfailing regularity. Before the First World War, St Panteleimon's gave food to 800 of them; by 1917, the monastery had resources only for 250, and for just 125 from the 1920s. Nevertheless, in November 1921, Patriarch Tikhon of Moscow and All Russia issued an appeal for help for those dying of starvation in his country. St Panteleimon arranged for a collection on Athos and handed the Sacred Community 10,000 drachmas to be passed on to the Russian Patriarchate.

Despite all the woes inflicted by nature and man, the aging monks of St Panteleimon's monastery continued to live a peaceful ascetic life in preparation for their imminent demise. St Silouan the Athonite describes the stoic calm of the brethren:

On September 14th 1932, there was a strong earthquake on Mt Athos. It happened [at 9 p.m.], during the vigil before the Exaltation of the Cross. I was standing in the gallery, close to the confessional of [Fr Ioanniky], the Abbot's designated successor, who was next to me, just outside the confessional. A brick fell from the ceiling onto the confessional and there was a shower of plaster. At first I was a little startled, but I soon calmed down and said to [Fr Ioanniky], "That's our merciful Saviour who wants us to repent." And we watched the monks below and in the gallery; few were frightened, about six left the church and the rest stayed put. The vigil continued in an orderly fashion, and so quietly, as if nothing had happened. And it occurred to me how much grace of the Holy Spirit there is in the monks: in such a strong earthquake, when the whole vast monastery building shook, the cement crumbled, the chandeliers swung, the lamps and candle stands swayed, the bells in the belfry rang and even the great bell struck on account of the mighty tremors—nevertheless, they remained calm.[27]

The stability and peace of the monastery was in large part due to the patience, resilience, and prayerful strength of the abbot. The greatest test of his leadership had been the Name of God rebellion. After the deportations in 1913, nothing more could disturb him.

On May 31, 1926 Priest Schema-Monk Ioanniky (Kutyryov) had been chosen by apostolic ballot to succeed Archimandrite Misail. Fr Ioanniky died on September 11, 1937; on December 12, after another ballot, Priest-Schema-Monk Iustin (Solomatin) became the abbot's successor.

On January 22, 1940, Fr Misail died. Two years before his death, on December 28, 1937, he wrote a final testament to the brethren: he forgave everyone and asked for forgiveness; he wished not to be forgotten in their prayers, and urged all to be at peace and maintain brotherly love.

Chapter 12

The Next Four Abbots: From Iustin to Avel' (1940–1978)

Their Biographies

Archimandrite of the Great Schema Iustin (Solomatin) was born in the Ryazan'skaya Guberniya in 1878. He arrived at St Panteleimon's in December 1896, aged eighteen, and did his obedience in the silversmith workshop for forty-one years, eventually rising to the position of *starets* / master craftsman. During this period he kept his own counsel; only his spiritual fathers (Frs Agafador [Budanov] and then Kirik [Maksimov]) "knew the depths of his soul."[1] In 1924 he was ordained priest by Metropolitan Anthony (Khrapovitsky); he was tonsured to the Great Schema in 1938.

Upon the death of Archimandrite Misail's designated successor, Fr Ioanniky (Kutirev) (December 12, 1937), Iustin was proposed as one of the three candidates to succeed the abbot and his name was selected by Apostolic ballot. For almost three years, Fr Iustin acted as *namestnik* / *locum tenens*. In January and February 1940 the St Panteleimon *Sobor startsev* / Council of Elders asked for confirmation of Iustin's abbacy from the patriarch and the Sacred Community. The Council was repeatedly told that no confirmation would be forthcoming unless the monastery signed its assent to the new Canons of the Constitutional Charter of the Holy Mountain.[2] The Council withheld its signature but promised to "live according to the new Charter."[3] The Council also pointed out that according to the Charter, "the enthronement of a [new] abbot cannot be postponed for more than a month."[4] On April 1, 1940, Fr Iustin, his abbacy having been eventually confirmed, was elevated to the rank of archimandrite.

During his reign the monastery continued its rapid decline: its increasingly aging brotherhood dwindled; poverty and hunger increased. In desperation, Abbot Iustin appealed for help in February 1945 to the patriarch of Moscow. This was the first official contact between St Panteleimon Monastery and the Russian Orthodox Church in Russia since 1917. The abbot died on August 3, 1958.

He was succeeded by Fr Ilian (Sorokin), who was born Ivan Mikhaylovich in 1885 in a merchant family, in the Yaroslavskaya Guberniya. Having received a sound primary school education, he entered the Glinskaya Pustyn' Hermitage "for reasons unknown,"[5] rather than continue his schooling according to his parents' wishes. Inspired by the *Pis'ma / Letters* of the popular Athonite writer Svyatogorets,[6] he dreamt of going to the Holy Mountain, and arrived at St Panteleimon's in August 1905. He was tonsured to the Great Schema in 1922 and Metropolitan Anthony (Khrapovitsky) ordained him to the priesthood in 1932. Having served in the monastery's *arkhond-arik / guest quarters* and *kantselyariya / office*, he was assigned to the St Panteleimon Constantinople dependency from 1911 to 1914. Upon his return he was assigned to the vestry and became *ekleziarkh / ecclesiarch*.[7] From 1932 to 1933 he was in Serbia gathering alms, after which he went to Constantinople as the dependency's superior. The Turks, however, refused him residency, so he returned to Athos. In September 1958 Deacon David (Tsuber) was elected abbot by apostolic ballot, but he begged to be excused from taking up the post, so another ballot was held. Finally, on October 3, 1958, Ilian (Sorokin), having been elected abbot, was enthroned as archimandrite. The monastery continued to suffer great material hardship and its brotherhood was dying out. Abbot Ilian therefore sent urgent appeals to the Moscow Patriarchate for help, and during his reign the first new recruits arrived at St Panteleimon's from the USSR. In June 1962, on the occasion of the millennium of the Holy Mountain, Patriarch Aleksey I awarded him the St Vladimir Medal. Abbot Ilian died on January 5, 1971.[8] He was remembered as a gentle, otherworldly figure, who, like Abbot Makary (Sushkin), "exhaust[ed] himself at church services."[9] Fr Ioann (Abernethy) remembers "the ascetic figure of Fr Ilian the Abbot."[10]

The next abbot was Fr Gavriil (Legach), who was born Georgy Vasil'evich in Carpathian Ruthenia, in 1901. He quickly learnt to read and write, and excelled at primary school. He arrived at St Panteleimon's in June 1924 with a sizeable group of compatriots, among the last of the Slavs officially allowed by the Greeks to visit the monastery. He was tonsured in March 1930 and ordained to the priesthood in 1949. His first obedience was as a roofer, at which task he worked diligently and fearlessly. In the 1930s he was sent to Serbia to gather alms for the monastery. He was chosen as Archimandrite Ilian's successor in 1965 and made abbot on April 9, 1971. Metropolitan Nikodim (Rotov) of Leningrad enthroned him with the title of archimandrite eleven days later. In his fifty years at the monastery he was never known to say an idle word. He liked conducting services in Greek and fluently read the Gospels in Greek. By July 4, 1975, he was too infirm to continue as abbot, so he ceded his post to Archimandrite Avel' (Makedonov). Abbot Gavriil died on June 26, 1976.

His successor, Archimandrite Avel', was one of the first monks to arrive at the monastery from the USSR. He was born Nikolay Nikolaevich in a large peasant family, in the Ryazan'skaya Oblast', in 1927. Having spent his childhood suffering from privation and hunger, he became orphaned at the age of sixteen. He sought solace in the church and was nicknamed Kolya the Monk.[11] Two years later he was tonsured, and in October 1947 ordained to the priesthood. With Metropolitan Nikodim (Rotov)'s help, he entered St Panteleimon's in February 1970 where he fulfilled the obediences of librarian, office worker, and manager of the Pokrov Central Church vestry. He was tonsured to the Great Schema on March 23. Although he had been designated abbot on March 13, 1971, the Sacred Community refused to recognize his appointment "because he had not lived long on Athos."[12] Continuing as Archimandrite Gavriil's deputy, Fr Avel' worked hard to bring new monks to the monastery from the USSR, where he went in 1974 to negotiate with the Moscow Patriarchate concerning this. When he returned to Athos, Fr Gavriil was too sick to continue as abbot. On July 4, 1975, Avel' was appointed abbot for the second time, but he did not stay long at his post. On October 1, 1978, he left for the USSR to attend the funeral of Metropolitan Nikodim, who had died on September 5 while visiting the Vatican. Avel' never returned to Athos.

The Second World War: Mount Athos Occupied (1941–1944)

As long as Greece remained neutral, the Second World War did not affect Athos. In a bid to impress Hitler, however, Mussolini decided to invade Greece, which he saw as easy prey. Having already occupied Albania in 1939 the Italians crossed the border into Greece on October 28, 1940. The Italians were repulsed, and so the Germans (via the territory of their Balkan ally Bulgaria) invaded Greece on April 6, 1941. A German captain and five officers arrived on Athos on April 22; having expelled the Greek civil governor and his entourage, he assumed command of the Mountain and set up his headquarters in Karyes. Franz Dölger, a German academic, became the new civil governor.[13] "By the beginning of June 1941 the whole of Greece was under a tripartite German, Italian, and Bulgarian occupation."[14]

Rumors spread that the Bulgarians intended to seize Athonite property belonging to them; the Greeks feared expulsion by them from the Mountain. Athos remained secure, however. On April 29 a decree was signed by Generalmajor Arenzen: "The region of the Holy Mountain comes under the protection of the German armed forces. Without the written permission of the military commandant, nobody may enter this region."[15]

St Sophrony (see previous chapter) accompanied the German officers in their first inspection of the Mountain and served as their interpreter. The Germans, impressed with this educated Russian polyglot, spoke of him favorably in dispatches to the Führer. It was thanks largely to St Sophrony that the Twenty Monasteries were able to preserve their independence during the occupation. The occupiers behaved respectfully. They did not enter a monastery armed and refused the Bulgarians military access to Athos.

In April 1941, the abbots of the Twenty Ruling Monasteries wrote a letter: "To the Chancellor of the Glorious German State, Mr Adolph Hitler …. We have the exceptional honor to present to your Excellency our earnest plea to vouchsafe to take under your personal protection and care this sacred place." The letter concluded:

> We implore the King of Kings and the Lord of Lords from all our soul and hearts to grant your Excellency health and length of days for the wellbeing of the glorious German people, and we sign with deep respect [followed by the signatures and seals of the Twenty].[16]

Some Athonites believed that the Germans would protect them from the Soviet threat. R. M. Dawkins, the British archaeologist (1871–1955) and Director of the British School in Athens (1906–1913), saw a portrait of Hitler in Konstamonitou Monastery. Dawkins commented on "the admiration felt by the monks for Hitler, regarded by them as the High Protector of the Holy Mountain in the new world order," and on "the rather silly remark of a monk that the Virgin was protecting the Germans in their struggle against Bolshevism."[17]

In June 1942, a year after the German invasion of the USSR and two months before the Battle of Stalingrad, representatives of the DNB[18] visited the Mountain. They were greeted enthusiastically:

> The Synod of the Sacred Community most heartily thanks the German occupying forces in Greece for their defense and recognition of the Sacred Community's former rights, which the German authorities have promoted in every manner. We follow with great amazement the brave struggle of the German army and its allies for the liberation of Russia from godless Bolshevism …. The Sacred Community of the Holy Mountain of Athos confidently awaits the victory of the defender of Christianity, the German Reich and its allies.[19]

Expecting widespread Athonite condemnation of the Bolsheviks, the Germans hoped to exploit the lack of unity affecting the Russian Orthodox Church Outside Russia (ROCOR) and the Church in Russia's compromised position.[20] In the

Autumn of 1943 the APA (Außenpolitisches Amt, the Nazi Foreign Policy Office) asked the Sacred Community to sign a condemnation of the election of Metropolitan Sergy (Stragorodsky) as patriarch of Moscow.[21] Neither the Sacred Community nor the Russian Athonites responded.

During the German occupation of the Mountain, rations in St Panteleimon's had to be reduced drastically. Owing to hyperinflation of the drachma the gold coins accumulated in the abbot's safe had to be sold. This enabled Monks Vasily (Krivoshein) and David (Tsuber) to go on several trips to Bulgaria to buy provisions.[22] The Holy Synod of the Bulgarian Patriarchate donated 35,000 levs[23] to the Russian Athonites, and in 1944 the Bulgarian Red Cross brought in more supplies. The Germans, meanwhile, demanded that all the monasteries hand over 400 *oka* / 512.8 kg of oil. The monasteries were also obliged to sell their timber to the German army. Athonites were forbidden to buy provisions on German-occupied territory in Northern Greece. As a result of pressure by the Bulgarians, Romanians, and ROCOR, however, Athonites were allowed to barter the timber left over, as well as nuts and olive oil for essential foodstuffs such as wheat, beans, and other vegetables. Despite the increasing austerity, St Panteleimon's continued to make charitable donations. In May and September 1943, and April 1944, it gave money for poor orphans in Thessaloniki and elsewhere in Greece; in October 1944, it donated clothing and food to Serbian partisans.

Life on Athos was considerably less harsh than in other parts of Greece. The *Megalos Limos* / the Great Greek Famine (1941–1944) claimed some 100,000 victims.

In May 1944, the German occupiers left the Holy Mountain. Soon the first Greek civilians arrived, of whom ten were assigned to Karyes. Ten soldiers each were billeted in Daphne and the Great Lavra. On October 12, 1944, the communist-backed Greek Liberation Army, ELAS, and its political wing, EAM, having waged guerrilla warfare against the Germans, took control of most of Greece, and occupied the Holy Mountain from November 1944 to March 1945.

Certain Athonites were suspected of collaboration with the Nazis. The hermits of Karoulia, on the southwestern tip of the peninsula, would therefore not speak to St Sophrony. For reasons unknown, he left St Panteleimon's and moved to Aghiou Pavlou Monastery, but in 1946 he moved again to the St Andrew Skete. The next year he left the Mountain for good and emigrated to France. One of his spiritual children, Fr Irinaios of Karakallou Monastery, commented:

> The ill-educated, venal nationalist monks (or rather, those who backed them) began to spread rumors of Fr Sophrony's collaboration with the Germans. In

so doing they unjustly besmirched his name. Instead of receiving gratitude for helping to preserve the holy things of Athos—which the Athonites themselves requested—he was accused of secretly helping the occupiers. This merciless slander was the main but largely unknown reason for the Fr Sophrony's forced abandonment of the Holy Mountain.[24]

Monk Vasily (Krivoshein)'s fate was harsher. On September 26, 1947, he was tried in Thessaloniki, having been expelled from Athos. Along with some Bulgarian and Russian Athonites he was accused of collaboration: the prosecution claimed that he was secretly working with the Bulgarians, for he had visited Bulgaria several times (with Fr David [Tsuber], to buy provisions). He was condemned to two years imprisonment and incarcerated on the island of Makronisos (off Cape Sounion), where he lost half a finger from frostbite.[25]

The Establishment of Links between St Panteleimon Monastery and the Moscow Patriarchate

Patriarch Sergy (Stragorodsky) died in May 1944. In February 1945 he was succeeded by Aleksey I (Simansky), who was his *locum tenens* for a year. It was to Patriarch Aleksey that Abbot Iustin first wrote, in June 1945. The letter was handed to the Yugoslav consul in Thessaloniki by Monk Vasily (Krivoshein) and reached Moscow via diplomatic post.

Archimandrite Iustin told the patriarch about the Greeks' plans:

Their clear aim is to stifle all the non-Greek houses on Athos (and above all those of the Russians), to wipe out the national minorities there, and to convert the Holy Mountain from a Pan-Orthodox center, where monks of all Orthodox nationalities live, into a purely Greek region inhabited by Greeks alone.[26]

Iustin complained that in every way possible the Greek government was hindering settlement on the Mountain by non-Greeks. There had been 800 brethren in the monastery in the 1920s, but today there were just 215.

Iustin seemed naively unaware of the realities of Stalinist Russia; perhaps in desperation he resorted to flattery:

With still greater joy we hear from every quarter that the Orthodox faith and Church in Russia now enjoy complete freedom, and that the rulers of mighty Russia regard the Church of Christ with fitting respect and benevolence ....

We firmly believe that … the Russian government, continuing the age-old tradition of Russia's defense of Orthodoxy in the East, will be able honorably and successfully to defend both Russian and Pan-Orthodox interests on Mount Athos.[27]

Nonetheless, the wheels of the Soviet government machinery were set in motion. On September 26, 1945, G. Razumovsky, an official of the Department of External Church Relations (DECR) sent a *spravka* / note of reference to Metropolitan Nikolay (Yakushevich) of Krutitsk and Kolomna: "The Russian Orthodox Church must insist on the return to the three Russian monasteries [*sic*] and sketes[28] of their property so that the Church's outpost at the entrance to the Mediterranean be restored."[29]

For all its belligerent Stalinist rhetoric, a more astute observation was voiced by another member of the DECR, Archpriest Veniamin (Platonov). He understood that much of Russian Athos had become amenable to the USSR:

The mood of the Athonite monks is interesting insofar as, being for the most part apolitical, they have not yielded to those fragments of anti-Soviet propaganda which have managed to reach them … and they have not been inclined to lean towards the militant "Crusade" of Hitler against the USSR in 1941–1945. Rather, the heroic struggle of the USSR against the German invaders and their brutality in the occupied regions, not to mention the restoration of the Patriarchate in Moscow, have fundamentally altered the attitude of a significant proportion of the monks to Soviet power. For these monks it has become clear that the Soviet Union's policy is to defend the traditional interests of the Motherland throughout the world, and in particular in the Balkans and the Near East.[30]

Ironically, coming to the aid of what was seen as the oppressed Russians on Athos had become something of a crusade. In Aleksey I's words:

Reviving the traditional Russian policy of protecting Russian Athonites can significantly strengthen their position, at the same time increasing the influence of the Soviet Union on the peoples of the Balkans and the Near East. The Soviet Union alone can hinder the Greek chauvinists from laying their hands on the Russian houses.[31]

It seems that the worst fears of the Greeks about Russian expansionist aims in the Near East before the Bolshevik Revolution were at last being realized. Whereas in the age of Ieronim and Makary Russian Athonites were intent on merely establishing strong monastic communities on the Holy Mountain, often despite hindrance from the motherland, the Soviets were beginning to understand the tactical importance of their representatives' holding on to a key position in the Mediterranean.

St Panteleimon Monastery was, it seems, becoming increasingly pro-Soviet. On July 21, 1946, the Second Secretary to the Soviet Embassy in Athens, B. D. Karmanov, was invited to visit St Panteleimon's. At his arrival he was greeted with a peel of bells. Many were shocked, however, that this Soviet functionary did not show sufficient respect to cross himself upon entering church.

Fortunately, the Holy Mountain was out of the USSR's reach. Political and expansionist aims were irrelevant; all that mattered was the survival of the Russian Athonite community. As Vasily (Krivoshein) repeatedly wrote to Metropolitan Nikolay (Yakushevich): "We must achieve only one thing—the sole matter of importance at present: Russian monks must be allowed to go to Mount Athos, otherwise Russian monasticism will die out there."[32]

At first Patriarch Aleksey's pleas to Greek hierarchs fell on deaf ears. He first wrote to Archbishop Damaskinos of Athens, Head of the Church of Greece, on May 15, 1947. The patriarch asked why the Slav monks of Athos were being cut off. He sent the same letter two days later to Patriarch Athenagoras of Constantinople, and to others. Damaskinos replied that he was sorry, but he had "nothing to do with the autonomy of the Holy Mountain …. which, according to its Charter, enjoys the privilege of independence and autonomy in its own administration." He added that he had it on competent authority that no injustices had been committed against the Slav brethren; and that in view of the "the general political situation," stricter controls were necessary.[33]

A colloquium entitled *O slavyanskom monashestve na Afone / About Slav Monasticism on Athos* was held in Moscow July 5–8, 1948, coinciding with the celebrations for the 500 years of the Russian Orthodox Church's autocephaly. Representatives of the Church of Greece and the Ecumenical Patriarchate, present as honored guests, heard of the parlous state of St Panteleimon's and of the suppression of the non-Greek Athonite population. Owing to civil war in Greece,[34] and poor relations between Greece and the USSR, however, nothing was achieved to ease the plight of St Panteleimon's.

On March 7, 1953, Patriarch Aleksey wrote to Patriarch Athenagoras complaining that Russian Athos had been cut off for more than three decades. Aleksey continued in his unfortunately hostile vein: "The present unjust position of the Russian monks on Athos cannot be tolerated any longer." He threatened to take measures to "return the property confiscated from the house of St Panteleimon;" he demanded that Russian monks be freely allowed to settle on the Mountain and that their rights be defended.[35] Seemingly unaware of the thin ice he was treading on, Aleksey wrote another letter to Athenagoras, also in 1953, complaining that the 1926 Charter was "in diametric contradiction to both the traditions of the Holy Mountain and international law."[36] He then reiterated his plea that monks and scholars of the Russian Orthodox Church be granted free access to St Panteleimon's. Athenagoras did not reply and the Greeks hardened their stance.

On September 7, 1954, St Panteleimon Monastery again extended hospitality to Soviet officials. The Soviet ambassador in Athens, Mikhail Sergeev, and three of his colleagues visited, although the Greek Foreign Ministry disapproved. In the monastery's guest book Sergeev enthused: "I am grateful to the monastery's abbot, Archimandrite Iustin, and to all the brethren for the gracious reception afforded to me and the embassy staff."[37] As had been the case eight years before with Mr Karmanov, some were shocked that the Soviet officials did not cross themselves upon entering church. The Sacred Community wrote a letter to St Panteleimon's objecting to the visit; this provoked a testy reply from the monastery's Council of Elders.[38]

Fr Vasily (Krivoshein) understood the situation better than most. On his visit to the USSR in August 1956, he told Metropolitan Nikolay (Yakushevich) that the Moscow Patriarchate must moderate its tone; it must cease its political hectoring and avoid mentioning constitutional rights: it should instead ask for nothing more than the free entry to Athos of ten Russian monks.

Patriarch Aleksey duly wrote to the Greek Foreign Ministry and Athenagoras on March 12, 1957, for permission to let in ten Russian monks. Another letter followed a year later to Athenagoras. The ecumenical patriarch eventually replied, but merely to point out that all those wishing to enter the Mountain must obtain six different sets of documents.

In 1958 Abbot Ilian (Sorokin) wrote to Patriarch Aleksey begging for material aid. The monastery's numbers, wrote Ilian, had dwindled to fifty; the youngest monk was fifty-four years old, whereas most of the brethren were into their eighties.

Just when the situation at the monastery seemed hopeless, the head of the Russian Orthodox Spiritual Mission at Jerusalem, Archimandrite Nikodim (Rotov) arrived, on February 9, 1959. He saw for himself the state of St Panteleimon Monastery and reported back to Moscow. Later to rise meteorically to the rank of metropolitan of

Fig 2.1 Novaya Fivaida Skete, built at the behest of Frs Ieronim and Makary for the wandering beggar monks, the *siromakhi*. The skete was one of the centers of the Name of God rebellion.

Fig 2.2 Ilarion Domrachov, monk of the New Athonite Monastery of St Simon the Canaanite, author of *On the Mountains of the Caucasus*, which sparked off the Name of God Rebellion.

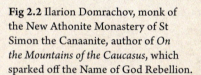

Fig 2.3 The platoon of the 50th Belostoksky Regiment at St Panteleimon's with sailors from *SS Donets* brought in to quell the Name of God Rebellion.

Fig 2.4 The *SS Donets* and *SS Kherson* anchored off St Panteleimon's, ready to deport the Name of God rebels.

Fig 2.5

Fig 2.6

Fig 2.7

Fig 2.8 The central courtyard between the refectory and the *Kato Katholikon* / the Lower Central Church of St Panteleimon (1880s).

Fig 2.9 Greek soldiers stationed at the Preobrazhensky Korpus, turned into an army sanatorium, 1923–1924.

Fig 2.10 St Sophrony (Sakharov) (1st left, back row), Monk Vasili (Krivoshein), later Archbishop of Brussels (3rd right, back row), and St Silouan (1st left, front row).

Fig 2.11

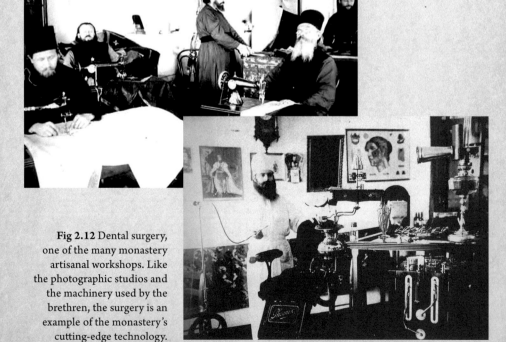

Fig 2.12 Dental surgery, one of the many monastery artisanal workshops. Like the photographic studios and the machinery used by the brethren, the surgery is an example of the monastery's cutting-edge technology.

Fig 2.13 The great bell being hoisted onto the belfry. The bell arrived by ship in 1894 and took eight days to be transported into the monastery and put in place.

Fig 2.14 Fr Vasili (Krivoshein) showing German officers round St Panteleimon's. He and St Sophrony, the only ones with fluent German, looked after and liaised with the occupiers.

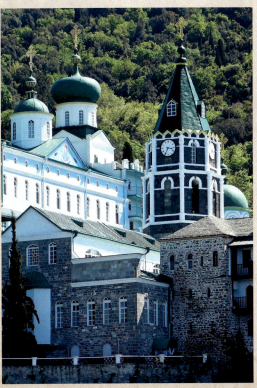

Fig 2.15

Fig 2.16 The refectory of St Panteleimon's Monastery circa 2015.

Fig 2.17 A festive meal in the refectory, 1912.

Fig 2.18 The consecration of the shrine to the Mother of God of the Drawn by Light Icon (2011). The icon has been reproduced as a marble plaque to the right of the fountain. See detail on the right. Fig 2.19

Fig 2.20 Abbot Ieremiya (left) and Fr Makary (Makienko) with Putin, 2005.

Fig 2.22 His All-Holiness Ecumenical Patriarch Bartholomew and Abbot Ieremiya, October 2013.

Fig 2.21 Metropolitan Nikodim (Rotov) of Leningrad (1929–1978), who was instrumental in getting new recruits and material aid from the USSR to St Panteleimon's.

Fig 2.23 A fragment of an icon given by Patriarch Kirill to the monastery in 2014 showing the Mother of God as Abbess of Athos with all the Russian Athonite Saints.

Fig 2.24

Fig 2.25 Abbot Ieremiya clearing the snow.

Leningrad, here at last was someone who had the energy and common sense to make things happen.

In 1959 there was a serious fire at the monastery. Machinery and other material aid were sent from Russia. These were blocked, but on November 11–15, 1959, a Moscow Patriarchate delegation was visiting Thessaloniki for the 600th anniversary of St Gregory Palamas and managed to get some of the goods through. By the 1960s calendars from the Moscow Patriarchate, its magazine, *Zhurnal Moskovskoy Patriarkhii / The Journal of the Moscow Patriarchate*, and letters were being delivered to the monastery. There were attempts by Russian émigrés to block what they saw as the godless influence of the Soviet Church on the monastery. One such opponent was an American millionaire named Semenenko, who angrily asked Abbot Ilian why he was "conducting a lengthy correspondence with the Church of Moscow."[39]

The breakthrough came in June 1962, when Nikodim (Rotov), now an archbishop, visited the monastery again. On September 1, he wrote to DECR recommending that a minimum of ten monks be sent from Russia. The main thrust of his letter, however, was about solidarity the Moscow Patriarchate must be seen to have with the beleaguered Russian Athonites. The monastery needed parcels of goods, a lorry, and a tractor:

> Although these parcels attract heavy duty, they are essential not so much for their material worth, which is minimal. The Russians' mood is lifted because they realize that after decades of isolation they have a Motherland and compatriots. The Greeks, on the other hand, are now beginning to respect the Russians, whom they hesitate to upset, knowing that the Moscow Patriarchate backs the Russians.

Having discussed the practicalities of acquiring the heavy machinery for the Monastery, the archbishop explains the impact a new tractor would have:

> In the final analysis, it will play an important part in what [people say] in both the Athonite community and the regions of Northern Greece close to Athos. Such was the case with the Serbs, who sent a tractor to [Hilandar]. It was the talk of not only all of Athos but Northern Greece.[40]

A year later, a lorry was delivered to St Panteleimon's.

Better lines of communication were at last being established between Moscow and Constantinople. Having joined the World Council of Churches in 1961, the Russian Orthodox Church sent its representatives to the 1963 Pan-Orthodox Conference on Rhodes. On June 23, 1963, Archbishop Nikodim attended the millennial celebrations of the founding of the Great Lavra, at which Patriarch Athenagoras announced that he would guarantee the acceptance of new Athonite recruits sent by the heads of the autocephalous churches.

In October 1963 Aleksey I sent Athenagoras a list eighteen candidates for St Panteleimon's. The following summer the ecumenical patriarch granted permission for five members of the Pskovo-Pecherskaya Lavra to join the brotherhood.[41] Two years later, Greek citizenship was granted to the five, thanks in part to the efforts of the Slavicist, Professor A.-E. Tachiaos of Thessaloniki University.[42] At last, in July 1966, just four monks from the Pskovo-Pecherskaya Lavra arrived at St Panteleimon's. In 1967 one of the new recruits returned to the USSR "owing to illness and complications of a personal nature," and one of them asked for political asylum. Nonetheless, "from henceforward the Moscow Patriarch became an official benefactor of the monastery, since he was now genuinely able to help it."[43]

With the establishment of the military Junta in Athens and the deposition of the king of the Hellenes in April 1967, St Panteleimon Monastery enjoyed a brief period of closeness with the Sacred Community. The Junta issued Decree 124. It aimed to subjugate the Holy Mountain by giving control to the civil governor over the property of the Twenty Monasteries, the decisions of the Sacred Community, and over all Athonite legal matters. The Moscow Patriarchate fully supported the Sacred Community in its opposition to Decree 124. Patriarch Alexy and his Synod protested to Colonel Papadopoulos, the Junta's leader, and to Patriarch Athenagoras. In August 1967 Archbishop Ieronimos of Athens came out in support of the Decree, which, he claimed, did not interfere with Athos. Patriarch Aleksey fell out with him over this, but the Sacred Community became well disposed to St Panteleimon's because of Moscow's stance.

A devastating fire broke out in the monastery on October 23, 1968. Heavy machinery was needed for refurbishment, but it was not until four years later that a lorry and bulldozer got through. Numbers in December 1968 were down to a mere fifteen, but in March 1969 permission was granted for four new recruits. Of these two did not make the journey to Athos; one of those who did was Archimandrite Avel' (Makedonov), the future abbot.

There was a change of personnel in the patriarchates. On April 17, 1970, Alexy I died. He was replaced by Pimen, who, between October 23 and 25, 1972, was the first Patriarch of Moscow to visit the Holy Mountain. Meanwhile, Patriarch Athenagoras, with whom Moscow had spent decades building a working relationship, died on July 7, 1972. Metropolitan Nikodim, followed by a DECR representative, visited the Greek ambassador in Moscow to ask for six more new recruits to be sent to the monastery. They were told that visas would be granted, but the new ecumenical patriarch would have to give his blessing.

Patriarch Dimitrios, enthroned in Constantinople on July 7, 1972, did not reply to Pimen. The latter was upset; he sent Dimitrios a telegram expressing his bewilderment at the "inexplicable silence, which we interpret as Your Holiness shunning us."[44] Eventually, in March 1974, Dimitrios gave his blessing for two new recruits.

The Junta fell on July 23, 1974, and Decree 124 was annulled. Thereafter there was a thaw in the relations between the Greek government and the Russian Church; visas were granted more easily to Soviet citizens wishing to go to the Mountain. Of the two new recruits to whom Patriarch Dimitrios had given his blessing, only one came to St Panteleimon's, in April 1975: he was Priest-Monk Ieremiya (Alyokhin), who was to succeed Abbot Avel'. This was hardly enough, for between 1970 and 1974 a further eight fathers had died; now only fourteen, mostly infirm old men, remained. Nonetheless, life was becoming easier. From 1975 Russian delegations arrived at the monastery annually. In June 1976 the first Athonites, a group of nine representatives of the Greek monasteries, visited the USSR. In August 1976 Archbishop Vasily (Krivoshein), after an absence of twenty-seven years, came to the Holy Mountain. On October 12–19, 1977, Patriarch Pimen visited Constantinople; as a result, five new recruits arrived in May 1978.

Archimandrite Avel' Leaves

The short reign of Abbot Avel' was problematic. As in the case of Abbot Andrey (Veryovkin) (Chapter 8), whose abbacy was overshadowed by the powerful Fr Pavel (Durnev), Avel' lacked the strength of character possessed by the monastery's leading light—the experienced and popular steward, secretary, and one-time monastery representative in Karyes, Deacon David (Tsuber). The Greek Slavicist A.-E. Tachiaos assessed Tsuber thus: "Everyone on the Holy Mountain loved and respected him for his gentle and accommodating nature, which excelled in discretion and sagacity."[45] Archbishop Vasily (Krivoshein), with whom Fr David had traveled during the War to Bulgaria for supplies, knew his worth: "He knows everything going on with the Greeks—the Sacred Community, the governors etc."[46]

Unfortunately, once he became abbot, Fr Avel' seemed to resent David, who complained about this to the Archbishop. In a letter to Metropolitan Nikodim, Vasily said: "I am just saddened that [Archimandrite Avel'] has developed poor relations with Fr David, for the abbot does not yet know enough and underestimates the experience of Fr David." Archbishop Vasili knew that Avel' was generally disliked: "Some criticize him for his lack of firmness, for his inability to enforce discipline and to cope with the brethren."[47]

Although few in number, the brethren desperately needed strong leadership. Deacon David explained:

> There are now eighteen brethren, of whom two are Greek, as well as one Bulgarian, and one a Serb. We have a total of fourteen Russians, but some are quite elderly, while others don't know Greek. The young ones show no initiative. Their sole wish is to live comfortably; they are not in the slightest concerned how everything has to be obtained, cooked, and served at table; we simply cannot make them realize that as the monastery is our home we must take responsibility for everything .... The worst thing is that there is no brotherly love among them. They often fight—even in church—and twice two of them pulled each other's hair out. Avel' is agitated, and we're all upset that we cannot knock sense into them, and kicking them out is inconvenient. Quite simply, they're abnormal people. It's really bad that the whole of Athos will find out, the Russian Church and its monks will get a bad reputation, and our [erstwhile] well-wishers will gleefully point a finger at Soviet monasticism.[48]

Fr David spoke of a young Priest-Monk Sergy, an "outright drunkard," whose behavior was horrendously inappropriate in the refectory and church. The brethren tried in vain to send him to other monasteries because of his insubordination, so they had to bring in the police to calm him down.[49] It seems that the rotten apples were just three or four in number. They were "mentally unstable. It's become clear that over there, in Russia, they had been locked up in mental hospitals."[50]

During Avel''s troubled reign, the St Andrew's Skete became empty and derelict. Writing in 1978, the Karyes representative of St Panteleimon's and one-time dean, Archimandrite Misail (Tomin), described how he was suddenly summoned to the civil governor at Karyes:

> He proposed that I select two of our Russian monks and move into the St Andrew Skete. Vatopedi Monastery [the skete's Ruling Monastery] was giving

the skete away so that services could be conducted in it; and Vatopedi promised to offer every assistance. Fr Avel', however, reacted completely differently to the Governor's summons, and was stunned. He is extremely mistrustful and thinks very highly of himself.[51]

Abbot Avel"s lack of popularity was largely due to his unwillingness to commit to his abbacy. In a statement starkly at odds with the selfless dedication of the likes of Abbot Makary (Sushkin), Avel' complained:

Church at night. In the day it's either domestic matters or reception of visitors. And so it goes on, day in, day out. It's hot almost the whole year round. And what heat! It's damp. If I serve at the altar, everything is wet on me and sweat pours down. I come back from church to my cell, change and think: well, perhaps nobody will come today, let's try. No sooner have I soaked my laundry than people start coming—from the Governor and the ministry, or ambassadors turn up, and businessmen, or someone else. I say goodbye to one lot and others immediately arrive. By now the bells are being rung; it's time to go to vespers, and then the night services begin.[52]

Archimandrite Avel"s departure on October 1, 1978, to attend Metropolitan Nikodim's funeral was an embarrassing inconvenience. The monastery's Council of Elders asked Metropolitan Yuvenaly (Poyarkov) of Krutitsk and Kolomna, the Chairman of the DECR, to send them a written certification of Avel"s resignation from the abbacy.

In a letter to Patriarch Pimen, Fr Ieremiya, the Abbot's *locum tenens*, said: "Fr Avel' has left his brotherhood, and the whole monastery is upset. When he was leaving for the funeral … as he was saying goodbye to the brethren he intimated that perhaps he might return to Athos, but perhaps not."[53] Writing to Archbishop Vasily, Deacon David summed up the Avel' debacle thus:

We now have no abbot. Archimandrite Ieremiya has been elected *locum tenens*. No outsider could have so upset the monastery as Avel' managed to do. He had categorically demanded that the keys to all the moneyboxes, the vestry etc. be handed over to him, and nobody suspected that he was an outsider and that he even harbored hostile feelings to the monastery. We noticed this, but unfortunately, it was already too late; nonetheless, no one could believe that he was from the KGB. When he left, he entrusted the keys neither to the *locum tenens*, nor the stewards, nor anyone else; he left them to his cook and cell attendant, Filaret—a fellow of the vilest demeanor, whom [government representatives] told me to warn Avel' to expel from the monastery, but Avel' would not hear of this.[54]

Patriarch Pimen asked for a full report on Avel' from St Panteleimon's. As a pro-tégé of Metropolitan Nikodim (Rotov's), Avel' was said to be lined up for a bishopric. Now that the metropolitan was dead, and on account of the doubtlessly far from glowing report, the former Athonite was never elevated in rank. He became abbot of the Ioanno-Bogoslovsky Monastery in Ryazan', where he died on December 6, 2006.

Chapter 13

From Abbot Ieremiya to Abbot Evlogy

Abbot Ieremiya (1978–2016)

Priest-Monk of the Great Schema Ieremiya (Alyokhin) was unanimously elected abbot, "since there was simply no other candidate."[1] On June 9/22, 1979, he was enthroned as the monastery's archimandrite.

One of Fr Ieremiya's more detailed biographies was written by Priest-Monk Makary (Makienko), until recently the *obschy dukhovnik* / general spiritual father of St Panteleimon Monastery and deputy to the abbot.[2] Fr Ieremiya was born Iakov Filippovich on October 22, 1915, in the Novorussky Khutor, Rostovskaya Oblast' (today Ukrainian Donbass). His family were pious peasants who attended church regularly, and chanted and sang from the service books at home. He had two elder brothers.

At the end of the 1920s the Alyokhins suffered from the anti-kulak pogroms.[3] Iakov's father was arrested and was about to go to prison, but Iakov's brother Ivan voluntarily went to prison in his stead. In 1928/1929 the whole family was "dekulakized" and deported to the Urals. Having arrived at a desolate bank of the River Kama, "they made the sign of the cross and eked out a living by building huts out of pine and by heavy labor."[4] The following year, Iakov's mother, Tatyana, died of cold and starvation. His father disappeared; the brother who had been imprisoned escaped back to Mariupol', close to his home village. Over the next three years Iakov also made his way home. In 1935 he was working as a crane operator at the Donbass Il'ich metallurgic plant, having met up with his other two brothers.

By the start of the Second World War, the brothers had volunteered to fight in the Red Army.[5] Iakov himself was spared military service because the Il'ich plant, which produced T-34 tanks and Il-2 fighter 'planes, was essential to the war effort, and he was a skillful and valued worker. In February 1941 Mariupol' was taken by the Germans. The twenty-six-year-old Iakov was deported by train to Bavaria where he worked for three years, again as a crane operator. In 1945 he was back in the USSR, earning his keep for the next eleven years at the Lugansk bread factory.

Throughout Iakov's life in the Soviet Union, he openly professed his Christianity, refusing to join the Komsomol and attending church whenever possible. Miraculously, and perhaps because he was an excellent worker, he was not persecuted for his faith. In 1956, aged forty-one, he joined the Odessa Seminary. He was tonsured with the name of Ieremiya in January 1957, at the Odessa Monastery of the Dormition. There he was ordained to the priesthood a year later.

Fr Ieremiya performed the obedience of cellarer. His spiritual father was St Kuksha (Velichko), who in the last forty days of his life received Communion only from Fr Ieremiya.[6] Before he died (1964), the saint prophesied to him: "How can I thank you, my child? You will become an abbot on Athos."[7]

From then on Fr Ieremiya yearned for the Holy Mountain, but he had to wait. It was only on April 26, 1974, that he made it to St Panteleimon's. He was one of the six candidates who had applied to go to Athos. The other five were from the Pskovo-Pecherskaya Lavra, of whom only two were selected but none left the Soviet Union.[8] Now an archimandrite and almost sixty, Fr Ieremiya said to the brethren upon his arrival: "Forgive me for coming at such an [advanced] age."[9]

Fr Ieremiya initially worked as a cellarer, as he had done in Odessa. He was then put in charge of vestments and was soon promoted to membership of the Council of Elders. On April 10, 1976, less than two years after his arrival, he was made *obschy dukhovnik* / the monastery's general spiritual father.

Ieremiya was appointed *namestnik* / *locum tenens* following Archimandrite Avel''s departure on October 1, 1978, to attend Metropolitan Nikodim's funeral. Archbishop Vasily (Krivoshein) had warned:

> Do not expect that a ready-made abbot be sent to you from Russia; this would not be desirable: rather choose for yourselves an abbot from one of your own Athonite monks, whom you already know, for whom the monastery's matters will be of paramount importance, and who will not be constantly leaving for Russia. It seems to me that such a person is Archimandrite Ieremiya.[10]

The archbishop was right. Fr Ieremiya's harsh life in the Soviet Union, during which he had spent twenty years in camps and in captivity, and sixteen working in factories, had instilled in him resilience, single-mindedness, and industry. One of the senior St Panteleimon brethren, Archimandrite Misail (Tomin), assessed him thus: "an excellent monk, hard-working, humble, and quiet."[11] Some twenty years later Priest-Monk Kirion (Ol'hovik) enthused:

Fr Ieremiya does not like giving orders; he simply gets on with a job himself and leads by example. You'll sooner find him with a saw, spade, paintbrush or brick in his hands than with his abbot's staff. Once … he and Fr Iona, the caretaker of Old Mountain Rusik, painted the roof of the skete's *kyriakon* / central church.[12]

Not everyone approved of the new abbot, however. Deacon David (Tsuber) wrote to Archbishop Vasily (Krivoshein):

Many brethren are now highly displeased with Fr Ieremiya's behavior, and rightly so. As a monk, Fr Ieremiya is an example to all: he is industrious to a fault, he fasts, and is a man of prayer and compassion, etc. As a leader, however, owing to his buttoned-up character, he has turned out really rather negatively. Nobody could imagine that such a humble man should be so attached to power. As soon as he became abbot, he gradually and discreetly grabbed hold of all the keys and rights; so now he is both abbot, spiritual father, treasurer, librarian, in charge of vestments, clothing, food stores (but not the wine cellar), and buyer and seller of all goods, etc. At first I kept quiet; I thought, let him toil for the glory of God; but the junior brethren grumbled, for they saw that they were being ignored, and they were right: he trusts no one with anything. Then I noticed that harm was being done. This is because he cannot look to everything and hasn't the time. I've found out that the library manuscripts and books have holes bored in them by moths and worms; rats and mice have made nests in the vestries, etc. No accounts are being kept and there is no record of any kind of transaction. As the senior member of the brotherhood, I upbraided [him], because we are [all] responsible. Unfortunately, instead of listening to me and thinking things over, he got angry with me and grumbled that I purportedly wanted to dismiss him from the abbacy—such an idea never occurred to anyone. The point is, none of us is suitable to fulfil the obedience of abbot; we merely aim to remedy the situation. Recently at our [Council of Elders] gathering I absolutely insisted that a report be written by the end of the year and that he appoint as his deputy one of the younger brethren who could get used to running things. In the New Year I'm thinking of adding new members to the Council. If he doesn't agree, steps will have to be taken, but I hope that he'll make concessions. It's obvious that for all his meekness he is influenced by his lust for power. Let us hope that for the sake of power he gives up some of his stubbornness. Personally, I have to say that such a man can be tolerated up to a point as his hard work for the monastery cannot be matched.[13]

Deacon David's assessment is somewhat harsh. He was, of course, not bitter that he himself had not become abbot, for, as we saw at the beginning of Chapter 10, he had refused the post upon his election by apostolic ballot in 1958. That Abbot Ieremiya did not deputize and seemed suspicious of everyone, however, was not due to his lust for power, as Deacon David claimed. Ieremiya was a product of imprisonment, the War, camps, and hard labor; he had had to stand up to authority in defense of his religion. Unsurprisingly therefore, he withdrew into himself, trusting only himself. Apart from Fr David, the brethren, were, as we have seen, unreliable.[14] Furthermore, the abbot is head of everything at St Panteleimon's: he is, for instance, officially though only nominally the chief librarian.

For a time it seemed as if the abbot could not cope. Discipline went from bad to worse. Archimandrite Misail (Tomin) wrote:

> We have no elder in the house. Our Father Abbot is uncommunicative; he is always silent and never says a word to anyone—not a word of instruction or of reprimand for any of the brethren's misdemeanors. Complete absence of order reigns here; anybody can do as he pleases. Some wander freely about the monasteries of the Mountain, others lie blotto in their cells or get up to the most frightful shenanigans. And all this is seen by pilgrims and tourists who come to us. Practically nobody goes to church, and if they do, it's at the end of the Liturgy .... Father Abbot doesn't say a word to anyone, and he won't send … anyone to work. He himself works day and night. So the situation in our house is very bleak.[15]

In judging Fr Ieremiya, Deacon David, the immensely experienced former steward and Karyes representative, was really voicing his own grave concerns for the terrible state of his monastery, which had not recovered from the 1968 fire. In Fr Makary (Makienko)'s words:

> When Fr Ieremiya arrived at the Holy Mountain, the Great Russian House—the adornment of the whole of Athos, the glory of the Russian Land—was in a truly sorry state. Of its former magnificence not a trace remained: its extensive lands were overgrown with wild shrubs; its numerous houses and churches had been ruined by the merciless march of time and by inclement weather, and above all by the lack of timely upkeep and refurbishment, for nobody could take care of such things.[16]

In short, St Panteleimon Monastery had reached its nadir. On finding the St Panteleimon library now shut, Professor Tachiaos complained[17]:

The spiritual condition of the monastery is going from bad to worse; God alone knows what lies in the future. Owing to a lack of spiritual leadership, instead of flourishing, especially after the arrival of the new monks, the monastery is sinking ever deeper into decrepitude. I've been visiting the monastery for more than thirty years now and cannot remember anything akin to its present spiritual decline.[18]

Every last scrap of salvageable goods and materials had been removed from Novaya Fivaida. The skete was left to decay. A similar fate befell the buildings of Krumitsa (but not its vineyards), and the monastery's hermitages. Only one monk, priest of the Great Schema Iakov (Polyansky), was left in Xylourgou, and the caretaker, Deacon Iona, lived alone at Old Mountain Rusik.[19]

Although new recruits, nearly all from Pskovo-Pecherskaya Lavra, had continued to arrive in dribs and drabs, several returned to the USSR. For instance, in May 1978 five monks arrived, including Priest-Monk Nikolay (Generalov), the future Karyes representative, but three left for home.[20] The brotherhood was again becoming depleted: "A significant proportion of the newcomers left for their home country. Thus, although there were twenty-seven brethren in 1979 ... and twenty-six on November 1st 1980, by 1981 twenty-two were left, and in 1982 there were just twenty."[21]

Fr Ieremiya, however, was not a quitter. He continued petitioning the Moscow Patriarchate and others for new recruits and material aid.[22] On January 8, 1984, a Greek named Stavros Pasaleris became one of the monastery's first novices for decades, and in July that year an electric generator was installed. A significant breakthrough came in 1987, when seven new monks arrived. Although four of them subsequently left, two of the rest were to become key players in the house's history: Priest-Monks Makary (Makienko) and Kirion (Ol'hovik). The future abbot, Monk Evlogy (Ivanov), arrived in 1988; he was followed in 1991 by Frs Pyotr (Pigol'), and Ioakim (Sabel'nikov). Sabel'nikov and Pigol' were the authors of *Velikaya Strazha*, the first detailed modern history of the monastery based on hitherto unpublished archival sources. It was printed without the monastery's permission. As a result, Ioakim was exiled to Xylourgou and then Krumitsa, and Fr Pyotr left the brotherhood.[23]

It seems that anyone who showed too much independence or initiative in the monastery was considered to be stepping out of line. Fr Nikolay (Generalov), the Karyes representative, spoke up at a meeting of the Sacred Community in May 1992 following the expulsion of the brotherhood of the Prophet Elijah Skete.[24] He had been repeatedly asking Fr Ieremiya for support and advice during the Prophet Elijah

Skete crisis. The abbot told him to proceed with caution and seemed to be in a quandary about the best course of action. Eventually, Fr Nikolay's protest and refusal to sign any protocol in Karyes was deemed to be bordering on disobedience. He was relieved of his post as representative and exiled to Xylourgou.[25]

Meanwhile, Deacon David (Tsuber), having been tonsured to the Great Schema with the name of Dimitry, died on June 12, 1987. Fr Ieremiya's governance of the monastery was now unchallenged. Numbers gradually increased, and in 1989 there were thirty-two brethren. The first two Russian novices joined in 1990. Owing to difficulties in obtaining permission from the Ecumenical Patriarchate, one of them had to wait nine years and the other over ten before tonsure. From now on, however, new recruits arrived from Russia with greater regularity and numbers continued to grow:

Year	Total Number of Brethren
1994	44
1996	57
2002	67, including 20 novices
2003	70
2005	78
2009	82, of whom 5 settled in Krumitsa, 4 in Xylourgou, and 3 in Old Mountain Rusik.[26]

Despite the revival of St Panteleimon Monastery, due to evidently improving relations with Constantinople and with the Greeks in general, the Moscow Patriarchate bore a grudge for the years of opposition it had faced in the twentieth century. Moscow's displeasure was publicly voiced at a conference held in the Russian capital on October 1–4, 2006, entitled *Rossiya-Afon: tysyacheletie dukhovnogo edinstva / Russia–Athos: A Millennium of Spiritual Unity*. Some eighteen Greeks delivered papers and Abbot Efraim (Kutsu) of Vatopedi was a guest of honor. There was an embarrassing showdown at the opening plenary session. A bishop representing Constantinople was sitting on the dais along with Patriarch Aleksey II, several Russian metropolitans, a representative of the Russian government, and Archimandrite Efraim. The bishop objected to be given the floor after one of the metropolitans because, he reminded everyone, Constantinople is senior to Moscow.

Then Metropolitan Yuvenaly (Poyarkov) of Krutitsk and Kolomna spoke. Midway through his speech the simultaneous translation was no longer audible on the delegates' headphones, but by this time everyone had heard enough: Yuvenaly had pulled no punches in his description of the "disgraceful" and "illegal" Greek opposition to the Russian Athonite community. That evening at dinner in the dining room of the Danilov Monastery Hotel, where most of the conference delegates were housed, the Greeks held an impromptu meeting. They were scandalized by the metropolitan's hostility; some even suggested walking out of the conference, but the moderates among them prevailed. Yuvenaly, they said, was a "silly old Jew," who did not necessarily reflect official Moscow Patriarchate opinion; he had apparently taken fright and "barricaded himself" in his residence. So the conference continued as planned, but Yuvenaly's paper was printed not at the beginning of the published proceedings, but tucked away on pp. 236–40. His text contains none of the inflammatory statements that caused such offense.

At length, Moscow and Constantinople seemed to bury the hatchet. In October 2013 Ecumenical Patriarch Bartholomew visited the monastery. He awarded Abbot Ieremiya a pectoral cross and an episcopal staff, and spoke in a spirit of genuine reconciliation and warmth:

> We find this famous house at the height of renovation and reconstruction. This fills our paternal heart with joy, emotion, and satisfaction. We congratulate [its] dearly beloved brethren and invoke God's mercy, and the Protecting Veil of [His] Mother …. Thus [the brotherhood] will ever be a source of joy and godly pride for the Mother Church.[27]

The brotherhood of the monastery now numbered a hundred.

Three Moscow patriarchs have visited St Panteleimon's: Pimen was the pioneer back in 1972; he was followed by Aleksey II in 1996, and by Kirill, who first came four months before the ecumenical patriarch in 2013. The senior hierarchy of the Moscow Patriarchate make regular pilgrimages. His Beatitude Metropolitan Onufry, Head of the Autonomous Ukrainian Orthodox Church of the Moscow Patriarchate, has been coming every year since 1995. In 2014 no fewer than sixty-five Moscow Patriarchate bishops visited the monastery.

Senior Russian government representatives have also been regular visitors to the monastery. President Vladimir Putin first came on September 9, 2005; he was accompanied by Prime Minister Dmitry Medvedev. This was the president's third attempt at reaching Athos: in December 2001, he had been prevented by bad weather, and by the Beslan terror attack on September 4, 2004.[28] The 2005 visit is described with characteristic exuberance by "the monastery chronicler": "For the first time in the entire history of Russian Athonite monasticism the Russian Sovereign visited the monastery."[29] Ever more in the limelight, Fr Makary (Makienko) met the guests at the monastery's wharf and led them to the main gates.[30] The chronicler continues: "The President was in his usual good spirits, but was also modest and humble, and spoke little."[31]

As we have seen, especially in Chapter 4, there were plenty of high-profile visits and solemn festivities at the monastery in the nineteenth century, notably those of the Grand-Princes. All were depicted with joyful elation. Reports of the important twenty-first-century occasions, on the other hand, are drearily wordy. The account of Patriarch Kirill's 2013 visit is a case in point:

> Having arrived at the monastery and walking along a path strewn with laurel, his Holiness proceeded with the brethren to the Central Church dedicated to the Holy Great Martyr Panteleimon. In the Central Church, the Abbot of the Russian Athonites, 98-year-old Elder Priest-Monk of the Great Schema Archimandrite Ieremiya, the oldest abbot of the Holy Mountain, awaited the Primate of the Russian Church and greeted him with filial love. The Representative of the Russian Church bowed down at the main altar table of the house and venerated the sacred skull of the monastery's heavenly patron, the Holy Great Martyr Panteleimon. The monastery choir sang the church's troparia and the troparion to Kirill, the holy Enlightener of the Slav peoples, whose name His Holiness bears; it also sang the *velichaniya* / hymns of praise to the holy saints of God venerated in the Central Church. His Holiness then addressed words of greeting and patriarchal instruction to the brethren, after which he blessed his fellow countrymen who were living as monks in the Garden of the Mother of God.[32]

Distinguished guests in the nineteenth century were presented with special photographic albums, which were highly prized and much appreciated. Recently, a jubilee album has come out to mark the millennium of the Russian presence on Athos.[33] It is a fine edition, printed on expensive, glossy paper. The photographs are in superb color, several opening out to a triple-page spread. On page 101, however, the pictures become official: they feature state visits, of Patriarch Kirill and President Putin in 2016, and of the chair of the Russian Federation State Duma, Sergey Naryshkin. Page 151 is a good, close-up portrait of the president; everything else is out of focus, so in itself the picture is irrelevant to St Panteleimon Monastery. On pages 152–5, civilian bodyguards are prominent; squiggly wires attached to their earpieces are clearly visible on pages 158–9.

The millennium of the Russian presence on Athos was to be the grand culmination of six years' preparation, as well as proof to the world that St Panteleimon

Monastery had been restored as a major presence on the Mountain. The precise date of the jubilee in 2016, however, remained a mystery until the last moment. On March 10, 2016, Patriarch Kirill announced: "For a long time the Church and State have been preparing for this wonderful day. It is assumed that the main celebrations will take place on Mount Athos by the end of May this year."[34] The embarrassing delay was over when President Putin arrived on the Holy Mountain, on May 28, 2016. His visit coincided with that of Patriarch Kirill and he was met in Karyes with the full honors due to a head of state. The jubilee celebrations on Athos at last took place.

The Greeks were unenthusiastic. On March 3, 2016, Greek Athonites claimed that they knew nothing about the proposed visit of Patriarch Kirill to the Holy Mountain for the jubilee. The Sacred Community stated that the patriarchal visit breached protocol because the ecumenical patriarch would have to be approached first and he in turn ought to let the Sacred Community know. Meanwhile, the Sacred Community proposed to invite the then president of Ukraine, P. Poroshenko, to the jubilee celebrations.[35] He declined, but the mischievous intention of inviting the president of a country at war with Russia was clear.[36]

Some members of the Sacred Community were openly hostile. They brought up the old complaints voiced in the previous century: St Panteleimon Monastery had always been Greek until the 1830s; then the Russians settled there, took it over and by cunning installed their own abbot; the monastery had never been Russian, for its designation, *Ton Ros* or *Rossikon*, had nothing to do with the Russians.[37] That the Greek and Russian Athonites did not see eye-to-eye was also apparent because the new St Panteleimon Monastery librarian had no access to the 1016 act held in the Great Lavra.[38]

Furthermore, yet again a new version appeared of the discredited Esphigmenou legend about the tonsure of St Anthony Pechersky. The historian and Indrik editor, Kirill Vakh, observes:

> A new, unannounced version of the legend has [recently] appeared: St Anthony was tonsured in Esphigmenou monastery in 1016. There is no explanation offered either for this date … or for the basis (or revelations) of the sources upon which this date is grounded. One has the impression that the date was artificially connected with the millennium year of Russian Athonite monasticism.[39]

***

Three months after the millennial celebrations at the monastery, on August 4, 2016, Abbot Ieremiya died, aged 101. He was buried by the south sanctuary wall of the *Kato Katholikon* / the Lower Central Church dedicated to St Panteleimon. His remains will be exhumed in August 2021.

Fr Ieremiya had reigned for thirty-six years with admirable tenacity and patience. For all his faults, much had been achieved during his time: "The old buildings were refurbished, twenty chapels and two churches were restored, and six brand-new chapels were built."[40]

The abbot's spiritual legacy was more important. He gave a part of the relics of St Silouan to Simonopetra's Elder Emilianos, upon whose insistence the saint was canonized by the Ecumenical Patriarchate in 1988. In 1999 the Church of Elijah the Prophet at the monastery mill was refurbished. It was here that St Silouan encountered Christ in front of the Saviour's icon on the iconostasis. In 2003 the commemoration of the Icon of the Mother of God Drawn by Light (see Chapter 8) became one of the monastery's main feasts, on August 21/September 3. A fountain was built to the left of the main gate, in front of a marble fresco of the Virgin; on the wall to the right of the gate a large marble plaque of the Icon was fixed.[41]

The St Panteleimon brethren remember Archimandrite Ieremiya with affection bordering on reverence.[42] A whole corner of the monastery museum's first hall,[43] *Igumensky zal* / the Abbot's Hall, is dedicated to him. Ieremiya is thus given almost as much prominence as Archimandrite Makary. There are several websites of Ieremiya's sermons and spiritual instructions, which have also been printed.

Abbot Evlogy (from 2016)

In October 2016 the election for Fr Ieremiya's successor was held. Only those of the brethren who had been monks at the monastery more than eight years were eligible to participate, so thirty-four of the one hundred brethren did so. Spiritual Father Makary (Makienko) received eleven votes; the winner, with twenty-three votes, was Deacon Evlogy (Ivanov).

Fr Evlogy was born Mikhail Ivanovich on September 12/29, 1958 in the Town of Emanzhelinsk, Chelyabinskaya Oblast'. He was tonsured in the Trinity-St Sergius Lavra in 1986 and ordained deacon two years later. Upon his arrival at St Panteleimon's on May 15, 1988, his first obedience was that of *ogorodnik* / vegetable gardener, and then of woodsman. He was next appointed steward of Xylourgou before being transferred to the monastery's Constantinople dependency.

On the Feast of *Pokrov* / the Protecting Veil, October 1/14 2016, Deacon Evlogy was ordained priest by Archbishop Ionafan of Abakan and Khassk. Nine days later, a special Sacred Community commission accompanied by the governor of Athos, A. Kasmiroglou, and the Thessaloniki Russian consul, A. A. Popov, arrived at the monastery. Between the Sixth Hour and the start of the Liturgy, Evlogy was enthroned as archimandrite. Having placed on him a bishop's *mantiya* (blue-and white monastic cloak) and archimandrite's cross, Priest-Monk Nikodimos of the Great Lavra entrusted him with an abbot's episcopal staff. He addressed the new archimandrite, emphasizing the importance of following regulations and tradition to the letter:

> In the name of the Sacred Community we convey with brotherly love to Your Reverence, o beloved of the Lord, that we, representing the Sacred Community of the Holy Mountain of Athos, were informed of the ... legal election of the Most Venerable Archimandrite Evlogy, successor to the deceased Abbot Archimandrite of the Great Schema Ieremiya. Having been informed in our Sacred Assembly of the above-mentioned event, and having found the said event legal and worthy of recognition, we inform you that ... it is the duty of none other than the Representative of the Megisti Lavra to offer the episcopal staff to the newly appointed Abbot .... It is incumbent on us to remind you ... of your spiritual responsibilities to be loyal and devoted to the Mother Church, of your immutable obedience to our Archbishop, Kyrios Kyrios Bartholomew. [I must also remind you of your duty] to fulfill the Heavenly Edicts, the Sacred Canons of the Orthodox Church, the laws of our [monastic republic], and the Constitution of the Holy Mountain of Athos. All this is based on the fundamental premise that Your Reverence cooperate harmoniously with the most honorable members of the Sacred Community, with the Ecumenical Patriarch, and with the Greek State.[44]

It is too early to assess the abbacy of Archimandrite Evlogy, but so far the signs are good. In 2017 he paid an official visit to Patriarch Neofit of Bulgaria together with Fr Nikolay (Generalov), with whom he had evidently come to some sort of a reconciliation on behalf of the monastery.[45] Another olive branch was extended by Fr Evlogy to Schema-Monk Gerasim, a Russian monk who had long lived on the Mountain illegally and had been repeatedly expelled from St Panteleimon's. Now a legally registered Athonite, and living in a Koutloumousiou *kellion* outside Karyes, he received a friendly visit from the St Panteleimon abbot.

Fr Evlogy also granted the historian and authority on St Seraphim of Sarov, Priest Georgy (Pavlovich) of Diveevo, Russia, permission to study a rare nineteenth-century manuscript. On the point of giving up hope, Pavlovich had been asking to see the document for many years. I too have benefited from the Abbot's generosity enabling me to complete this book.

Conclusion

St Panteleimon Monastery is once again an imposing presence on the Holy Mountain. A Greek travel guide—refreshingly free of phyletic bias—sums up the impression a visitor has on approaching the monastery for the first time by sea:

> The … monastery with its emerald-green roofs comes slowly to view and, like a small city state, towers over the visitor ….. Its architectural styles and cupolas are in stark, imposing contrast with all that we know of the Holy Mountain ….. All seems overpowering, huge and numerous ….. Everything in the monastery is on an immense scale ….. The colors stand out; they are a far cry from what we are used to in our familiar East.[1]

The refurbishment of the entire monastery is approaching completion. Novaya Fivaida, Krumitsa, Xylourgou, Old Mountain Rusik, the hermitages, and outlying buildings—nearly all are as new. Since 2015 the remaining half of the vast Preobrazhensky Korpus has been rebuilt. Renovation has progressed at speed.[2]

Watching the builders, bulldozers, and cement mixers, one wonders why everything is being so meticulously restored. Athelstan Riley's observation (see Chapter 8) again comes to mind: "The whole place is more like a small town than a monastery ….. and still the monks are building, so that the great monastery is increasing in extent year by year."[3]

St Panteleimon's can now house large numbers of visitors: there is room for 600 in the Preobrazhensky Korpus alone.[4] The ordinary Russian lay pilgrim finds getting to Athos relatively easy. Before the 1990s, non-Greeks had to get Greek ministerial permission, which was to be presented first to the police upon boarding the Ouranoupolis or Ierissos ferry, and then at the Protaton in Karyes where it was exchanged for a *diamonitirion* / Athonite pass. The Greek government did not issue permission freely and could limit the daily numbers of visitors. In 1993 *diamonitirion* offices were set up in Thessaloniki and Ouranoupolis; the trip to the Greek ministry and to Karyes was no longer necessary. Matters were further simplified by the opening of St Panteleimon dependencies in Moscow (1992) and Kiev (2012).[5] Professor Shkarovsky, the Athonite historian, explains: "From then on citizens of Russia, Ukraine, Byelorus', and other [CIS] countries could reserve their *diamonitiria* ... at their own convenience, [up to] several months in advance ... by applying to the Pilgrims' Bureau at the Moscow and Kiev dependencies."[6] On my last three visits (in April and October 2019) to the monastery I counted fifty to ninety new pilgrims arriving at the monastery every day.

The vast majority of pilgrims are Great and Little Russians, other Slavs, and Romanians. There are very few Greek visitors, perhaps because applying for permission to stay is difficult for the outsider. Each Athonite monastery has a telephone number and email address, but attempting to contact the St Panteleimon authorities via them is problematic. A visitor not having access to the Pilgrims' bureau in Moscow has to write to the *Palomnicheskaya sluzhba RPMA* / the St Panteleimon's Pilgrims' Bureau. He then has to fill in a form, stating, among other things, which church he belongs to and the name of his bishop. This is because of the schism between Moscow and Constantinople.

It is not within the scope of this book to deal in depth with this sorry state of affairs, for the schism has affected St Panteleimon's only tangentially. On October 11, 2018, Patriarch Bartholomew granted autocephaly to a newly created Orthodox Church of Ukraine (OCU) formed by merging two previously independent Ukrainian Orthodox Churches that until that time were not recognized as such by any of the Orthodox Churches: Moscow did not accept that Constantinople had the authority by itself to take these actions. Patriarch Bartholomew explained that the intention of his actions was to heal the rift between Russia and Ukraine, and to include all Orthodox believers in Ukraine in his fold.[7] Moscow responded by breaking communion with Constantinople on October 15, 2018.[8] Constantinople did not, however, break communion with Moscow. From then on Moscow forbade the clergy and laity of the Moscow Patriarchate Russian Orthodox Church to take Communion in Ecumenical Patriarchate parishes. The interdiction is often ignored. Although Patriarch Bartholomew is no longer being commemorated by the Russian Orthodox Church, in St Panteleimon's both the ecumenical patriarch and the patriarch of Moscow continue to be commemorated— Bartholomew first.

On Saturday February 9, 2019, however, a delegation of pilgrims headed by Metropolitan Pavel of Odessa from one of the Autocephalous Ukrainian Orthodox

Churches recognized by Constantinople came to the monastery. They found the gates shut and were not allowed entry.[9]

***

Life in St Panteleimon's continues to be physically hard for the brethren. On May 19, 2019, a fire destroyed the monastery's electrical generators and no pilgrims could be accepted for a while; but the hordes of visitors are now back. In general, the monastery is a comfortable and civilized place to stay for the outside visitor: accommodation is spotless and generally up to basic hotel standards, and the food served in the refectory is varied and plentiful. Despite the many pilgrims who give of their time and effort to help with general tasks (e.g., in the kitchen, harvesting olives, working in the candle factory) the brethren are burdened with relentless hard work. They have to look after all the fine, restored buildings, which once housed up to five thousand monks and laymen, and to cope with the numerous new arrivals.[10]

Toil for a monk is, of course, an essential part of an Athonite's life: it is what distinguished and sanctified Abbot Ieremiya's contribution to the monastery; and the first thing that all who enter a cenobium are given is an obedience—a job of work to be completed. No monk, however, is merely a worker in the physical sense. Prayer is his primary task.

Metropolitan Kallistos of Diokleia analyzes a monk's duty to pray.[11] In the *Lausiac History of Palladius*,[12] St Makarios of Alexandria declared that he was "guarding the walls." The Metropolitan explains:

> We may think of monks as sentries, watchmen, on the walls of the spiritual city; and because of them, the inhabitants of the city within the walls are able to continue their lives in greater peace and security. Against whom do the monks guard the walls? The early monks and the Athonite monks today would have quite a clear answer there: "Against the demons, against the forces of evil." How do the monks guard the walls? Through prayer! This is how the monks help the world, whether Athonite or otherwise. Not actively, but existentially; not primarily though preaching, teaching, and writing, through outward works of mercy: but through prayer of the heart. It is this that upholds the universe.[13]

Writing in 1957, Abbot Ilian expressed the same thought: "Our task is to pray for the peace of the whole world and to be ready for everything that the Lord should determine for us by his holy will."[14]

As well as toil and prayer, endurance is an essential part of an Athonite's life. Metropolitan Sergy of Voronezh understood the role of endurance in the monastery's history. Addressing the congregation after the Liturgy in the *Kato Katholikon* / Central Church dedicated to St Panteleimon, he spoke of the Myrrh-Bearing Women's[15] obedience—*poslushanie*—which he likened to that of the monastery's brethren: the duty of enduring, of keeping going. The Metropolitan marveled at the excellence of the two choirs, the orderliness of the brethren, and the beautifully restored buildings. All this he compared with the state of the monastery thirty years before, when the meagre brotherhood, mostly from the Pskovo-Pecherskaya and Trinity-St Sergius Lavras, had been struggling to keep the lamp burning.

Perhaps St Panteleimon's is becoming too big, and the intensely ascetic spirit of Ieronim and Makary's golden age is in danger of being lost. Spiritual Father Agafodor (Budanov) feared that this had already been the case even before Elder Ieronim (Solomentsov)'s death:

> The very best defense in the avoidance of falling into sin or into devilish temptation is *starchestvo*—i.e. revelation of your [innermost] thoughts to your *starets* / elder and guide: you must do nothing without his blessing and advice. This is the very *starchestvo* that existed in our house, and it was thanks to it that our house flourished, especially in the beginning. [In those early days] there were few brethren and Fr Ieronim accepted all for confession and revelation of thoughts; no day or night was his door locked. But when the brotherhood became more numerous and Fr Ieronim fell ill, he received visitors more seldom ….. Father Abbot Makary [helped as he could], but he was not [physically] capable of taking lengthy confessions and listened only to what was essential. For [Fr Makary] confessed all the brethren and all the pilgrims.[16]

Today the two to three *dukhovniki* / spiritual fathers on duty hear the confessions of some hundred pilgrims a week. The Sacrament is taken kneeling throughout, but the process has to be brief, owing to lack of time. Nonetheless, nobody is refused. At the end of the Liturgy, once the fathers have come up to the Cross and taken *antidoron*, there is a great queue of lay pilgrims. The morning meal cannot start until everyone has left church, and then the refectory doors are shut. Lay pilgrims are therefore hurried along in church, and asked to make the sign of the Cross well before venerating the Cross and icons. They are also asked to move along briskly when coming up for Communion.

Why, then, do pilgrims continue to flock to St Panteleimon's? One Russian visitor, clad in battle fatigues[17] and waiting to be registered by the *fondarichny* / guestmaster in the Preobrazhensky Korpus with me recently, had the answer. "How wonderfully peaceful it is here!" he exclaimed; "I can feel the grace—*blagodat'*."

Pilgrims seeking refuge from the harshness of civilian and military life find solace in a place especially favored by the Mother of God. As elsewhere in her Garden,[18] she is omnipresent. In the two central churches her icons are especially prominent and numerous. The Mother of God is said to have visited the Pokrov Central Church twice in Ieronim Solomentsov's time during all-night vigils, when nearly all the faithful felt her presence, experiencing a lightness and joy rather than the fatigue of a twelve-hour service. As we have seen, she again visited the monastery in 1903 when her photograph was taken. Finally, both the Pokrov Central Church and Xylourgou, the oldest Russian Athonite house, are dedicated to her feasts.

The problems of today threaten the peace of St Panteleimon's. Yet despite the political crises impinging from the outside world and the seemingly insurmountable tasks facing the brethren, the monastery continues to be a center of prayer and silence. The schism between the Ecumenical Patriarchate and the Patriarchate of Moscow is unfortunate, but it cannot prevent the brethren from getting on with their monastic existence. As we have seen, most of the monastery's brethren during the Name of God Rebellion patiently and quietly got on with their ascetic lives. There must have been and probably still are many virtually unknown St Panteleimon saints.

One such was Schema-Monk Memnon (Tyurin), who died aged ninety in March 1967. As a boy he was troubled by the verse, "Therefore you shall be perfect, just as your Father in heaven is perfect" (Matthew 5:48). He asked the priest of his village church how it was possible to attain sanctity by being perfect. The answer was: "To be a saint means to love others as the Lord loves us. He created us that we may learn to love in this world and, by gradually perfecting ourselves in brotherly love, we may reach the level of Christ's love."[19] Tyurin entered St Panteleimon's in 1901 and zealously fulfilled his obediences. After he had been in the monastery just three months, during the Liturgy, when the priest proclaimed "Let us lift up our hearts!" the young man was so overwhelmed with joy that he sobbed: "His tears flowed copiously, but they were so sweetly comforting that [he] shuddered from an excess of delight." His Spiritual Father, Elder Agafodor (Budanov), warned: "What you have experienced you must earn over many long years through hard toil; and then this experience will remain with you forever."[20] In his subsequent sixty-year life at St Panteleimon's, Memnon had two more visitations of grace at the same point in the Liturgy. On the last occasion, he exclaimed: "I give thanks, but I beg you, do not visit me again, else my heart cannot bear such joy and will burst."[21] In March 1928 he was tonsured to the Great Schema. His last obedience was that of *ekkleziarkh* / ecclesiarch. This enabled him to spend all his time outside services in church, reciting the Jesus Prayer. He was universally loved. When he was advanced in years he would often tell the brethren:

> How easy it is to live with love. You have no need to deceive, betray or humiliate anyone: just ask with love and all will be given to you. Why harm yourself with sinful subterfuge when it is so easy to be happy? Love selflessly and everyone will love you.[22]

Afterword

Many who visit the Mountain are aware of the immediacy and importance of the past. On Athos history is not remote or confined to academic study, but an integral part of the present; it explains why and how things stand, and how they develop. Since this book was submitted to the publishers much has happened, but the Russian monastery has once again become largely inaccessible, and travel to Athos has become problematic. The afonit.info site has ceased to produce new stories and some of its links, including many cited in this book, have become invalid.

A new chapter in the history of St Panteleimon's needs to be written. For this to happen someone has to be favored enough to go to the monastery, see for himself, and gain access to the library and its archives, which are again closed.

This book has dealt with the main events, but certain questions remain unaddressed. What, for instance, is the significance of the monastery's meteoric growth and vast size in the nineteenth and twentieth centuries in the wider context of Russian political expansion in the Near East? Such demographic and political questions are beyond the scope of this book.

Frustratingly, precise figures about the rises and falls of the numbers of the St Panteleimon brethren and of the Russian Athonite community in general have been unavailable. A precise table describing the numbers inhabiting St Panteleimon Monastery during most of the years between from 1996 to 2009 is given in Chapter 13. These statistics are clear and easy to verify because the numbers are low. Earlier statistics, especially pre-1914, however, are as contradictory and fluctuating as Turkish,

Greek, or Russian currency values over the last hundred years. A clear, authoritative chart giving statistics about Russian monks and Athonites of other nationalities during different historical periods is needed. That is for another researcher, one who has the time and exceptional resources to get hold of more precise data, if such can be found.

Timeline

The entries listed within gray boxes refer to events in world history, not events on Mount Athos. Unless otherwise indicated, the patriarchs listed are from either Moscow or Constantinople.

Xylourgou

1016	first Russian Athonite monastery, Bogoroditsa Xylourgou, already in existence, according to document found in Great Lavra
1048	Xylourgou granted Royal Lavra status
1051	St Anthony Pechersky tonsured in Xylourgou

Nagorny / Old Mountain Rusik

1161	move to Nagorny Rusik dedicated to St Panteleimon
1191	tonsure of St Stefan (Nemanja)
1347–1348	Stefan Dušan and family on Athos; gift of skull of St Panteleimon to Old Mountain Rusik
1355	death of Stefan Dušan; Serbian patronage of Athos ends
1497	in earliest recorded alms-gathering mission Rusik delegation receives gifts from Ivan III
1533	Grand-Prince Vasily III donates 15,000 gold coins to Rusik and Hilandar
1568	mainland *metochia* / dependencies confiscated by Porte; Athonite tax imposed of 14,000 gold pieces: Rusik ruined
1571	Ivan IV grants 350 rubles to Rusik
1574–1584	Rusik deserted
1626	Rusik debt-ridden; alms-gathering missions in Russia arranged every four years
1709	Ippolit Vishensky reports Rusik thriving; Danubian *gospodars* donate to Rusik Doamna Monastery in Botoşani
1725	after the first visit Barsky reports that Rusik brotherhood just four, of whom two are Russian
1730	Rusik monks chased out; minaret installed in central church

1744	during the second visit Barsky finds Greeks in charge of Rusik; Russians encamped elsewhere on the Holy Mountain; "Dark Period" until 1804: Russians homeless; unable to communicate with Greeks plague in Constantinople: St Panteleimon's skull effects miraculous cures, e.g., in the household of Moldavian *Gospodar* Ioannis Nikolau Kallimakh; Kallimakhs now give yearly grants to Rusik
1754	donation of *metochion* by Patriarch Kyrillos
1757	St Paisy Velichkovsky, who takes traditionalist stance in Kollyvades Dispute (1750–1820), founded Prophet Elijah Skete, the only Russian Athonite house
1760	*Gospodar* Alexander Kallimakh and wife Roxandra give generously
1762	Patriarch Ionnikios III intervenes for Rusik in property dispute with Vatopedi
1773	Old Mountain Rusik deserted

St Panteleimon's-By-The-Sea

Circa 1773	Rusik brethren (all Greeks) move to site of St Panteleimon's-By-The-Sea
1774	Treaty of Kuchuk-Kainarji after Russia's victory over the Turks; Russia's prestige at its height: Nicholas I protector of Balkan Orthodox Christians
1803	Sacred Community proposes to strike St Panteleimon's off the list of Twenty; Patriarch Kallinikos V issues charter protecting monastery: to become cenobium led by Savvas (Peloponneseos)

Abbot Savvas (AS)

Post-1803	AS in Constantinople with miracleworking skull of St Panteleimon raising funds for monastery
1806	AS confirmed abbot by patriarchal charter Skarlat Kallimakh cured of the plague by St Panteleimon relics; becomes munificent benefactor: AS now has enough money to build monastery
1814	formation of Philiki Hetaireia in Odessa
1812–1821	St Panteleimon's built from scratch
1821	AS dies
	Greek uprising; Skarlat Kallimakh and Patriarch Grigorios V executed in Constantinople
March 1821	Emmanouil Pappas sails with arms to Athos
October 1821	Pappas and insurgents defeated at Battle of Kassandra
December 15, 1821	Turks invade and occupy Athos; exodus of Athonites

1828–1829	war: Russia defeats Turkey
1830	last of Turkish troops leave; Athos semi-autonomous again

Abbot Gerasimos (AG)

1830	AG returns to Athos from Morea; confirmed abbot of St Panteleimon's
June 9, 1835	Anikita (Shikhmatov-Shirinsky) arrives on Athos; based at Prophet Elijah Skete
June 18	Anikita to St Panteleimon's; then back to Prophet Elijah Skete
July 2	Anikita's second visit St Panteleimon's; leaves money to build St Mitrofan Church
July 29	Anikita's third visit St Panteleimon's; then off to Holy Land with Elder Arseny
May 9, 1836	Anikita's fourth visit St Panteleimon's
May 18	Anikita's fifth visit St Panteleimon's; discovers St Mitrofan Church project abandoned
July 8	Anikita to Athens, via Prophet Elijah Skete; appointed head of Russian Spiritual Mission, Athens
1836	Prophet Elijah Skete stricken with plague; Priest-Monk Pavel, a Great Russian, becomes new prior; deposed three times in skete quarrels between Great and Little Russian brethren
1839	Pavel with fellow Great Russians expelled from skete and move to Karyes; St Panteleimon Greeks beg Pavel to move to monastery
November 21, 1839	Pavel and fellow Great Russians solemnly received at gates of St Panteleimon's
	Greek Deacon Venediktos says *Nunc Dimittis* and dies, knowing monastery will be saved by Russians and their wealth
July 29	Pavel dies
October 10, 1840	arrival at St Panteleimon's of Fr Ioanniky (Solomentsov) (IS)
1841	IS, now ordained priest, tonsured to the Great Schema with the name of Ieronim: becomes *Dukhovnik* / Spiritual Father and leader of the Russian brotherhood
	Tsar permits alms-gathering missions in Russia; IS sends Parfeny Ageev
1843	Parfeny Ageev returns to St Panteleimon's empty-handed
October 1843	Arrival at St Panteleimon's of Serafim Svyatogorets
July 16, 1845	Grand-Prince Konstantin Nikolaevich visits

March 1846	Spiritual Father Arseny dies
1848	Parfeny Ageev persuaded to write; huge success of his *Skazanie o stranstvii / Tale of Wanderings* brings Russian Athos to public attention
	Svyatogorets in St Petersburg for publication of his *Letters*: First and second editions in 1850; eight editions by 1895
October 1849	IS sends Monk Sil'vestr (Trofimov) on successful alms-gathering mission: sent again in 1857
November 3, 1851	arrival of millionaire Mikhail Sushkin (MS) who becomes Abbot Makary
November 27	MS dangerously ill and tonsured Makary of the Great Schema
January 1852	MS miraculously recovers
October 1852	first of gifts from Sushkin family
February 1853	Greek rebels arrive in Halkidiki; Russian brotherhood's safety threatened: 10 opt to leave for Russia, including Svyatogorets, who is unable to leave owing to bad weather and dies December 1853
1854	start of Crimean War
April 1854	Greek guerillas under Cham arrive on Athos
May 1854	1,600 Turkish troops, later reinforced by a further 2,000, march on Cham, who flees with his guerillas: bloodshed avoided
March 30, 1856	Treaty of Paris concludes Crimean War; defeated Russia loses standing in Orthodox Balkans
June 3, 1856	MS ordained priest; becomes Deputy Spiritual Father
August 3, 1856	Russian Steam Navigation and Trade Organization (RSNTO) was founded
July 1857	B. N. Mansurov of Imperial Marine Ministry with distinguished group arrives on maiden RSNTO voyage—first Russian ship since start of Crimean War; from now on Russian pilgrims arrive in droves
1858	Turkish quarantine hut erected at St Panteleimon *arsanas* / wharf to deal with huge numbers of Russian pilgrims
1859	Archimandrite Antonin (Kapustin) visits
1861	Vakhtang Barklai, later Priest-Monk Venedikt, arrives on Athos: beginning of the Georgian Affair; IS continues to give material aid to Georgian kellion well into 1870s
1862	Priest-Monk Arseny (Minin) to Russia on successful alms-gathering mission; returns in 1867

1863	Twenty-six dissenting Greek brethren leave St Panteleimon's monastery debts now liquidated; visit of N. P. Ignat'ev, newly appointed ambassador to the Porte
	Romanian Prince A. I. Cuza secularizes Greek Athonite metochia / dependencies in Wallachia and Moldavia
June 1867	visit of Grand-Prince Aleksey Aleksandrovich; lays foundation stone to Serai Central Church
1868	IM made archimandrite by Bishop Aleksandr of Poltava
1866	beginning of Greek-Russian brotherhood dispute: Greeks reluctantly agree to 1857 proposal of alternating refectory readings in Slavonic and Greek
1871	death of Prophet Elijah Skete Prior Paisy II; dispute with Pantokratoros about his successor; unwelcome Russian diplomatic pressure applied
1872	the Revenikia affair
1873	contentious instatement of new abbot of Aghiou Pavlou Monastery
	contentious instatement of new abbot of Xenophontos Monastery
	Serai dispute with Vatopedi: Patriarch Anthimos VI elevates St Andrew Skete to stavropegic status and its prior to rank of Abbot
	Bulgarian schism: Ecumenical Patriarchate breaks communion with Bulgarian Exarchate
	Alexander II *ukaz* / decree: all Greek Athonite Bessarabian and Caucasian dependencies to be administered by Russia
July 27, 1873	a reluctant MS appointed AG's successor
January 1874	AG issues written formalization of division of brotherhoods
	Greeks appoint three *sympraktores* / consular leaders to run monastery, undermining authority of ailing AG
March 15, 1874	MS secretly goes to Constantinople to enlist Ignat'ev's help
April 23, 1874	Sacred Community draws up written *kanonizmos* / charter to resolve Greek-Russian St Panteleimon dispute; Greek brotherhood approve, but not the Russians
May 22, 1874	Consul Yakubovsky buried within monastery walls, contrary to AG's wishes; Greeks scandalized and even Ignat'ev disapproves
May 9, 1875	AG dies
September 24, 1875	MS returns in triumph from Constantinople; final Greek dissenters leave St Panteleimon's
September 26th	MS made archimandrite (second time!) and installed as abbot

Abbot Makary (MS)

August–November 1875	Fr Arseny (Minin) and small group from St Panteleimon's, including Fr Ieron (Nosov) start building New Athonite Monastery of St Simon the Canaanite in the Caucasus
April 12, 1877–February 18, 1878	*Russo-Turkish War*: New Athonite Monastery abandoned, then razed by Turks; St Panteleimon's, under threat, visited by Turkish delegation (September 1877) but spared; monastery representatives in Thessaloniki imprisoned
Autumn 1878	Arseny (Minin)'s group return to site of New Athonite Monastery and start rebuilding
November 15, 1879	First abbot of New Athonite Monastery, Arseny (Minin), dies; succeeded by Ieron (Nosov)
December	New Athonite Monastery granted full legal rights and imperial sanction
1881	Novaya Fivaida *Kyriakon* / Central Church consecrated; the skete has been housing former desert-dwellers and *siromakhi* / wandering beggar-monks since 1879
1882	Krumitsa *Kyriakon* / Central Church consecrated; skete cultivated as vineyard, produces fine wine for export to this day
Summer 1883	Athenian Professors Damalas and Pavlidis visit Athos; proposals to strengthen Greek Athos in the face of Russian supremacy
1884	Abbot Ieron masterminds building of New Monastery; work on upper monastery starts (completed 1911)
November 14, 1885	IS dies
1887	Thessaloniki Consul Dokas visits Athos; proposes to Foreign Minister Dragoumis further plans to strengthen Greek Athonites: Athoniada School to be upgraded to university
1888	Alexander III and Imperial Family visit the New Athonite Monastery and lay foundation stone for its new Central Church
August	*Ano Kathonikon* Central Church of the Protecting Veil of St Panteleimon's gutted by fire Krumitsa fire extinguished after four days; later another fire followed by shipwrecks of monastery vessels
Easter 1889	MS's successor, Andrey (Veryovkin) (AV), chosen by apostolic ballot
June 19, 1889	MS dies

Abbot Andrey (AV)

August 4, 1889	promulgation of *Ustav* / Rule written by IS and MS

1894	Preobrazhensky Korpus completed
May 31	great new bell hoisted in belfry
April 1895	AV backs down in disagreement with Steward Fr Pavel (Durnev)
December	Fr Pavel (Durnev) dies
5, 1895	Synaxis of monastery fathers and abbot reaffirms IS and MS's *Ustav / Rule*
February 11, 1896	Priest-Monk Nifont (Chetverikov) chosen as AV's successor by apostolic ballot
August 21, 1903	Sacred Community wants distribution of alms to *siromakhi* / beggar-monks at the monastery gates stopped; Icon of Mother of God Drawn by Light: distribution continues
October 30, 1903	AV dies

Abbot Nifont (AN)

November 3, 1903	AN enthroned abbot
November 8	AN made archimandrite
May 26, 1905	AN falls ill; Priest-Monk Misail (Sapegin) chosen as AN's successor by apostolic ballot
October 24	AN dies
1904–1905	Russo–Japanese War
1905	Revolution in Russia

Abbot Misail (AM)

1906	Nicholas II becomes constitutional monarch
March 30, 1909	Fr Iakinf chosen as *namestnik* / *locum tenens* and deputy to AM
1910	Venizelos Prime Minister
November 6, 1911	Sacred Community votes in new Athonite canons; St Panteleimon's refusing to sign, resolutely opposes them
September 25, 1912	First Balkan War; Greece's sweeping gains
October 26	Greece beats Bulgaria to Thessaloniki
October 31, 1912	Second vote on new canons and on patriarchal charter: opposed by St Panteleimon's
November 1, 1912	Athos liberated by Greece from Turks

1913	plans to build new Holy Trinity Central Church and ask Nicholas II to lay foundation stone
October	Sacred Community hands over patriotic letters on behalf of Athonites to king of Hellenes and Metropolitan Theoklitos; St Panteleimon's representative and signature absent
January	Second Balkan War
August 17	Greek forces leave Athos, after objections from Russian Foreign Ministry and diplomatic corps

Name of God Dispute

1907–1911	
1907	*On the Mountains of the Caucasus* by Ilarion Domrachov
1908	Domrachov's book to Agafodor, St Panteleimon father-confessor and Karyes representative; asks Agafodor sends book on to Fr Khrisanf of Prophet Elijah Skete for assessment
	Agafodor also sends copy to St Andrew Skete Prior Ieronim (Silin), who asks Antony (Bulatovich) to read book and comment
	Bulatovich becomes ardent admirer of book
	Fr Khrisanf's excoriating review incenses Fr Ilarion (Domrachov), who drums up support among Novaya Favaida brethren
	Simple, uneducated monks of St Panteleimon's, St Andrew Skete and Novaya Fivaida support *On the Mountains of the Caucasus*
	Aleksey (Kireevsky), educated, influential monk of St Panteleimon's, and prominent opponent
Autumn	AM to Novaya Fivaida to placate Domrachov's supporters
1911	(Kireevsky) stays AM's hand from signing placatory statement about name of Jesus
1912	
February	second excoriating review: in *Russky Inok*, by Archbishop Anthony (Khrapovitsky)
	entrenched opposing camps: Name-Glorifiers vs Name-Haters
Easter	AM threatens Fivaida Name-Glorifiers with excommunication, but unheeded
April–May	Antony (Bulatovich) publishes Name-Glorifying articles; writes open letter to Archbishop Anthony
	Archbishop Anthony writes excoriating review of *On the Mountains of the Caucasus*

July	copies of Bulatovich's *Apology* circulated
	Prior Ieronim and Bulatovich become enemies: Prior visited by Aleksey (Kireevsky) with letter from Agafodor about the Archbishop's anger
	Prior hostilely asks Bulatovich to burn *Apology*
	Bulatovich leaves skete for Kellion of Annunciation to continue writing
August	Bulatovich asks Patriarch Joachim II for support
	Aleksey Kireveevsky to Constantinople, to petition Joachim for Name-Haters support
	Joachim commissions Halki Seminary to examine Name-Glorifiers' doctrine
August 20	AM draws up *A Directive Against the Veneration of the Name of Jesus*, which is read aloud in monastery; rejected by many of the brethren
August 27	Halki Seminary declares Name-Glorifiers' doctrine heretical
September	Joachim's encyclical condemning as heretical "new false doctrine"
December	meeting in Novaya Fivaida declaring Khrisanf's review of *On the Mountains of the Caucasus* heretical
1913	
January 12	Bulatovich's coup: Prior and eighteen senior St Andrew Skete fathers expelled
January 13	David (Mukhranov) declared new head of skete
January 19	Vatopedi reluctantly confirms Mukhranov's appointment, but postpones his enthronement
January 18–29	Sacred Community declares Bulatovich a heresiarch and excommunicates other Name-Glorifiers
	Ambassador Giers has St Andrew Skete blockaded
	Name-Glorifiers' public meeting at St Panteleimon's in presence of Scherbina; AM feels impelled to sign their *Confession of the Name of God*
	constitutional regime at Monastery: governance by council of elders elected triennially
January 23	Name-Glorifiers expel eight senior Name-Hating fathers from monastery
February 12	Bulatovich leaves Athos
February 15	Patriarch summons Bulatovich and Mukhranov to explain themselves
March 7	Mansurov's placatory mission to monastery a failure
March 19	Greece military detachment arrives at monastery and restores calm
Beginning of April	Igumen Arseny arrives; stirs up Name-Glorifiers
	Archbishop Nikon (Rozdestvensky) sends ineffectual conciliatory letter to monastery

April 5	Patriarch's encyclical condemning pantheistic heresy of Name-Glorifiers; Mukhranov appears before patriarch and Synod; promising not to become prior of St Andrew Skete, Mukhranov is allowed to go home
6th week of Lent	Sacred Community demand reinstatement of expelled fathers at St Panteleimon Monastery
April 29	Name-Glorifiers cut St Panteleimon telegraph wires; failed attempt to oust AM and seize treasury; new arrival of Greek peace-keeping force
May 1	Name-Glorifier Iriney (Tsurikov) summons public meeting at monastery; asks for pledge of allegiance
May 3	AM invites Sacred Community delegation to monastery; patriarch's encyclical read to brethren in Pokrov Central Church and brethren asked sign as proof of renouncing Name-Glorifying dogma; chaos ensues
May 4–8	chaotic second and third public meetings; Sacred Community delegation returns to Karyes
May 15	Iriney (Tsurikov) to Novaya Fivaida; appoints prior
May 23	Archbishop Nikon, Scherbina, and Prof. Troitsky set sail for monastery
May 26	Greek military detachment leaves monastery AM's telegram to Nicholas II: "Your Majesty, save our monastery from revolution"
June 5	AM about to be apprehended by rebels; Archbishop Nikon, Scherbina, and Prof. Troitsky arrive in the nick of time Archbishop Nikon, Scherbina, Prof. Troitsky, Shebunin, Serafimov, ship's captain, and crew land at St Panteleimon Monastery Archbishop Nikon retreats to SS *Donets* for safety; Troitsky and diplomatic officers conduct fruitless interviews with Name-Glorifiers eight fathers expelled on January 23 return to monastery
June 7	rebels heckle Shebunin's meeting and try to lock monastery gates; Troitsky shouted down
June 8	Shebunin and Serafimov's attempted arrest of Iriney (Tsurikov) ends in brawl
June 9	challenged by Iriney, AM declares: "The name *Jesus* is not God"
June 11	Archbishop Nikon confronts hostile brethren in Pokrov Central Church; heckled and beats hasty retreat rebels refuse to sign written compliance with patriarchal encyclical and letter from Greece Holy Synod rebels seize keys to treasury, larder, and vestry; threaten to start fire
June 18	SS *Tsar'* arrives; Platoon lands at monastery and mans key positions

June 14–19	Archbishop Nikon's census of brethren to gauge obedience to patriarchal encyclical and synodic letter: 700 obedient vs 1,000 rebels
June 29	during Vigil of Saints Peter and Paul Feast Archbishop Nikon retreats to SS *Donets*
	Archbishop Nikon's fruitless negotiations
July 2	SS *Kherson* anchors next to *Donets*
	Shebunin's ultimatum to rebels, who demand compensation
	rebels barricade themselves in monastery corridors
July 3	military attack; rebels hosed down, beaten, and arrested
July 4	four hundred St Panteleimon rebels frog-marched to ship
July 6–7	One hundred and eighty-three St Andrew Skete rebels peacefully board *Kherson*
July 9	SS *Kherson* sails for Odessa carrying 621 Name-Glorifiers; SS *Chikhachev* transports more rebels
July 17	by now, over 1,000 rebels deported
End of July	ecumenical patriarch protests at brutal treatment of rebels, who are tonsured Athonite monks; Alexandria and Jerusalem patriarchs join in protests
1914–1918	
February 13, 1914	Nicholas II and consort sympathetically receive Name-Glorifier delegation
Easter	warning from Nicholas II: Name-Glorifiers should be forgiven; public opinion in their favor
November– December 1917	meeting of *Pomestny sobor* / Local Church Council chaired by Patriarch Patriarch Tikhon to discuss Name-Glorifiers' rebellion
September 1918	Bolsheviks close Local Church Council: Name-Glorifiers' case unresolved

The Rest of AM's Reign

August 1914	First World War; able-bodied St Panteleimon Monks to the front as hospital orderlies, chaplains, and ambulance workers
January 4, 1917	Franco-Greece detachment on Athos
July 2	detachment leaves Athos
March– October	provisional government in Russia

October/ November	Bolshevik Revolution
August 10, 1919	A. A. Pavlovsky and Archimandrite Sergy (Dibich) arrested and deported from Athos
1922	clothing and food shipments paid by US scholar and industrialist C. R. Crane to St Panteleimon's, also in 1923 and 1926
1923	Archbishop Anthony (Khrapovitsky) refused permission to go to Athos, thwarting his plans to retire in St Panteleimon's
March 4, 1924	USSR officially recognized by Greece
May 10	New Athonite canons incorporated into *K.H.A.O.* / Constitutional Charter of the Holy Mountain, confirmed by Greece State in 1926; St Panteleimon's refuses to accept charter
	Exchange of Populations
1924	St Panteleimon's loses Sikia, Kalamaria, and Kassandra dependencies
1925	St Sophrony (Sakharov) and Vasily (Krivoshien) join St Panteleimon
March 25/7, April	Patriarch Tikhon dies; Sergy Stragorodsky appointed namestnik / locum tenens; Metropolitan Evlogy, supported by Moscow, splits from ROCOR 1926
June 18	Sacred Community in debt for 99,000 drachmas; St Panteleimon's to pay major part; AM objects
August 27	St Panteleimon Representative Fr Pinufry (Erofeev) expelled from Karyes; St Panteleimon's forced to pay for Sacred Community debt, but Pinufry not reinstated
May 31, 1926	Ioanniky (Kutyryov) chosen by apostolic ballot to succeed AM
1927	Metropolitan Sergy (Stragorodsky), patriarchal namestnik / locum tenens compromises himself with his Declaration praising Soviet state
1928–1929	League of Nations makes Greece compensate Athos for loss of dependencies; St Panteleimon's receives small compensation
1929	St Panteleimon's appeals to king of Serbs and Croats for help; by 1934 1¼ million dinars collected for monastery
1931	Paisios Ypsilantis affair
November 1935	AM suffers stroke
September 11 1937	AM's successor, Ioanniky (Kutyryov), dies
September 24, 1938	St Silouan dies, as predicted by AM

December 12	Priest Schema-Monk Iustin (Solomatin) (AI) elected AM's successor; acts as AM's *namestnik* / *locum tenens*
January 22, 1940	AM dies

Abbot Iustin (AI)

January and February 1940	Sacred Community declines AI's confirmation as abbot because St Panteleimon's refuses to sign *K.H.A.O* / Athonite Constitutional Charter
April 1	AI confirmed abbot; raised to rank of archimandrite
1941	Megalos Limos / Great Famine in Greece, until 1944
April 6, 1941	Germans invade Greece
April 22	Germans occupy Athos; Franz Dölger new ivil governor; St Sophrony accompanies and interprets for German officers on tour of Athos
April 29	Generalmajor Arenzen's decree protecting Athos
June 22	Germany invades USSR
June 1942	Nazi news agency enthusiastically greeted on Athos
August	Battle of Stalingrad
1943	Metropolitan Sergy (Stragorodsky) becomes Patriarch of Moscow
1944	Germans leave Athos
May 1944	Patriarch Sergy dies
November 1944–March 1945	ELAS/EAM occupy Athos
February 4, 1945	Aleksey I enthroned patriarch of Moscow
June 1945	AI writes to Patriarch Aleksey for help: first ever contact of St Panteleimon's with Moscow Patriarchate
July 21, 1946	B. D. Karmanov visits St Panteleimon's
September 26, 1947	Monk Vasily (Krivoshein), now expelled from Athos, tried in Thessaloniki for collaboration with Bulgarians; condemned to two years imprisonment on Makronisos
July 5–8, 1948	Moscow colloquium on 500th anniversary of Russian Orthodox Church autocephaly
March 7, 1953	Patriarch Aleksey writes to Patriarch Athenagoras about Russian Athos

September 7, 1954	Soviet Ambassador in Greece, M. Sergeev, visits St Panteleimon's
March 21, 1957	Aleksey asks Athenagoras and Greek Foreign Ministry for permission to send ten monks from Russia to St Panteleimon's
August 3, 1958	AI dies

Abbot Ilian (Sorokin) (AIS)

September 1958	Steward David (Tsuber) elected by apostolic ballot to succeed AI, but refuses
October 3	AIS enthroned abbot and elevated to archimandrite
1959	fire at monastery
February 9	Archimandrite Nikodim (Rotov) visits St Panteleimon's
1961	Moscow Patriarchate joins World Council of Churches
June 1962	Patriarch Aleksey awards AIS Order of St Vladimir Archbishop Nikodim (Rotov) visits St Panteleimon's; writes to DECR and succeeds in helping the monastery
1963	new lorry arrives at St Panteleimon's from USSR
	Moscow Patriarchate representatives at Pan-Orthodox Conference, Rhodes
June 23	Archbishop Nikodim (Rotov) attends millennium celebrations of Great Lavra; Athenagoras promises acceptance of new Athonite recruits sent by heads of autocephalous churches
June 19–July 2	Athos Millennium celebrations
1965	Priest of the Great Schema Gavriil (Legach) appointed *namestnik* / *locum tenens* of AIS
July 1966	first new recruits from USSR arrive at St Panteleimon's
April 1967	King of Hellenes deposed; Junta takes over
	St Panteleimon's opposes Junta's Decree 124, in solidarity with rest of Athos
October 23, 1968	serious fire at monastery
January 5, 1971	AIS dies

Abbot Gavriil (Legach) (AGL) and Abbot Avel′ (Makedonov) (AA)

| February 1970 | two new recruits arrive, including AA
AA tonsured to the Great Schema |

April 17	Patriarch Aleksey I dies
March 13, 1971	AA designated abbot, but not recognized by Sacred Community; continues as AGL's deputy, although AGL now infirm
April 9	AGL made abbot and elevated to archimandrite on the 20th
1972	
July 7	Patriarch Athenagoras dies; succeeded by Patriarch Dimitrios
October 23–25	Patriarch Pimen becomes, first Moscow patriarch to visit Athos
July 23, 1974	Decree 124 annulled
April 1975	Arrival at St Panteleimon's of Archimandrite Ieremiya (Alyokhin) (AIA)
July 4	AA appointed abbot second time
August 1976	Archbishop Vasily (Krivoshein) visits
May 1978	five new recruits arrive, including future antiprosopos / Karyes representative, Priest-Monk Nikolay (Generalov)
September 1978	Metropolitan of Leningrad Nikodim (Rotov) dies in Vatican City
Second half 1978	civil governor proposes on behalf of Vatopedi to Archimandrite Misail (Tomin) that St Panteleimon repopulate Serai with Russian monks
October 1	AA leaves for Metropolitan Nikodim's funeral, never to return

Abbot Ieremiya (Alyokhin) (AIA)

October 1, 1978	AIA appointed *namestnik* / *locum tenens*
January 8, 1984	Stavros Pasaleris becomes one of first novices in decades
1987	arrival of Frs Makary (Makienko) and Kirion (Ol'khovik)
June 12	Deacon David / Great Schema-Monk Dimitry (Tsuber) dies
1988	arrival of Monk Evlogy (Ivanov) (AE), future abbot
1990	first Russian novices join
May 3	Patriarch Pimen dies
June 10	Aleksey II enthroned new patriarch of Moscow
1991	arrival of Frs Pyotr (Pigol') and Ioakim (Sabel'nikov), later expelled for publishing *Velikaya Strazha*
October 2	Patriarch Dimitrios dies
November 2	Bartholomew enthroned patriarch of Constantinople
1992	St Panteleimon *podvor'ye* / dependency opens Moscow

May	expulsion of last Russian representatives from Prophet Elijah Skete; Fr Nikolay (Generalov) speaks up for them in Sacred Community meeting and exiled to Xylourgou
1993	*diamonitirion* office opens in Ouranoupolis
1995	first of yearly visits by Metropolitan Onufry of Ukraine
1996	Patriarch Aleksey II visits
September 9, 2005	V. Putin and D. Medvedev visit
October 1–4, 2006	Moscow conference on Athos and spiritual unity; walk-out of Greek delegates narrowly avoided
December 5, 2008	Patriarch Aleksey II dies
February 1, 2009	Kirill enthroned patriarch of Moscow
June 4–8, 2013	Patriarch Kirill visits
October 2013	Conciliatory visit of Patriarch Bartholomew
May 28, 2018	Putin arrives on Athos and celebrates Russian Millennium with Patriarch Kirill at St Panteleimon's
August 4	AIA dies
June 19–26, 2016	Pan-Orthodox Council on Crete, boycotted by Moscow Patriarchate

Abbot Evlogy (Ivanov) (AE)

October 1/14, 2016	AE enthroned abbot
2017	AE's official visit to Patriarch Neofit of Bulgaria, accompanied by Fr Nikolay (Generalov)
October 11, 2018	Patriarch Bartholomew grants autocephaly to independent Ukrainian Orthodox Churches
October 15	Moscow Patriarchate breaks communion with Constantinople
February 9, 2019	Metropolitan Pavel of an autocephalous Ukrainian church refused entry to St Panteleimon's

Acknowledgments

My father was my teacher and mentor. I dedicated my doctoral thesis and first monograph to him; I am ever in his debt for my endeavors as a researcher and historian. My mother shared my interest in Mount Athos from the beginning. She read all my work, corrected my Russian and French scripts, and longed to see this book, but died just months before it was published.

Metropolitan Kallistos encouraged me in my writing for some forty years; he advised me and his scholarship inspired me. David Holloway kept me going from page one, checking through each chapter, weeding out my typos, helping me keep my narrative chronological, and pointing out my illogicalities. I was also supported and encouraged by Graham Speake, with whom I have enjoyed twenty happy years of academic cooperation. I thank Fr Andrew Louth for his advice and careful reading of my script.

I owe a debt of gratitude to Archimandrite Evlogy, abbot of St Panteleimon Monastery, and its brethren. They were most generous hosts on my numerous visits, put their library at my disposition, and allowed me to use their archival photographs.

My sister-in-law, Lina, provided me with my home-away-from-home in Yannitsa whenever I set off on my Athonite trips. On these I was supported by my brother-in-law, Archimandrite Silouanos, Gerontas Maximos, and the brethren of the ever-hospitable monastery of St Dionysios on Olympos. Finally, I thank my wife. I have run past her every word I have written; she has put up with my absences at conferences and on the Mountain, and supported me unfailingly.

Notes

Introduction: The Russian Monastery on Mount Athos

1. For definitions of *isihastirion, kathisma, kalivi, kellion,* and *skiti/skete,* see Dorotheos Monahos (Vatopedinos), *To Aghio Oros, Miisi stin Istoria tou kai ti Zoi tou, B'* (Katerini: Tertios, 1985), pp. 5–81. Before the Second World War there were more categories of Athonite houses: see *Sentences arbitrales rendues par les membres neutres de la Commission Mixte en vertu de l'article 32 de la Convention signée à Ankara le 10 juin 1930 et relatives aux cas de certains moines et monastères du Mont Athos ayant demandé l'admission au bénéfice des articles 9 et 29 de la même Convention* (Ankara: Tsitouris, 1930), pp. 57–9. My definitions of Athonite houses and organizations are a simplification.

2. July 1 according to the Julian Calendar—"Old Style"—which is thirteen days behind the Western Gregorian Calendar.

3. Until the late twentieth century a full sequence of services in both Slavonic and Greek was maintained in St Panteleimon's. When I visited in 1982, services in the *Kato Katholikon*/the Lower Central Church dedicated to St Panteleimon were in Greek; those in the *Pokrovsky sobor*/Central Church of the Protecting Veil were in Slavonic.

4. The monastery of St John the Baptist, founded in Constantinople by Flavius Stoudios in 462, was perhaps a thousand-strong at the time of its abbot, Theodoros (759–826), but this high figure is doubtful: https://www.thebyzantinelegacy.com/stoudios (accessed December 15, 2020).

5. https://athosfriends.org/pilgrims-guide/ (accessed July 5, 2018): "Mount Athos needs to protect its seclusion, without which it would lose its *raison d'être*. For this reason it has to impose strict entry regulations."

6. He told me this with sadness when I visited him at his home some ten years later. The professor, who died in 2018, was an eminent Russian Athonite scholar. Along with the former Athonite civil governor, K. Papoulidis, he was the only Greek historian who read Russian and wrote sympathetically about Russian Athos. I met him at his home in Thessaloniki in 1984 and photocopied the texts he lent me. He also gave me some of his own publications on Athos and the Slavs.

7. *ISRA 6* (Moscow: Indrik, 2010), p. 18, fn. 10. For more about the difficulties in accessing the St Panteleimon library, see N. Fennell, "The Garden of the Mother of God Revisited," Friends of Mount Athos *Annual Report 2017*, pp. 47, 52–3.

8. http://afonit.info/novosti/1000-letie-russkogo-afona/glava-pravitelstva-rf-i-patriarkh-moskovskij-proveli-zasedanie-obshchestvenno-popechitelskogo-soveta-afonskogo-panteleimonova-monastyrya-video-i-foto (accessed March 22, 2018).

9. "Russky Afonsky otechnik XIX–XX vekov ili izbrannyya zhizneopisaniya russkikh startsev i podvizhnikov, zhivshikh na Afone v XIX–XX vekakh," *SRA 1* (Mount Athos: RPMA, 2012). An edition of this volume has also appeared in Greek.

10. In the Cold War years, such publishers as YMCA and Posev Press published mainly anti-Soviet works and used pre-revolutionary script as a statement of protest; *Pravoslavnaya Rus'*, the journal of the Russian Orthodox Church Abroad, published by the Holy Trinity Press, Jordanville, continued to use the script into the '70s. The *Russky Afonsky otechnik XIX–XX vekov*, however, has nothing to do with anti-Soviet protest. The anonymous author is probably Priest-Monk Makary (Makienko), the principal editor of the series. He was the monastery's *dukhovnik* / spiritual father until 2018, when he was transferred to Karyes as the monastery's *antiprosopos* / representative at the Sacred Community.

11. "Monakhology Russkogo svyato-Panteleimonogo monastyrya na Afone," *SRA 2* (Mount Athos: RPMA, 2013).

12. "Katalog slavyano-russkikh rukopisey," *SRA 7/1* (Mount Athos: RPMA, 2013) and "Katalog arkhivnogo fonda Russkogo svyato-Panteleimonogo monastyrya na Afone," *SRA 7/4* (Mount Athos: RPMA, 2013).

13. http://afonit.info/biblioteka/knigi/afonskij-panteleimonov-monastyr-goto-vit-k-izdaniyu-ne-imeyushchuyu-analogov-25-ti-tomnuyu-seriyu-russkij-afon-kh-ikh-khkh-vekov (accessed July 7, 2018).

14. "Istoriya russkogo svyato-Panteleimonogo monastyrya na Afone s drevneyshikh vremen do 1735 goda," *SRA 4* (Mount Athos: RPMA, 2015).

15. It is based in Russia but collaborates with the monastery. Zubov is an economist by training. Along with the other directors, V. I. Pirogov and D. V. Kostygov, he revived the monastery's magazine, *Dushepolezny sobesednik*, the publication of which had been interrupted in 1918.

16. Institut russkogo Afona published this last section of *SRA 4* as a separate book, entitled *Rosikon: Afonsky russky paterik* (Mount Athos: Institut russkogo Afona, 2015). The hagiographies listed in the back are in alphabetical order.

17. "Istoriya russkogo svyato-Panteleimonogo monastyrya na Afone s 1912 do 2015 goda," *SRA 6* (Mount Athos: RPMA, 2015).

18. "Istoriya russkogo svyato-Panteleimonogo monastyrya na Afone s 1725 do 1912 goda," *SRA 5* (Mount Athos: RPMA, 2015).

19. Fennell, pp. 47–57. See also fns 8 of Introduction and 2 of Chapter 1.

20. In October 2019, however, it and some fifteen other volumes of the SRA series were on sale at the St Panteleimon bookstore on Athos at the reduced price of €40 per volume.

21. *SRA 6*, p. 714.

The Monastery's Early History: From Xylourgou to the Old Mountain Rusik

1. Also known in Greek as *Thessalonikeos*: See Dorotheos Monahos, A', p. 417; also Gerasimos Smyrnakis, *To Aghion Oros* (Mount Athos: Panselinos, reprint edition, 1988), fn. 2 p. 68.

2. Priest-Monk Kirion (Ol'khovik), "Istoriya svyatogorskikh monasheskikh traditsiy v Ksilourgou, Starom Rusike i Svyato-Panteleimonovom monastyre," *Rus'–svyataya gora* Kirion (Ol'khovik), "Istoriya Svyatogorskikh monasheskikh traditsiy v Ksilurgu, Starom Rusike i Svyato-Panteleimonovom monastyre," *Rus'—Svyataya Gora Afon: tysyacha let dukhovnogo i kul'turnogo edinstva* (Moscow: Danilov Monastyr', 2017), p. 170. Fr Kirion was moved to Xylourgou at the same time as Fr Makary's transferal to Karyes.

3. M. V. Bibikov, "Russkie monastyri na Afone i v Svyatoy Zemle v svete novykh i maloizvestnykh istochnikov," *Rus'—Svyataya Gora Afon: tysyacha let dukhovnogo i kul'turnogo edinstva*, p. 19.

4. S. V. Shumilo, "The First Russian Monks on Mount Athos," in *Mount Athos and Russia*, eds. Nicholas Fennell and Graham Speake (Oxford: Peter Lang G, 2018), pp. 26–7. It is probable that no Russian researcher, certainly for the last fifty years, has seen this document.

5. I.e. not merely a skete or *kellion*, but a house the head of which is an abbot or *igoumen*. S. Shumilo ("The First Russian Monks on Mount Athos,"), p. 26, says that Xylourgou had become an *Hegoumenarion*.

6. Ibid., pp. 28–9. See also Ol'khovik, p. 171.

7. The year 1051 is the date given in the *Russian Primary Chronicle*: Shumilo, p.32. Shumilo and most Russian historians today along with the brethren of St Panteleimon Monastery give no credence to the Esphigmenou legend, according to which the saint was tonsured not in Xylourgou, but in Esphigmenou Monastery: ibid., pp. 33–40.

8. Shumilo, Ibid.

9. A.-E. Tachiaos, "Nachalo dukhovnykh svyazey Rusi s Afonom," http://afonit.info/biblioteka/russkij-afon/prof-a-takhiaos-nachalo-dukhovnykh-svyazej-rusi-s-afonom-1000-let (accessed November 26, 2019).

10. Bibikov, p. 35.

11. Speake, p. 79. Responding to the letter, Stefan set off for Athos, where he joined Savva and was tonsured at Vatopedi. Father and son, who were both canonized, later founded the Serbian brotherhood of Hilandar. Compare Speake, *Mount Athos: Renewal in Paradise* (New Haven, CT and London: Yale University Press, 2002), p. 67; it refers to D. Obolensky, according to whom Savva received his tonsure at Vatopedi.

12. At Easter 1846 he gathered in Skopje his courtiers, and Serbian, Bulgarian, and Greek clergy, and the Athonite *Protos* / Sacred Community Head, abbots, and elders. In front of them the Serbian archbishop was declared autocephalous patriarch, independent of Constantinople. On Athos Stefan Dušan now took the place of the Byzantine emperor.

13. *SRA* 4, p. 154. Compare Smyrnakis, fn. 2 p. 68.

14. Patriarch Cyril of Bulgaria, *Contribution to the Bulgarian Church Problem (Documents from the Austrian Consulate in Salonika)* (Dublin–Vienna: Mosaic Publications, 1998), p. 40.

15. *SRA* 4, p. 210.

16. Alexandar Fotić, "From Mount Athos Stories: An Unusual 'Union' between Hilandar and St Panteleimon in the 16th and 17th Centuries," *Philosophy, Sociology, Psychology and History*, Vol. 17, No. 2, 2018, p. 120.

17. Ibid., p. 27 and fn. 54.

18. Dorotheos Monahos, *A′*, pp. 418–9.

19. Fotić, p. 122.

20. Priest-Monk Ioanniky (Abernethy), "K Tysyacheletyu russkikh na Afone," unpublished MS, p. 28. Fr Ioanniky was until 1992 the Prophet Elijah Skete librarian. After the expulsion of the skete brethren from the Mountain (https://www.rocorstudies.org/2019/11/21/the-ever-burning-lamp-a-reassessment-of-the-expulsion-of-the-last-russian-representatives-from-the-prophet-elijah-skete/, accessed March 17, 2020) he joined the brotherhood of the Saints Kyprianos and Iustini in Attica, and was tonsured to the Great Schema with the name of Ioann.

21. Patriarch Cyril, p. 41.

22. Ibid., p. 30.

23. Dorotheos Monahos, *A′*, p. 419.

24. Four of them took place in the eighteenth century: 1710–1712, 1735–1739, 1768–1774, 1787–1791.

25. Quoted by Dorotheos Monahos, *A′*, p. 419, and ref. *B′*, p. 194, from an MS of the Great Lavra archive (Κώδ. Μεγ. Λαύρας Ω 47 φ. 287 α.). The Ishmaelites are the Turks, and the monastery in question is St Panteleimon's.

26. Vasily Grigorovich-Barsky, *Vtoroe Poseschenie svyatoy Afonskoy gory Vasiliya Grigorovi-cha-Barskogo im samim opisannoe* (Moscow: Indrik, 2004), p. 296.

27. Inok Parfeny (Ageev), *Skazanie o stranstvii i puteshestvii po Rossii, Moldavii, Turtsii i Svya-toy Zemle, vol. 1, Chast′ II, § 148* (Moscow: Novospassky monastyr′, 2008), p. 391.

28. Ol′khovik, p. 175.

29. *SRA* 5, p. 11. Cf. "Vvedenie," *SRA* 5, p. 5, where this period is referred to as the dark ages.

30. Barsky, pp. 297–8. He does not explain what the "above-mentioned good reasons" are—*radi predpisannykh blagoslovnykh vyn [vin]*. He also records a bloody confrontation between the Greeks and Russians at the beginning of the eighteenth century. Another clash was reported after he left, in 1765; perhaps it was the same as the one briefly referred to by Archimandrite Anikita (Shirinsky-Shikhmatov), *ISRA*, Vol. 4, p. 65. Neither incident is given much credence by scholars, but the fact remains that Russians no longer lived in the Russian monastery: *SRA* 5, p. 11.

31. The dispute split (1750–1820) Athonite society. The Kollyvades were committed to reviving hesychasm and returning to the teachings of such fathers as Saints Symeon the New Theologian, Gregory of Sinai, and Gregory Palamas. Contrary to the normal practice of the time, the Kollyvades advocated frequent communion, and were against the commemoration of the dead on Sundays rather than on Saturdays. They aroused strong opposition but their standpoint was eventually endorsed by Patriarch Grigorios V.

32. N. Fennell, *The Russians on Athos* (Oxford and Bern: Peter Lang, 2001), pp. 61–9.

33. Tachiaos, in *O Paisios Velitskofski kai i Askhitikophilologiki skholi tou* (Thessaloniki: Institute for Balkan Studies, 1964), p. 36, argues that the skete began its existence in 1761.

34. *SRA* 5, p. 21.

35. In 1796, a gift of Gospodar Alexios Kallimakh.

36. The *kellion's* church was rededicated to the Ascension: *SRA* 5, fn. 44, pp 27–8.

37. *SRA* 5, p. 130.

38. Under Empress Anne (1730–1740) royal alms were stopped; instead, a new department was created in the Holy Synod called the *Palestinskie Shtaty*, which allocated a mere 3,000 rubles a year to all Orthodox churches in the East.

39. *SRA* 5, p. 31.

40. The Ottoman piaster or kuruş was a silver coin and until 1844 the standard denomination of Ottoman currency (See note 1 in Chapter 2 "From Abbot Savvas to ...").

From Abbot Savvas to Abbot Gerasimos

1. By the reign of Mahmud II (1808–1839) the silver content and thus the value of the Ottoman piaster/ kuruş was diminishing. In 1808 it would have been worth approximately ¼ franc. One franc was worth about ¢20, the equivalent of $3.70 today. Thus 20 piasters would today be roughly equivalent to $18.(https://ru.wikisource.org/wiki/%D0%AD%D0%A1 %D0%91%D0%95/%D0%9F%D0%B8%D0%B0%D1%81%D1%82%D1%80_%D1%82%D1 %83%D1%80%D0%B5%D1%86%D0%BA%D0%B8%D0%B9); and (https://www.google. com/search?sxsrf=ALeKko1p-fAbfSwOztzoPX7s1MxcThgSmQ%3A1607685261114&ei= jVTTX4-7BvK78gKq3KvYCQ&q=how+much+was+a+french+franc+worth+ in+1800&oq=how+much+was+a+french+franc+worth+in+1800&gs_lcp=CgZwc3kt YWIQAzIFCAAQyQM6BwgAEEcQsANQ5T1YiT9g8opoAXACeACAAWSIAbkB kgEDMS4xmAEAoAEBqgEHZ3dzLXdpesgBCMABAQ&sclient=psy-ab&ved= oahUKEwjPtZin5sXtAhXynVwKHSruCpsQ4dUDCAo&uact=5).

2. *ISRA* 6, pp. 80–1.

3. According to Ageev, *Book I, Part 2, § 148*, p. 392, he had inherited considerable wealth from his parents, but it was not enough.

4. Ibid., p. 135.

5. *Russky Monastyr' sv. Velikomuchenika i tselitelya Panteleimona na sv. Gore Afonskoy* (Moscow: Podvor'e Russkogo na Afone svyato-Panteleimonova monastyrya v Moskve, 2005), p. 55.

6. Ibid., p. 56.

7. The Doamna Monastery in Botoşani given as a dependency to St Panteleimon by the Kallimakhs in 1709. It had lain empty and neglected for some time.

8. The Straits, or the Dardanelles, were the strategically important passage through which Russian Black Sea shipping could gain access to the Aegean.

9. *SRA* 5, p. 126.

10. *SRA 2*, p. 12: "Abbot Savva[s] was the renewer and builder of this house after the ruin of the Old Rusik. For this reason, he is considered to be the founder [of St Panteleimon Monastery]. On the day of the founder's death the brethren are served in the refectory honey and pancakes called *talanta* in Greek."

11. From "up to 40,000 to no more than 1,000," according to *SRA 1*, p. 25.

12. *ISRA 4*, p. 65.

13. Episkop Porfiry Uspensky, *Pervoe puteshestvie v Afonskie monastyri i skity arkhimandrita, nyne episkopa, Porfiriya Uspenskogo v 1845 godu* (Kiev, 1877), p. 79.

14. Dorotheos Monahos, *A′*, p. 419. Monk Dorotheos refers to the Old Mountain Rusik Monastery of St Panteleimon as *Thessalonikeos* / The Thessalonian Monastery.

15. *Perigraphikos katalogos ton en tis kodixi tou patriarhikou arheiophylakeiou sozomenon episimon ekklisiastikon engraphon peri ton en Atho Monon (1630–1863)*, quoted in *SRA 5*, p. 44. The archimandrite later became a metropolitan and had access to the patriarchal archives in Constantinople.

16. Nikiphoros Mylonakos, *Aghion Oros kai Slavoi* (Athens: Eisagoghi, 1960), pp. 78–9. The last of the Iviron Georgians died in 1955, although the monastery was Georgian only in name since the fourteenth century.

17. A. Soloviev, *Histoire du monastère russe au Mont-Athos* (Belgrade: Slavija, 1933), p. 2 and fn. 3, p. 4. The arguments about *Ros* and its derivatives are reminiscent of the so-called Normanist Controversy about the *Rus'*, the Varangian settlers mentioned at the beginning of the Russian Primary Chronicle. According to the traditionalist Soviet anti-Normanists, who dismiss the Primary Chronicle version as a myth, the Rus' were native Slavs, not Varangian outsiders. See J. L. I. Fennell, *A History of the Russian Church to 1448* (London: Longman, 1995), pp. 3–5.

18. Smyrnakis, p. 663.

19. *SRA 2*, p. 11.

20. Serafim Svyatogorets (Vesnin), *Pis'ma Svyatogortsa o svyatoy Afonskoy gore* (Moscow, 1895), Part 1, §14, p. 161. Ageev, who also knew him, merely says of him: "He was of Macedonian origin:" Ageev, Book 2, part IV, § 180, p. 352.

21. Uspensky, p. 58.

22. "His abbacy was confirmed by Patriarch Konstantios only in 1832–3 because during the Greek uprising the patriarch was also in exile in the Morea for ten years," *SRA 1*, p. 46.

The Return of the Russians in the Reign of Abbot Gerasimos

1. "Svytogorets" is literally "of the Holy Mountain." It's the Slavic/Russian equivalent of "Hagiorite."

2. Svyatogorets, pt. 1, §5, p. 46.

3. Ageev, vol. 2, pt. 4, § 180, pp. 352–3.

4. Metropolitan Kallistos (Ware), "St Nil Sorsky: A Hesychast Bridge between Byzantium and Russia," in *Mount Athos and Russia*, p. 79. The term *Non-Possessor* refers to the

monastic group headed by St Nil Sorsky (*c.* 1433–1508) in Russia "opposed to large-scale landowning by the monasteries." Since then the term has come to mean an adherent of ascetic poverty and non-reliance on material possessions.

5. Ibid., p. 354. In his practical attitude to wealth the abbot was like St Paisy Velichkovsky (on Athos 1746–1753), who was an exemplary non-possessor. He abandoned the destitute and debt-ridden Simonopetra entrusted to his care because creditors were demanding payment and he wished to avoid living with his brotherhood in grinding poverty.

6. Archimandrite Anikita was a member of the Russian Academy and the Imperial Academy of Sciences. He had a working knowledge of Demotic and Byzantine Greek, and was probably well versed in Classical Greek. His brother, Platon Aleksandrovich, was Nicholas I's minister of education and a senator, and was also a poet.

7. *ISRA 4*, p. 64.

8. Ibid., p. 70.

9. Ibid., p. 65.

10. It is not clear whether this was Archimandrite Prokopios (Dendrinos) mentioned at the beginning of this chapter.

11. Ibid., p. 66.

12. Ibid., p. 70.

13. Ibid, pp. 69–70.

14. On the ship from Thessaloniki to Jaffa he paid 300 leva for his cabin; the rest of his party paid 180: ibid., p. 73.

15. Sorokoust is the practice of serving forty (usually consecutive) Divine Liturgies with special commemorations for the ill or for those who have died during the proskomodi / preparatory service.

16. Ibid., p. 115.

17. Ibid., pp. 116–17.

18. Anikita's letter to A. S. Sundy, Commissioner of the Black Sea Fleet; quoted by P. Troitsky, the editor of Anikita's diary, *ISRA*, Vol. 4, fn. 149, p. 154.

19. Ageev, book I, Chast' 2, § 151, p. 397.

20. Ibid., § 152, p. 398.

21. *ISRA 4*, p. 117. According to Russian Athonites at the time, it was believed that the Greeks had been guilty of this murder, but modern scholarship has discredited the legend, as we have seen in Chapter 1, fn. 30.

22. Ageev, pp. 396–7. Parfeny's chronology is confused. According to him, they processed from the skete to the monastery, where he stayed for a month.

23. Quoted in *ISRA 8*, p. 89.

24. This happened before Arseny and Nikolay's tonsure to the Great Schema. At the time, they were called Monks Avel' and Nikandr. Ageev, book II, Chast' 4, § 157, p. 314.

25. Ibid., p. 318.

26. At the end of his life, when Monk Nikolay died, Elder Arseny moved to a *kellion* belonging to Stavronikita and accepted disciples to live with him.

27. Ibid., book I, Chast' 3, § 98, p. 328.

28. Ibid., book I, Chast' 3, § 151, p. 396.

29. *ISRA 8*, pp. 91–2.

30. *Russky Obschezhitel'ny skit svyatago Proroka Ilii na Svyatoy Afonskoy Gore* (Odessa, 1913), p. 46.

31. Ageev, book I, Chast' 3, § 109, p. 338.

32. Ibid., §110, pp. 339–40.

33. Ibid., p. 340.

34. Parfeny was very emotional, but no doubt consciously emulated his spiritual father, Elder Arseny, and Schema-Monk Nikolay, whose liturgies ended in floods of tears. Nikolay had a divine gift of tears and wept constantly.

35. Ibid., §116, pp. 347–8.

36. Ibid., §§112, 114, pp. 341, 343.

37. According to Ageev, he died forty days after Pavel's arrival.

The New Spiritual Father and Leader of the Russian Brotherhood Is Chosen

1. *SRA 5*, p. 183.

2. *SRA 9/1*, p. 7. The writer and diplomat, Konstantin Leont'ev, expressed similar views in his description of the idealistic purity of young people from mercantile families living in the remote Russian provinces: *KNL 7/1*, p. 758.

3. Stary Oskol is some 600 km south of Moscow, in the Kurskaya Guberniya (today the Belgorodskaya Guberniya). According to his autobiography, Solomentsov was born "in 1805 or 1806": Priest-Monk Ioakim (Sabel'nikov), *Velikaya Strazha*, Book 1 (Moscow: Izdatel'stvo Moskovskoy Patriarkhii, 2001), p. 18.

4. Sabel'nikov, p. 21.

5. Ibid., p. 27.

6. *SRA 9/1*, p. 54.

7. Ibid., p. 55.

8. Sabel'nikov, p. 33.

9. According to Ageev, there were three disciples other than himself in Fr Ioanniky's *kellion*: Ageev, vol. 1, pt 2, §125, p. 360.

10. Ageev, vol. 1, pt 2, §134, p. 371.

11. Ibid., p. 372.

12. Ibid., §135, p. 372.

13. Ibid., p. 373.

14. Ibid., pp. 373–4. According to Fr Ioanniky's own autobiographical notes, Sabel'nikov, p. 36: "I left my *kellion* to live forever in the Russian monastery with my two disciples, Parfeny and Mitrofan."

15. Sabel'nikov, p. 37.

16. Sabel'nikov, pp. 76–7; fn. 1, p. 77: "Our Priest of the Great Schema Fr Mikhail testifies that he personally heard from *Batyushka* / Fr Ieronim about his vision."

17. *SRA 9/1*, p. 623.

18. In 1857, when the first ship of the Russian Steam Navigation and Trade Organization (see next chapter) docked at the St Panteleimon quay, which was an hour away from the *kellion*.

19. Sabel'nikov, p. 148.

20. On the Holy Mountain the midnight office, matins and hours are celebrated at night, the liturgy in the early hours. Fr Ieronim hardly slept at all, for in the few nocturnal hours at his disposal his hernia tended to be painful.

21. *SRA 9/1*, letter to his sister, Abbess Margarita, November 17, 1864, pp. 441–2.

22. He visited in 1883. Athelstan L. Riley, *Athos, or: The Mountain of the Monks* (London: Longman, Green & Co, 1887), p. 256.

23. Svyatogorets, pt. 3, §15, p. 469.

24. Uspensky, p. 59. Archimandrite Porfiry usually portrayed others uncharitably. Of Abbot Gerasimos he wrote (p. 58): "He is not in the least scholarly. He is taciturn and restrained either by nature or because he is aware of his lack of worth." He dismisses Archimandrite Prokopios (Dendrinos) (p.59): "It is good that he did not publish these thoroughly tedious Greek scholastics of his …. His pronouncements are about as tasty as acorns."

25. Leont'ev had recently been appointed consul in Thessaloniki (in office April–September 1871). There he fell ill, recovered, and decided to renounce everything and become a monk. Makary and Ieronim refused to tonsure him unless he retired from the diplomatic service. That Leont'ev had a wife was not an impediment to tonsure: wives usually released their husbands from their marital obligations if the latter set off on pilgrimages. Although Leont'ev agreed to retire, he left Athos after a year, owing to the indigestibility of the monastery diet and his bouts of sickness.

26. *KNL 6/1*, p. 760.

27. Ageev, vol. 1, pt. 2, §126, pp. 360–1.

28. Svyatogorets, pt. 1, §14, p. 165.

29. *SRA 9/1*, p. 123.

30. *KNL 6/1*, p. 760.

31. *SRA 9/1*, p. 122.

32. Riley, pp. 248–9.

33. "Dukhovnoe zaveschanie otsa Ieronima 1885 goda," *SRA 9/1*, pp. 302–3.

34. In the mid-nineteenth century the average unskilled laborer's wage in Moscow was 17 rubles per month. (https://bigenc.ru/domestic_history/text/3249696).

35. *SRA 5*, p. 210.

36. Svyatogorets, pt. 1, §5, p. 53.

37. Lazarus Saturday is the day before Palm Sunday, eight days before Pascha/Easter, and just over a week after Parfeny's tonsure to the Great Schema.

38. The Old Believers were members "of a group of Russian religious dissenters who refused to accept the liturgical reforms imposed upon the Russian Orthodox Church by the patriarch of Moscow Nikon (1652–58)": https://www.britannica.com/topic/Old-Believers.

39. Ageev, vol. 2, pt. 1, §69, p. 53.

40. Born in 1782, made metropolitan in 1826, died in 1867, and canonized in 1995, St Filaret was an influential enlightener who based his teaching on the Holy Fathers.

41. Quoted by S. Sheshunova, "Parfeny Ageev" in *Russkiye pisateli 1800–1917, Russky Biografichesky slovar'* [The Russian Biographical Dictionary], vol. 4, pp. 536–7 (Moscow: Terra-Knizhny klub, 1999).

42. F.M. Dostoevsky, *Polnoye sobranie sochineniy v tridtsati tomakh*, vol. 15, *Brat'ya Karamazovy*, vol. 1, "Startsy," p. 27. See also vol. 15, p. 528 (Leningrad: Nauka, 1976).

43. Located in the surrounds of what is today known as Kirov, in western Russia.

44. Svyatogorets, p. 512.

45. Ibid., p. 504.

46. Ibid., p. 508.

47. The general editor of the *ISRA* series. Both quotations are from *SRA* 5, p. 191.

48. Ageev, vol. 2, pt. 3, §78, p. 60.

49. *SRA* 5, p. 195.

50. See ch. 1, fn. 7. For a full discussion of the Esphigmenou legend of St Anthony, see Shumilo, pp. 32–40, and Kirill Vakh's explanation, in *SRA* 5, pp. 199–204.

51. Ageev, p. 63.

52. *SRA* 5, pp. 203–4.

53. *SRA* 1, p. 151.

54. At the beginning of the nineteenth century 1 ruble in silver was worth four times as much as a banknote ruble. An unskilled laborer's wage averaged 17 rubles a month in Moscow.

55. Ibid., pp. 151–2.

56. Dmitrievsky ascribes the success of the mission and the religious fervor it inspired to the fact that Arseny arrived shortly after the serfs had been liberated (1861). *ISRA* 6, p. 286.

57. Ibid., pp. 288–9.

58. *SRA* 9/1, p. 192.

59. *KNL* 6/1, p. 774. The italics are Leont'ev's.

60. *SRA* 9/2, p. 430.

61. I. F. Kraskovsky, *Makary Afonsky igumen i svyaschennoarkimandrit svyatogo Panteleimonogo monastyrya* (Moscow: 1889), pp. 20–3.

62. At the time it was the only Athonite church dedicated to the Protecting Veil and was unique for its wooden floor, which helped those suffering from colds and fevers. It was consecrated in 1853.

63. *KNL* 6/1, pp. 753 and 769.

64. Ibid., pp. 229–30.
65. Ibid., pp. 777–9.
66. *SRA 9/1*, p. 695.

The Crimean War

1. Odessa was established by a decree of the Russian empress Catherine the Great in 1794. During the course of the nineteenth century it became a major port for the Russian Empire on the Black Sea coast.
2. Theophilus C. Prousis, "Eastern Orthodoxy under Siege in the Ottoman Levant: A View from Constantinople in 1821" (2008), University of North Florida UNF Digital Commons, History Faculty Publications, 13. https://digitalcommons.unf.edu/cgi/viewcontent.cgi?article=1011&context=ahis_facpub.
3. A. J. P. Taylor, *The Struggle for Mastery in Europe 1848–1918* (Oxford: Oxford University Press, 1971), p. 60.
4. James J. Reid, *Crisis of the Ottoman Empire: Prelude to Collapse 1839–1878* (Stuttgart: Steiner, 2000), p. 251.
5. Quoted by Kraskovsky, p. 27, and in SRA 5, p. 231. Kraskovsky is unclear whether the excerpt from Makary's memoirs is dated 1833 or 1834, the year when Makary was ordained deacon.
6. *SRA 5*, p. 232; only five according to *KS 18*, p. 172.
7. According to *SRA 5*, but in *KS 18*, p. 172, the number is five.
8. *KS 18*, 172.
9. Ibid., p. 173.
10. Ibid.
11. Ibid., p. 174.
12. Ibid., p. 175.
13. Reid, pp. 252–3. It is likely that the Russians, only a few of whom knew Greek, misheard the name Tsamis, which they Russified as the easier to pronounce "Cham." Otherwise, most of Sapozhnikov's account and that of James J. Reid are similar.
14. Russkoe Organizatsiya Parokhodstva i Torgovli (ROPiT).
15. https://korvet2.ru/ropit.html (accessed March 26, 2016).
16. *SRA 5*, p. 283.
17. *SRA 5*, p. 284.
18. Ibid., p. 285.
19. Stephen Graham, *With the Russian Pilgrims to Jerusalem* (London: Thomas Nelson, 1913), pp. 36–43.
20. The ship, a steam-powered sailing frigate, had been salvaged from Sevastopl' Bay and refurbished. The final destination of this maiden voyage was Marseilles.
21. *SRA 5*, p. 289.
22. Ibid., p. 291.

23. Mansurov also saw the need of having a consular representative on the Mountain to serve the Russians, but realized that the Athonite community would baulk at what it would perceive to be outside interference. He therefore proposed that a resident RSNTO representative discretely carry out consular duties. This proposal also came to nothing.

The Greek and Russian Brotherhoods at Loggerheads

1. Svyatogorets, pt. 1, §5, p. 39.
2. Ageev, vol. 1, Pt. 2, §142, p. 379.
3. *ISRA 10*, pp. 42–53. Fr Antonin (Kapustin), a Greek scholar and archaeologist, was head of the Russian mission in Jerusalem.
4. *ISRA 6*, p. 155.
5. KS *18*, p. 103.
6. Ibid., p. 73.
7. See *SRA 5*, pp. 335–42 for a detailed description of the monastery's refurbishment and expansion. Most of the work was undertaken in the 1860s.
8. Smyrnakis, p. 216. Fr Gerasimos (Smyrnakis) was abbot of Esphigmenou 1906–1908. His monograph is a vast, seminal work, which has inspired most Greek historians of Athos, despite its chaotic structure and strong bias.
9. Count and General N. P. Ignat'ev (1832–1908), a devoted friend of St Panteleimon's, was Imperial Minister in Constantinople 1864–1866 and Russian Ambassador there 1866–1877. He negotiated skillfully with the Porte and representatives of the Powers, but with little backing from St Petersburg. At the conclusion of Russo-Turkish War of 1877–1878, he brokered the Treaty of San Stefano (January 1878), creating an independent Bulgaria and redrawing boundaries in the Near East. In July 1878 the Treaty of Berlin negated Ignat'ev's negotiations in favor of British and Austrian interests. Russia was weakened and the count was recalled.
10. KS *18*, p. 97.
11. The Serai *kyriakon*, not completed until 1901 owing to lack of funds, became the largest church in the Near East. The money was provided by the millionaire merchant, Innokenty Sibiryakov, who joined the skete in 1898. Bishop Aleksandr had prophesied to the Serai brethren in 1868 that a wealthy and saintly benefactor by the name of Innokenty would rescue the skete from its financial straits.
12. Patriarch Anthimos VI was on his way to Constantinople where he was to be elected for a third term in office (1871–1873).
13. *SRA 5*, p. 331.
14. Ibid., p. 332.
15. KS *18*, p. 104.
16. Cephalonia is an Ionian island south of Kerkira. The inhabitants were described by Russian historians like Lora Gerd and A. A. Dmitrievsky, as hot-headed—vspyl'chivogo

nrava. For their part, certain Greeks saw, and still see, the Russians as offensively wealthy, rapacious, tactless usurpers on Athos. Cretans were also phyletically labeled hot-headed.

17. *KNL* 7/1, p. 228.

18. *Sabel'nikov*, p. 208.

19. Greek historians are silent about the Aghiou Pavlou matter; with the exception of Leont'ev's (*KNL* 7/1, p. 227–9), Russian accounts are confused and vague.

20. Smyrnakis, p. 208. Presumably the "violation" was due to the Grand-Prince's taking center stage at the ceremony.

21. Revenikia is today called Megali Panagia.

22. Patriarch Cyril, pp. 66–8.

23. Smyrnakis, pp. 227–8. Sythonia is the second peninsula of Halkidiki, next to that of the Holy Mountain.

24. The Austrian was also wrong about Leont'ev's wife, who joined her husband in Constantinople after his stay in St Panteleimon's but never went to Halkidiki.

25. See, for example, Dorotheos Monahos, p. 185.

26. Patriarch Cyril, p. 44.

27. *ISRA* 6, p. 163.

28. *KNL* 7/1, p. 178.

29. Known as dedicated monasteries. See A. J. Bobango, "The Emergence of the Romanian National State" (New York: East European Quarterly, 1979), pp. 142–3.

30. Traian Nojea, *Secularization of Monastic Estates (1863): Some Legal–Historical Aspects*, https://www.academia.edu/30994454/Secularization_of_Monastic_Estates_1863_._Some_Legal_Historical_Aspects (accessed May 31, 2019).

31. The *Domnitor* / Ruling Prince of Romania 1861–1866. Romania was formed after the union in 1858 of the Danubian Principalities, Wallachia, and Moldavia.

32. Bessarabia, which had been part of the Principality of Moldavia, was acquired from the Ottoman Empire by Russia after the Treaty of Bucharest (1812). Part of Southern Bessarabia was ceded to Moldavia after the Treaty of Paris in 1856, but was repossessed by Russia in 1878.

33. For detailed descriptions, but differing views of the Georgian Question, see A.-E. Tachiaos, *To Georgianikon zitima (1868–1916)* ed. Theofanis G. Stavrou (Thessaloniki, 1962) and "Anekdota ellinika kai rossika eggrapha peri tou georganikou zitimatos," in *Aristoteleion Panepestimeion Thessalonikis Epistimoniki Epetiris Theologikis Skholis*, vol. 17 (Thessaloniki: Aristotle University of Thessaloniki, 1972); A. Natroev, *Iversky Monastyr' na Afone na odnom iz vysytupov Khalkidonskago poluostorova* (Tiflis: Tipografiya "Trud", 1909); also Smyrnakis, pp. 474–5.

34. Smyrnakis, p. 212.

35. Dmitrievsky, p. 164.

36. Sabel'nikov, p. 210.

37. Dmitrievsky, p. 173.

38. Sabel'nikov, pp. 212–13.

39. Ibid., p. 213.
40. Ibid.
41. Ibid., pp. 215–16.
42. Ibid., p. 222; *ISRA 6*, p. 174.
43. Ibid., p. 217.
44. This effectively halted building works in the Old Monastery, which remained unfinished until the twentieth century.
45. *SRA 9/1*, p. 593.
46. Ibid., p. 622.
47. Smyrnakis, p. 218.
48. Yakubovsky's grave is next to the Russian St Mitrofan Church in St Panteleimon's.
49. *SRA 9/1*, pp. 599–600.
50. Patriarch Cyril, pp. 108–9: "Malgré que nous [ayons] procuré par tous les moyens d'éviter un tel acte illégal ... pour éviter [de] plus grands désordres, nous [les] soussignés ... nous sommes retirés." / Although we have taken all possible steps to prevent such an illegal act ... to avoid greater disorder, we, the undersigned ... have withdrawn.
51. *SRA 12*, p. 675.
52. Smyrnakis, pp. 216–19.
53. Ibid., p. 221.
54. *SRA 9/1*, p. 594.

The Reign of Archimandrite Makary

1. According to St Varsonofy of Optina, quoted by Bishop Ilarion (Alfeev), *Svyaschennaya tayna tserkvi: vvedenie v istoriyu i problematiku imyaslavskikh sporov* (St Petersburg: Izdatel'stvo Olega Abyshko, 2007), p. 291.
2. The conversion of the Abkhazian population to Islam began in the fifteenth century.
3. Obschestvo vosstanovleniya pravoslavnogo khristianstva na Kavkaze.
4. *KS 16*, p. 10.
5. Ibid., p. 11.
6. Ibid., p. 12.
7. 327 *desyatiny*. One *desyatina* is equivalent to 1.09 hectares.
8. Ibid., p. 15.
9. The Russo-Turkish War (April 12, 1877–February 18, 1878) was sparked off by the 1875 Bosnia-Herzegovina uprising, which was brutally crushed by the Turks. Next year Serbia and Montenegro declared war on Turkey; they suffered a pogrom, forcing Alexander II to retaliate in their defense. The Treaty of San Stefano, masterminded by N. P. Ignat'ev, concluded the war.
10. *SRA 9/2*, pp. 218–19.
11. Austen Henry Layard (1817–1894), a distinguished archaeologist and leader of important excavations in Mesopotamia, was Her Majesty's ambassador to the Porte (1877–1894).

12. *The London Times*, November 22, 1877.
13. Trebizond is some 400 kilometers south along the Black Sea Coast from the New Athonite Monastery of St Simon the Canaanite. The ancient monastery of Panagia Soumela was closed in 1920, but was reopened for occasional services in 2010. The Pontic refugees, who came to Greece in the 1923 exchange of populations, founded in 1952 the Panagia Soumela Monastery in Kastania village on Mt Vermio near Veroia. Neither monastery is inhabited today.
14. *SRA* 9/2, p. 223.
15. *The London Times*, November 22, 1877.
16. *SRA* 5, p. 604. Cf. *KS* 16, p. 24.
17. The Exarch of Georgia was Archbishop Ioanniky (Rudnev, 1877–1882). He headed the Georgian Exarchate of the Holy Synod of the Russian Orthodox Church, which was in existence between 1811 and 1917.
18. *SRA* 5, p. 612.
19. The Red Cross is an international humanitarian organization founded by Henry Dunant following the Battle of Solferino in 1859, part of the Second War of Italian independence.
20. He was tonsured to the Great Schema in 1880 and made archimandrite in 1889. He was abbot of the Caucasian monastery for thirty-five years. Shortly before his death, August 15, 1912, he appointed his successor, Fr Ilarion (Kuchu). Archimandrite Ieron was buried by the ancient church of St Simon, but his grave has not been preserved.
21. *KS* 16, pp. 25–6.
22. Ibid., p. 27.
23. *SRA* 9/1, p. 286.
24. *SRA* 9/2, pp. 274–5.
25. *ISRA* 6, p. 317.
26. *SRA* 9/2, p. 247.
27. Kraskovsky, p. 42.
28. Riley, pp. 252–3.
29. Ibid., pp. 322–3.
30. *ISRA* 7, p. 51.
31. The embassy proposed to the Russian Holy Synod that after Makary a cleric should be appointed to act as Russian intermediary and representative on Athos. The idea was opposed by the civil head of the Synod, K. P. Pobedonostsev. This disagreement resulted in the government's having no clear-cut Russian policy or even idea about Russian Athos. The Constantinople Embassy and Thessaloniki Consulate repeatedly asked for an unambiguous statement from the Foreign Ministry about official policy toward the increase in the Russian Athonite community, but to no avail. See *ISRA* 7, pp. 51–2.
32. *ISRA* 7, p. 32.
33. Ibid., pp. 37 and 44.
34. Ibid., pp. 33–4.

35. The Phanariot Greeks were Ottoman subjects; they were the refugees who came to the Hellenic Kingdom in the 1923 exchange of populations. The Morea is another term for the Peloponnese, the main part of the Hellenic Kingdom.

36. A total of 18,600 Turkish lira was spent on the property from 1840 to 1874. According to Kraskovsky, the property had been mortgaged to release equity for the monastery when it was in financial straits before 1840; Makary paid off the mortgage himself. Krumitsa covers an area of a radius of 10 kilometers. It is located close to the Athonite land border with the mainland, 25 kilometers north-west of the monastery. The name "Krumitsa" is curious. Its Greek equivalent is Χρωμίτσα. According to Tasoula Eptakoili's article (http://www.oinoxoos.net/oinos/3916/tsantali-ae-i-oinobiomichania-ton-15-ekatom-murion-litron (accessed July 5, 2019), the place was originally called "Kormilitsa," which in Russian means "nurse," i.e. one who feeds, from the verb "kormit'"—for the vineyards and olive groves "fed" St Panteleimon's.

37. One *vedro* is equivalent to 12.3 liters. By 1970 Krumitsa was again abandoned and overgrown, but was discovered by the vintner Evangelos Tsantalis, who started commercial production of Athonite wines by agreement with St Panteleimon Monastery. The finest wine from here is the *Kormilitsa* Gold Label dry red, the official wine of the Kremlin, retailing at about $200 a bottle. Its label bears the name "Кормилица", not "Крумица."

38. Kraskovsky, pp. 76–7. I. F. Kraskovsky, a novelist and one-time contributor to the journals *Moskovskiye Vedomosti* and *Russky Vestnik*, stayed a year on Athos in the 1880s, befriended Archimandrite Makary, whom he admired, and wrote about in his monograph (see chapter 4, p. 31 fn. 57). Kraskovsky fell ill and was excellently treated in the Krumitsa hospital by its young resident doctor-monk.

39. Kraskovsky, pp. 135–6.

40. At the beginning of the twentieth century until the First World War, when the ruble was stable and inflation virtually non-existent, beer cost 10 kopeks (100 kopeks to a ruble), 1 kilogram wheat flour cost 24 kopeks and a parade uniform dress coat cost 70 rubles. According to an old pre-revolutionary Russian adage, one could buy a cow for 3 rubles: prices in the country were lower than that in the city. http://status-coins.ru/statji/article_post/rubl-chto-mozhno-bylo-kupit-na-nego-v-nachale-18-19-i-20-vekakh (accessed December 17, 2020).

41. The bejeweled wonderworking copy of the Panaghia Ierosolimitissa hangs over the Royal Doors and is ceremoniously descended during feasts of the Mother of God and readings of the Akathist Hymn.

42. *SRA* 9/2, p. 276.

43. Ibid., p. 279.

44. Igumen Pyotr (Pigol'), unpublished email to Nicholas Fennell, December 2, 2005: "According to Athonite rule, candidates for the abbot's succession are designated by him from among the most spiritually experienced brethren. Their names are written on slips of paper, which are placed in a reliquary with holy remains. Then a specially designated

monk, usually one of the oldest of the house, withdraws one of the slips. The name of the successor chosen by this ballot is solemnly declared." For more on Igumen Pyotr, see chapter 13.

45. Ibid., p. 283.

46. *Ustav Russkago na Afone svyatago velikomuchenika i tselitselya Panteleimona obschezhitel'nago monastyrya*, printed in Church Slavonic script and first used from 1889, by Makary's successor, Archimandrite Andrey (Veryovkin): Sabel'nikov, pp. 542–95.

47. Ibid., p. 304.

48. *SRA* 9/2, pp. 299–300.

49. Ibid., p. 297.

Makary's Successors: Abbots Andrey and Nifont 1889–1905

1. Riley, p. 241.

2. *SRA* 5, pp. 407–9. Today St Panteleimon Monastery houses an extensive museum, which is open to visitors by invitation only. The main part of the museum exhibits the workshops and their products, with hundreds of illustrative photographs on the walls. In a separate hangar, steam-driven machinery and other mechanical tools are on display.

3. The St Panteleimon vestments were renowned for their craftsmanship and precious materials. By the 1970s many had been sold. Some belong to the Greek Athonite houses and are worn on feast days. I found only one set still at St Panteleimon's: the archimandrite's festal liturgical robes, on display in the Abbots' Hall of the museum; it features crimson roses gorgeously embroidered in silk and gold thread. Today the clergy wear cotton and velvet vestments of Greek manufacture.

4. Fr Makary (Makienko) is the author of *SRA 1*, and editor-in-chief of the *SRA* series. While supplying the essential biographical facts, he writes uncritically reverential biographies, some of which border on hagiography.

5. In 1833, according to *SRA* 5, p. 388.

6. He read from the heart, clearly and loudly, as if he had written the text himself. This was especially true when he read the lives of St Alexios the Man of God and St Joseph the Beautiful of Egypt; those who heard these readings were moved to tears.

7. *SRA 1*, p. 259.

8. *SRA 16*, p. 46.

9. *SRA 1*, p. 260 and *SRA 16*, p. 45.

10. *SRA 5*, p. 395.

11. August 21 is now one of the monastery's nine *panigiry* / principal festivals. In the photograph a female figure on the left, dressed in monastic habit, with her head bent in sorrow and her feet amid flames, is walking away from the gates. The photograph is venerated as the miraculous *Svetopisanny Obraz Presvyatoy Bozhiey Materi u Bol'shoy Porty* / the Image Drawn by Light of the Mother of God at the Great Gates. In 2011, a sanctuary and fountain were built there and a plaque with the photograph has been put on the wall next to the gates.

12. *SRA* 5, p. 389.
13. Ibid., 396. Priest-Monk of the Great Schema Pavel, born Pyotr Mikhaylovich Durnev to a peasant family in the Voronezhskaya Guberniya. He entered the monastery in 1858, ordained priest in 1863, and tonsured to the Great Schema in 1882. He was steward and treasurer in the monastery's Moscow and Constantinople dependencies before becoming chief steward of St Panteleimon's.
14. *SRA* 16, p. 50.
15. An imposing residential block of 700 rooms, topped by the Chapel of the Transfiguration, outside the main gates by the sea.
16. *SRA* 5, pp. 389–90. The address was written on the eve of Lent 1898.
17. Ibid., p. 397.
18. *SRA* 16, p. 50.
19. *SRA* 5, p. 398.
20. In the mid-nineteenth century the average unskilled laborer's wage in Moscow was 17 rubles per month. (https://bigenc.ru/domestic_history/text/3249696).
21. Born into a merchant family in the small town of Peremyshl', Kaluzhskaya Guberniya, in 1842, he joined St Panteleimon's in 1870. He was ordained priest in 1876 and tonsured to the Great Schema shortly after his election as Andrey's successor, in 1896.
22. According to *SRA 1*, p. 264; *SRA* 5, p. 399, says that his illness was short.
23. *SRA 1*, p. 302.
24. Ibid., p. 302.

Archimandrite Misail

1. According to Moniale Pélagie, "L'higoumène Misaël," *Buisson Ardent*, 19 (Penthalaz and Dijon: Diffusion CRF, Cahiers Saint-Silouane l'athonite, 2013), p. 75. Cf. *SRA I*, pp. 305–7.
2. The Odessa dependency was more important than the one in Constantinople because nearly all Russian pilgrims set off from the Black Sea port to Palestine and Athos. Before embarkation, representatives of the Athonite houses would take them to their respective dependencies, house them and look after them. Once the pilgrims arrived in Constantinople and on Athos, they remained "loyal" to the house which looked after them in Odessa.
3. In a *kazyonnoe uchische* / a government-run public school: *SRA 1*, p. 252.
4. This is a strange exception. *Afonskaya tragediya. Gordost' i sataninskie zamysly* (Moscow: Institut Apostola Ioanna Bogoslova, 2005) p. 38. Igumen Pyotr (Pigol'), himself a one-time monk of St Panteleimon's, refers to Fr Misail as *skhiarkhimandrit* / Aarchimandrite of the Great Schema, although Misail was never tonsured to the Great Schema. Pigol''s mistake is surprising as he should have known better: he was a well-informed former monk of St Panteleimon's.
5. *ISRA* 3, pp. 23–5.
6. *SRA 1*, p. 311.
7. Ibid., p. 310.

8. *SRA* 2, p. 20. Most entries bear a similar laconic physical description, which was probably based on photographs and on the monk's mortal remains. Curiously, quite a number of monks are described as having gray eyes.

9. *ISRA* 3, p. 25.

10. "Igumen archimandrit Misail, vizantiyskoe vremya," www.isihazm.ru/?id=2048 (accessed April 2016).

11. Gardner and Mayevsky describe it as a bass.

12. *ISRA* 9, p. 235. *Eis polla eti Despota* / "Many years, o Master" is traditionally sung to bishops, but in the Twenty Ruling Monasteries the abbots are entitled to certain episcopal honors.

13. St Sophrony (Sakharov) of Essex, 1896–1993, the famous disciple, biographer, and compiler of the writings of St Silouan the Athonite, and founder of the Monastic Community of St John the Forerunner in Essex. He was canonized by the Ecumenical Patriarchate on November 27, 2019.

14. Pélagie, p. 76. Moniale Pélagie had been asked by St Sophrony to record his *Paroles à la communauté.* These are a record of the saint's words to the members of his monastic community; some of his words are about his time at St Panteleimon's and his discipleship to St Silouan the Athonite.

15. Ibid., p. 77. Moniale Pélagie is quoting from St Sophrony's *Starets Siluan Afonsky.*

16. Moniale Pélagie recorded St Sophrony saying, "à l'époque où je suis entré au monastère, il y avait plus de six cents moines—six cents rudes gaillards— craignant de faire quoi que ce soit contre sa parole." Ibid., pp. 77–8.

17. Ibid., pp. 79–80.

18. Ibid., p. 83.

19. Gold rubles were introduced to replace silver rubles during the Minister of Finance S. Vitte's monetary reforms (1897–1899). A gold ruble was composed of 0.77423g pure gold. https://www.krasplace.ru/ceny-1913-goda-v-sovremennyx-rublyax.

20. *SRA* 1, p. 311.

21. The same is true of Russian Athos as a whole. See L. A. Gerd, *Konstatinopol'sky patriarkhat i Rossiya 1901/1914* (Moscow: Indrik, 2012), pp. 189–90: according to the Bulgarian trade agent A Shopov, who was writing in 1900, the Holy Mountain had become entirely Russified—"Soon the Athonite peninsula will be politically Russian. Economically, it has long been in Russian hands."

22. According to *SRA* 1, p. 307. This is probably a rounded approximation. Compare the Athenian newspaper, *Skrip*, November 1912 (quoted in O.E. Petrunina's analysis, *SRA* 6, p. 16), according to which there were 1,928 monks in the monastery at its apogee.

23. *SRA* 6, p. 139.

24. Ibid., p. 401, but cf. p. 242.

25. So was Zograf. For Athonite population statistics, see O.E. Petrunina's analysis, Ibid., pp. 16–19.

26. Dorotheos Monahos, A', p. 156.

27. According to Dorotheos Monahos, ibid., p. 157, only 750 landed, "on the afternoon of the same day."

28. A. A. Dmitrievsky, *Afon i ego novoe politicheskoe mezhdunarodnoe polozhenie* (St Petersburg: offprint, 1913), p. 1.

29. http://agioritikesmnimes.blogspot.com/2011/11/134.html?m=1 (accessed September 27, 2018). Synaxis Meetings Nos 25 and 26, according to Meletios Metaxakis, *To Agion Oros kai i rosiki politiki en anatoli* (Athens: P.D. Sakellariou, 1913), pp. 13–21.

30. Dmitrievsky, p. 21.

31. *ISRA* 7, pp. 148–9.

32. D. Dakin, *The Greek Struggle in Macedonia 1897–1913* (Thessaloniki: Thessaloniki Institute for Balkan Studies, 1993), pp. 12–13.

33. In September 1913, the Sacred Community explained in a memorandum to the delegates attending the London Conference of Ambassadors that it could have no links with Bulgaria: "the schism also does not permit us Orthodox to enter into relations or have contact with the Bulgarian schismatics, on pain of incurring severe ecclesiastical penalties." See *Réfutation du mémoire soumis par les moines russes kelliotes à la Conférence des Ambassadeurs de Londres et contenant des propositions anticanoniques et subversives de toute notre constitution* (Karyes, 1913), p. 6.

34. According to the popular patriotic Macedonian rhyme, Pan-Slavism was a scabies:

I am proud to be Greek;	Είμαι Έλλην το καυχώμαι
I know my origins,	Ξέρω την καταγωγή μου
And my Greek soul	Και η Ελληνική ψυχή μου
Lives always free.	Ελευθέρα πάντα ζεί.
The scabies of Pan-Slavism	Του Πανσλαβισμού η ψώρα,
Does not infect the Macedonians,	Μακεδόνας δεν μολύνει
Nor does it remove them	Ούτε τούς απομακρύνει
From Hellenism.	Από τον Ελληνισμό.

35. Greece was counting on Britain, France, and Russia's support as her protectors, and Foreign Minister A. Skouzes begged them in vain to intervene. Eventually, Nicholas II obtained a cessation of hostilities followed by an armistice in May 1897.

36. The brother-in-law of Pavlos Melas, one of the principal Makedonomachoi.

37. I. Dragoumis, *Martyron kai Iroon Aima* (Athens: Malliaris-Paidia, 1903), p. 29.

38. Dmitrievsky, pp. 8 and 15.

39. Ibid., p. 7.

40. San Stefano (February 1878) Article XXII: "The Athonite monks of Russian origin will keep their properties and privileges, and in the three monasteries belonging to them … they will continue to enjoy those rights and prerogatives guaranteed also to the other spiritual foundations and monasteries of Mount Athos" (Sir Augustus Oakes, *The Great*

European Treaties of the Nineteenth Century (Oxford: Clarendon Press, 1938)), p. 388. Article LXII of the Treaty of Berlin (July 1878) refers simply to all monks of Mount Athos, but mentions no Russians (Oakes, p. 359).

41. Dmitrievsky, p. 10.
42. Communiqué from the Imperial Russian Foreign Ministry, quoted in *SRA 6*, p. 108.
43. Dmitrievsky, p. 11.
44. After the 1912 liberation of Athos, Macedonia, and Thrace, there were two Hellenic ecclesiastical jurisdictions: that of the Dioceses of the New Territories (newly liberated by Greece), under the Metropolitan of Thessaloniki and his council of bishops, who all answered to the ecumenical patriarch; and that of the Church of Greece. To this day, although this is sometimes disputed, the Holy Mountain remains under the aegis of the Patriarch.
45. *Réfutation* (Mount Athos, 1913), p. 26.

The Name of God Dispute

1. A renowned center of spiritual elders, visited by Dostoyevsky and Solovyov.
2. Priest-Monk Simeon (Kulagin), *"Monasheskie smuty" nachala XX veka: Afon, Optina, Solovki i Glinskaya pustynya*, http://www.orthedu.ru/ch-hist/14593-monasheskie-smu-ty-nachala-hh-veka-afon-optina.html (accessed April 2016).
3. Skhimonakh Ilarion Domrachov, *Na gorakh Kavkaza* (St Petersburg: Voskresen'e, Dioptra, 2002).
4. The prayer of the hesychasts, widely practiced on Mount Athos from its revival in the eighteenth century and championed by the early fathers and, among others, Saints Gregory Palamas and Gregory of Sinai in the fourteenth century: *"Gospodi Iisuse Khriste syne bozhii, pomiluy mya greshnogo* / Lord Jesus Christ Son of God, have mercy on me a sinner." The words *"greshnogo"* / "a sinner" are not always included; sometimes *"nas gresh-nykh* / us sinners" concludes the prayer.
5. *Imya Iisus est' Sam Bog* is the core of the book's message.
6. Tom Dykstra, *Hallowed Be Thy Name: The Name-Glorifying Dispute in the Russian Orthodox Church and on Mount Athos, 1912–1914* (St Paul, Minnesota: OCABS Press, 2013), p. 35.
7. *SRA 1*, p. 223.
8. Ibid., p. 224.
9. *SRA 16*, p. 102.
10. Bishop Ilarion (Alfeev), *Svyaschennaya tayna tserkvi: vvedenie v istoriyu I problematiku imyaslavskikh sporov*, p. 356.
11. He was head of the monastery's Constantinople dependency, from 1910, and then became father-confessor in the monastery's Odessa dependency before retiring to an eremitical life in Novaya Fivaida. See *SRA 1*, pp. 460–1.

12. *SRA 6*, pp. 23–4.

13. Dykstra, p. 44.

14. It is difficult to translate this last term. Dykstra, p. 58, adds, "Those siding with Khrisanf called their opponents *iisusane* (Jesusites), *iisustiki* (Jesusniks), or *imenopoklonniki* (name-worshippers)."

15. *SRA 6*, p. 23.

16. Ibid., p. 26.

17. In the west of the Russian Empire, now in western Ukraine.

18. *SRA 6*, p. 34.

19. Ibid., p. 36.

20. Alfeev, pp. 369–71. It should be noted, however, that prior to the 1917 revolution many Greek clergy studied in Russia, e.g., Chrysostomos Papadopoulos (the future archbishop of Athens) and Grigorios Papamihail (lay theologian and author of a book on St Maksim Grek).

21. *SRA 6*, p. 38.

22. He had become father-confessor and spiritual guide of the Siberian millionaire benefactor of the Serai, Innokenty Sibiryakov, who provided the funds to complete the building of the vast St Andrew *Kyriakon* / Central Church (see chapter 6). The two met in St Petersburg when Mukhranov was the prior St Andrew Skete dependency in the capital. They set off for the Mountain together in 1898.

23. Ibid., p. 43.

24. *SRA 6*, p. 45.

25. He was enthroned on November 12, 1912, at the death of Joachim III.

26. *SRA 6*, pp. 52–3.

27. He died in 1909 and was canonized by Patriarch Aleksey of Moscow in 1990. Vast crowds attended his funeral.

28. Alfeev, pp. 358–9. The letter was dated May 7, 1912.

29. Available in English: John of Kronstadt, *My Life in Christ: The Spiritual Journals of St John of Kronstadt* (Jordanville, New York: Holy Trinity Monastery, 2018) 9780884654650.

30. Ibid., p. 393. Inexplicably, Sabler's report with its sage underlined warning was probably not immediately read by Procurator Sazonov. The latter passed it on to the Holy Synod only a year later.

31. He was abbot of the Voskresensky Monastery in the Novgorod diocese. "Igumen" is an honorary ecclesiastic title in the Russian church.

32. "No 28: Zametki arkhimandrita o. Misaila, igumena Panteleimonovskogo monastyrya «Opisanie sobytiy v Panteleimonovskom monastyre za vremya religioznykh borzheniy v 1913 godu," *Zabytye stanitsy russkogo imyaslaviya* (Moscow: Izdatel'stvo Palomnik, 2001), p. 177.

33. Ibid.

34. His letter was dated January 19, at which time he was only a bishop. He was promoted archbishop shortly afterward.

35. Pigol', p. 9.

36. Alfeev, p. 394.

37. According to the deposed Prior Ieronim, he first renounced his Name-Glorifying views and blamed everything on Fr Antony (Bulatovich), then declared that he recognized Fr Ieronim as the rightful head of the St Andrew Skete. Bulatovich, on the other hand, claimed that Fr David was ordered neither to repent nor deny the Name-Glorifying "heresy"; he merely had to relinquish his claims to becoming prior, after which he was freely allowed home to Athos. Bulatovich believed that the patriarch was being pressurized by the Russian Embassy in Constantinople. Alfeev, p. 395; *SRA 6*, p. 56.

38. Zabytye stranitsy, p. 179.

39. Ibid.

40. Ibid., pp. 179–80.

41. *SRA 6*, p. 62.

42. Ibid., p. 65.

43. Zabytye stranitsy, N° 10, pp. 58–9.

44. *SRA 6*, p. 70.

45. Alfeev, p. 554.

46. Ibid., p. 555.

47. These are the Archbishop's figures. According to the monastery archive, of the 1,549 members of St Panteleimon's and Fivaida, 661 were opposed to the Name-Glorifiers; 517 supported the new doctrine; 360 brethren did not take part in the census and 11 could not make up their mind. It is likely that the 360 who did not take part were secretly Name-Glorifiers. *SRA 6*, p. 73.

48. A troop and supply ship of the Imperial Russian Volunteer Fleet.

49. Dykstra, p. 13.

50. *SRA 6*, pp. 76–7.

51. His version is corroborated by Priest Schema-Monk Nikolay (Ivanov), one of the victims of the attack. Fr Nikolay was concussed and dragged into the bakery. When he came to he thought he saw two killed monks being dragged in by soldiers. Alfeev, pp. 565–7.

52. Ibid., p. 564.

53. Zabytye stranitsy, pp. 98–9.

54. According to *SRA 6*, pp. 86-7, 833 left on the *Kherson* and *Chikhachev*; more left voluntarily over the next months: a total of between 1,000 and 1,500 Name-Glorifiers went to Russia.

55. It goes without saying that the ecumenical patriarch had nothing to do with the arrest and deportation of the Name-Glorifiers. The intervention by the Russian military, Holy Synod, diplomats, and Foreign Ministry were undertaken without his consent or prior knowledge.

56. *SRA 6*, p. 98.

57. I. K. Smolitsch, "Le Mont Athos et la Russie," *Le Millénaire du Mont Athos* (Chevetogne: Éditions de Chevetogne, 1963), pp. 317–8.

58. Pigol', Pyotr. *Afonskaya tragediya. Gordost' i sataninskie zamysly* (Moscow: Institut Apostola Ioanna Bogoslova, 2005).

59. The icon is to be found in the Church of the Holy Martyr Elizabeth Fyodorovna, of the True Orthodox Church / *Rossiyskaya Istinnaya Pravoslavnaya Tserkov'*, St Petersburg.

60. The book is very long; it contains 1,087 references. For all Ilarion's impressive scholarship (some of his quotations are in the original Greek, Hebrew, and even Syriac), his points are often obscured by excessively long quotations.

61. Alfeev, p. 843.

62. Now, as Metropolitan of Kolomna and Krutitsk and Head of the Moscow Patriarchate Department of External Church Relations (DECR), he is a senior member of the Holy Synod of the Moscow Patriarchate.

63. Unpublished email to Nicholas Fennell December 7, 2015.

64. *SRA 6*, p. 62.

65. See Alfeev, p. 485, fn. 36.

66. Ibid., p. 489.

67. unpublished email from Igumen Pyotr (Pigol') to Nicholas Fennell, December 2, 2005.

68. Dykstra, p. 224.

69. The Russian expression he uses is *Nel'zya rubit' suk, na kotorom sidish'* / [lit.] "You must not chop off the branch you are sitting on."

70. Bulatovich is cruelly satirized in Il'f and Petrov's novel *Dvenadtsat' Stul'ev* ("Chast' per-vaya, glava XII, 'Rasskaz o gusare-skhimnike*****,'" *Il'ya Il'f, Evgeny Petrov: Sobranie sochi-neniy, Tom pervy* [Moscow: Gosudarstvennoe izdatel'stvo khudozhestvennoy literatury, 1981]), pp. 122–7; see also Alfeev, p. 406, fn. 3.

71. A vestment worn by bishops and senior priests.

72. L. A. Gerd, *Konstatinopol'sky patriarkhat i Rossiya 1901/1914* (Moscow: Indrik, 2012), p. 235. Another modern Russian Athonite specialist, Pavel Troitsky (*ISRA 1*, p. 299), quotes a certain Rusinov, who also ascribes the Name of God dispute to the conflict between Little and Great Russians. Troitsky himself, however, considers this view a simplification and points out that both sides in the dispute consisted of Great and Little Russians.

73. Gerd, pp. 190–213.

74. St Sophrony (Sakharov), *Staretz Silouan* (Essex: Stavropegic Monastery of St John the Baptist, 1990), pp. 32–3.

75. *SRA 6*, pp. 663–4. The Fr V. who spoke to the Roman Catholic theologian was probably Monk Vasily (Krivoshein), the future archbishop, whom St Sophrony described as "a polyglot, well versed in theology, commanded in obedience to deal with visitors."

76. Pirogov et al., pp. 132–7, 205–6.

From 1913 to Abbot Misail's Death in 1940

1. See *ISRA* 7, p. 51.
2. The Russian Athonites asked, among other things: while keeping Athos under the aegis of the ecumenical patriarch, to establish a separate episcopal see on the Holy Mountain especially for the Russians; either to alter the composition of the Sacred Community to reflect the ethnic makeup of the Athonite community or free Russian Athonites from the authority of the Sacred Community; to allow the Russian houses to build a common warehouse, and to exonerate them from paying any taxes and duties. *SRA 6*, pp. 119–20.
3. Smyrnakis, p. 223.
4. Meletios Metaxakis (1871–1935), Patriarch of Constantinople (Meletios IV, 1921–1923); convened the Pan-Orthodox Congress May–June 1923, at which he introduced the revised church calendar in line with the secular Gregorian Calendar. Mount Athos, and the Patriarchates of Jerusalem, Moscow, Serbia, and Georgia have remained with the old Julian Calendar; Constantinople, Alexandria, Antioch, Albania, Bulgaria Cyprus, Greece, and Romania are now new calendarist.
5. *SRA 6*, p. 158.
6. The daily wages of carpenter workers in Greece: 4–7 drachmae in 1914; 18–25 drachmae in 1920 https://theodora.com/encyclopedia/w/wages_addition.html (accessed December 17, 2020).
7. Sof'ya Ilarionovna, a well-known philanthropist and representative of the Russian Red Cross.
8. The church of the Holy Trinity came under the jurisdiction of the archbishop of Athens.
9. *SRA 6*, p. 313.
10. A. A. Pavlovsky, *Afonskiya Izvestiya I*, p. 9.
11. *Afonskiya Izvestiya II*, p. 1. Fr Nikolay was a Bessarabian who had just returned from a visit to Russia; he went deaf as a result of the blow.
12. The *Katastatikos Hartis Aghiou Orous (K.H.A.O)* was ratified by the patriarch of Constantinople and, in 1926, confirmed by the Greek State.
13. *SRA 6*, p. 322.
14. Article XIII of the Treaty of Sèvres stated that, in accordance with Article LXII of the Treaty of Berlin, Greece undertakes to protect non-Greek Athonite communities and maintain their ancient rights. Greece was thus responsible for Mount Athos, which had become an integral part of it. The Treaty of Sèvres was not ratified, but it was incorporated into the Treaty of Lausanne, which was ratified. The USSR, of course, had at the time nothing to do with Russian Athos, whose interests it would certainly not defend.
15. Protoierey Pavel (Nedosekin), "O nekotorykh prichinakh krizisa «russkogo Afona» v XX veke," *Afonsky Arkhiv XX veka. Dokumenty Russkogo Svyato-Panteleimonovskogo monastyrya 1917–1941* (Moscow-Brussels: Arkhiv russkoy emigratsii, 2014), pp. 29–30.
16. Near Novi Sad, north of Belgrade.

17. Nedosekin, p. 14.
18. Owing to the Asia Minor defeats and Exchange of Populations, the Greek economy was in turmoil. Until May 1928, with the establishment of the Central Bank of Greece, the drachma was rapidly losing value and was not considered an internationally exchangeable currency: https://www.york.ac.uk/media/economics/documents/seminars/2012-13/GCRISIS_1932.pdf (accessed December 17, 2020).
19. See Chapter 8.
20. Archimandrite of the Great Schema Kirik and Abbot Misail's designated successor, Priest Schema-Monk Ioanniky.
21. *SRA 6*, p. 319.
22. In 1931 the dinar–Us dollar rate was fixed at 56 dinars to $ 1: https://en.wikipedia.org/wiki/Yugoslav_dinar#1920%E2%80%9341;_Serbian_dinar (accessed December 17, 2020).
23. Ibid., p. 316.
24. These gendarmes were armed civilians, sometimes referred to by the Ottoman title of "serdars." They wore traditional Macedonian costume and were armed with rifles, swords, or daggers.
25. Afonsky arkhiv XX veka: dokumenty Russkogo Svyato-Panteleimonobskogo monastyrya 1917–1941 (Moscow–Brussels: Arkhiv russkoy emigratsii, 2014), pp. 292–3.
26. Nedosekin, p. 19.
27. St Sophrony, p. 194. The saint's book has been published in English, but the translation is my own.

The Next Four Abbots: From Iustin to Avel' (1940–1978)

1. *SRA 1*, p. 476.
2. Katastatikos Hartis Agiou Orous (K.H.A.O.), confirmed by the Greek state in 1926: see Chapter 11.
3. *SRA 6*, p. 247.
4. Ibid., p. 246.
5. *SRA 1*, p. 495.
6. Chapters 4, 5, and 6.
7. The ecclesiarch is literally "one who rules in the church." The ecclesiarch is responsible for managing the schedule of services in the church and locating the appropriate texts and music to be used in their performance.
8. "In his 88th year," according to SRA 1, p. 498.
9. Ibid., p. 497.
10. Unpublished letter of Fr Ioann (Abernethy) to Nicholas Fennell, December 24, 2018.
11. Kolya is the diminutive form of Nicholas.
12. *SRA 1*, p. 510.

13. F. Dölger, author of *Mönschland Athos* (Munich: F. Bruchmann, 1945).

14. Richard Clogg, *A Concise History of Greece* (Cambridge: Cambridge University Press, 1992), p. 123.

15. *SRA 6*, p. 404.

16. *Afonsky arkhiv XX veka*, pp. 327–8.

17. https://www.cambridge.org/core/journals/journal-of-hellenic-studies/article/monchsland-athos-by-f-dolger-pp-303-pl-184-munich-f-bruckmann-1943/3DCF3BE-748D3E350D62DC6A4B53A7AD1 (accessed September 21, 2019).

18. Deutsches Nachrichtenbüro, the Nazi news agency.

19. *SRA 6*, pp. 406–7.

20. Metropolitan Anthony (Khrapovitsky), head of ROCOR, was one of the candidates for the headship of the church at the 1917 *Pomestny sobor Rossiyskoy Pravoslavnoy Tserkvi* / Local Council of the Orthodox Church of Russia, at which Metropolitan Tikhon (Belavin) was elected patriarch of Moscow and All Russia, the first patriarchal election in Russia since 1700. Metropolitan Evlogy (Georgievsky), also present at the Local Council, was put in charge of all the Orthodox Churches of Western Europe. Evlogy moved to Paris; Anthony stayed in Sremsky Carlovćy at the head of the *Arkhiereysky sobor* / Council of Hierarchs. In 1926 Evlogy split from Anthony and the Council of Hierarchs. He passed under the jurisdiction of Constantinople in 1931, but caused discord by returning to Moscow shortly before his death (1946). After the death of Patriarch Tikhon in 1925, Anthony had disassociated himself from Moscow.

21. A fearless man of principle, Patriarch Tikhon stood up to and was hounded by the Soviet state; the Russian Orthodox Church canonized him in 1989. Eighteen years after the saint's death, Metropolitan Sergy (Stragorodsky) became the next Moscow Patriarch, in 1943. He was considered to be morally compromised, having signed his infamous public *Deklaratsiya* / Declaration in 1927 decrying "the bitter and violently hostile activities of our foreign enemies .... It is essential to show that we men of the Church stand with neither the enemies of our Soviet Government nor with their mindless machinations, but with our people and Government" (https://drevo-info.ru/articles/2463.html [accessed September 15, 2019]). Many Orthodox, particularly outside the USSR, now believed that the Moscow Patriarchate was controlled by the godless Communists.

22. On Monk Vasily, (Krivoshein), later Archbishop, see fn. 22, below. Deacon David (Tsuber) was tonsured to the Great Schema toward the end of his life with the name of Dimitri. In *SRA 1* his surname appears as Tsubera.

23. After the communist coup in September 1944, owing to galloping inflation, the lev was no longer backed by silver or gold currency. Thus the relative value to today's currency is not clear.

24. *SRA 6*, pp. 525–6.

25. He was saved by Fr Nicholas Gibbes, the tutor of the Nicholas II's son, Tsarevich Alexey. In 1949, Fr Nicholas set up the Church of St Nicholas in Marston Street, Oxford. Fr Nicholas invited Monk Vasily, who moved to Oxford in February 1951. Although he

still considered himself a monk of St Panteleimon's and would not do anything without the abbot's blessing, Vasily was ordained priest in May 1951 and continued to serve in St Nicholas Church before becoming rector of the Moscow Patriarchate parish of the Annunciation at 1 Canterbury Rd, Oxford in 1959. Later that year he moved to Paris as a bishop. In 1960 he became bishop of Brussels, then archbishop. He visited St Panteleimon's in 1976, 1977, and 1979, and traveled some twenty times to the USSR. He died in Leningrad during his last visit, in 1985.

26. *SRA 6*, p. 437.
27. Ibid., pp. 437 and 439.
28. St Panteleimon's, The St Andrew Skete, and the Prophet Elijah Skete.
29. Ibid., p. 442.
30. Ibid., p. 445.
31. Ibid., p. 448.
32. *SRA 15*, p. 7.
33. *SRA 6*, pp. 454–5.
34. Between Communists and the Greek regular army, 1946–1949.
35. Ibid., p. 462.
36. Ibid., p. 463.
37. Ibid., p. 464.
38. Vasily (Krivoshein) did not like of the monastery's pro-Soviet stance. Some twenty years later and by then an archbishop, he wrote disapprovingly of representatives of St Panteleimon's who visited the Soviet Embassy in Athens to take part in celebrations to mark the 1917 October Revolution.
39. *SRA 15*, p. 219.
40. Both quotations from Archbishop Nikodim to Comrade Zelenkov, I. S., presumably of the DECR. The letter was on display at a private museum viewing in the Cathedral of Christ the Saviour, Moscow, in September 2016.
41. The Lavra, in the west of Russia, is one of only two monasteries which remained permanently open during the Soviet period.
42. Tachiaos, a friend and frequent visitor of St Panteleimon's, was to write on the monastery's archive in both Russian and Greek. As an influential Greek, he did much in aid of the monastery's cause in Greek government and ecclesiastical circles.
43. *SRA 6*, p. 476.
44. Ibid., p. 492.
45. Ibid., p. 616.
46. Ibid., p. 643.
47. Ibid.
48. *SRA 15*, p. 324.
49. Ibid., p. 334.
50. Ibid., p. 348.

51. Ibid., p. 356. Vatopedi's extraordinary offer to the Russians of the St Andrew Skete was thus never taken up. Today the skete houses the Athoniada School.
52. *SRA 6*, p. 643.
53. Ibid., p. 651.
54. *SRA 15*, p. 358. From a letter of David (Tsuber) to Archbishop Vasily, who replies that Avel' was hardly likely to be working for the KGB. Priest-Monk Filaret (Gachegov) was tonsured and ordained in the Pskovo-Pecherskaya Lavra came to St Panteleimon's in August 1976. After Avel'''s departure he left the monastery for Krumitsa. At some point, however, he came back to the monastery. I met him there in the mid-1980s.

From Abbot Ieremiya to Abbot Evlogy

1. Makary (Makienko): https://pravlife.org/ru/content/shiarhimandrit-ieremiya-ale-hin-podvizhnik-nashego-vremeni (accessed October 6, 2019).
2. Ibid. Although the biography is anonymous, Fr Makary's hand is obvious: as in *SRA 1*, he writes in pre-revolutionary script and indulges in the occasional hagiographic hyperbole. The biography can be found on other sites, but not in pre-revolutionary script. After the election of Abbot Evlogy (2016), Fr Makary became the monastery's Karyes representative instead of Kirion (Ol'khovik), who was moved to Xylourgou
3. A Kulak (Russian: "fist") was a wealthy or prosperous peasant. At the end of 1929 a campaign to "liquidate the kulaks as a class" ("dekulakization") was launched by the Soviet government. Most kulaks had been deported to remote regions of the Soviet Union or arrested, and their land and property confiscated: https://www.britannica.com/topic/kulak (accessed 14/10/2019).
4. Makienko.
5. Ivan was captured and deported to Germany, but at the end of hostilities was in Belgium, whence he emigrated to Canada. He visited Archimandrite Ieremiya at St Panteleimon's in the 1990s.
6. St Kuksha was tonsured in St Panteleimon Monastery, but, as we saw in Chapter 9, was deported in 1913, having been wrongly accused of involvement in the Name of God Rebellion.
7. Makienko.
8. See previous chapter, p. 155.
9. Makienko.
10. *SRA 15*, pp. 359–60.
11. Ibid., p. 363.
12. Makienko. When I first met Fr Ieremiya, at the end of the 1980s, he was just as described by Fr Kirion. I asked one of the monks offloading mattresses from a trailer at the main gates where I could find the abbot. "I'm the abbot," he replied.
13. *SRA 15*, p. 372.

14. Even Archimandrite Misail (Tomin), who was a gossip, was untrustworthy. When Tomin left for the USSR in 1980 never to return, Deacon David wrote to Archbishop Vasily that life had become easier in the monastery: *SRA 15*, p. 371.

15. Tomin to Krivoshein, Christmas 1981: Ibid., p. 367.

16. Makienko.

17. In the 1970s, he had had free access to the monastery archive where he worked with the cooperation and encouragement of Abbots Gavriil and Avel'. See Introduction (ii).

18. *SRA 6*, p. 655.

19. When I visited the Mountain Skete at the end of the 1980s, the buildings were in a sorry state, with many of their windows broken or boarded up. The caretaker was away; he had recently dug his own grave next to the *kyriakon* / central church.

20. He was appointed *grammatik* / the abbot's secretary and monastery scribe in 1983; a year later he joined the Council of Elders and became the St Panteleimon representative in Karyes, an appointment he held for the next decade.

21. *SRA 6*, p. 655.

22. Every Christmas in the late 1980s and early 1990s, the Church of the Annunciation and Holy Trinity at 1 Canterbury Road, Oxford, used to collect money for St Panteleimon's. I remember a thank-you letter to our parish written by Fr Ieremiya in biro on lined exercise book paper.

23. Igumen Pyotr, who left St Panteleimon's in 1997, was briefly in charge of the Moscow *podvor'ye* / dependency. He was appointed abbot of the New Athonite Monastery of St Simon the Canaanite in the Caucasus, but had to leave after the insurgency of armed Abkhazian separatists shortly after 1995. *Velikaya Strazha* is quoted from extensively in chapters 4–7. Although Pyotr (Pigol') is not officially its co-author, he collaborated with Sabel'nikov in sourcing the library's archives. Never afraid of official disapproval, Fr Pyotr took a brave stance over the Name of God dispute, as we saw in Chapter 10.

24. Archimandrite Seraphim (Bobich), the skete's prior, refused to commemorate the ecumenical patriarch. As a result, he and his small brotherhood, the last of the Skete Russian representatives, were summarily arrested and expelled from Athos.

25. According to *SRA 2*, p. 83, he eventually went to Krumitsa. In an interview (November 2008, https://pravoslavie.ru/28260.html [accessed September 2018]) entitled *Eto Bozhie blagoslovenie—byt' nasel'nikom na Afone*, the Ukrainian writer, Anatoly Kholodyuk, asks Fr Nikolay what he is doing in Xylourgou. Having asked whether Fr Nikolay is the skete's prior, Kholodyuk puts it to him: "Tell me, is it true that for the last two decades on Athos it has become customary to send to dilapidated or ruined sketes erring, or shall we say, 'inconvenient' monks?" Generalov gives an evasive answer, but admits that Fr Ioakim (Sabel'nikov) was at Xylourgou before him and is now at Krumitsa because of the publication of *Velikaya Strazha*, which "the monastery fathers did not like, so Fr Ioakim was in disgrace and exiled from the monastery."

26. *SRA 6*, p. 726. According to Metropolitan Yuvenaly (Poyarkov) of Krutitsk and Kolomna, there were sixty brethren in 2006: *Rossiya-Afon: tysyacheletie dukhovnogo edinstva*, "Vzaimootnosheniya Russkoy Pravoslavnoy Tserkvi i Afona v XX veke" (Moscow: Izdatel'stvo PSTGU, 2008), p. 240.

27. *SRA 6*, p. 747.

28. On September 1, 2004, some thirty armed individuals stormed a school in Beslan, North Ossetia, taking a thousand hostages. Three-hundred-and-thirty people were killed. The attack was linked with the separatist insurgency in Chechnya.

29. *SRA 6*, p. 700. Putin is referred to as *Rossiysky gosudar'*—the Russian sovereign or tsar.

30. Fr Makary was awarded the Order of St Sergy Radonezhsky 2nd Class on his sixtieth birthday in 2014 by Metropolitan Ilarion (Alfeev) on behalf of Patriarch Kirill.

31. *SRA 6*, Ibid.

32. Ibid., p. 710.

33. Russky na Afone Svyato-Panteleimonov monastyr': k 1000-letiyu russkogo monashestva na Svyatoy Gore Afon (RPMA: Izdatel'stvo Yulis, 2017).

34. http://afonit.info/novosti/1000-letie-russkogo-afona/glava-pravitelstva-rf-i-patri-arkh-moskovskij-proveli-zasedanie-obshchestvenno-popechitelskogo-soveta-afonsko-go-panteleimonova-monastyrya-video-i-foto (accessed March 2018). Patriarch Kirill's use of the expression "it is assumed"—*predpolagayetsya*—is a cautious admittance of his uncertainty.

35. http://www.romfea.gr/epikairotita-xronika/6830-agnoia-apo-tous-agiore-ites-gia-episkepsi-patriarxi-mosxas (accessed April 6, 2016).

36. A de facto war had been waged between Ukraine and Russia since the 2014 annexation by the latter of Crimea.

37. See Chapters 1 and 2.

38. During my stay at St Panteleimon's in April 2017, I visited Megisti Lavra. The newly appointed St Panteleimon librarian, Fr Martiry, asked me to have a look at the document and, if possible, photograph it. I was not allowed into the Lavra library.

39. *SRA 5*, pp. 199–200.

40. Makienko.

41. The original negative of the miraculous icon seemed to be lost among the thousands of archival photographs which were taking an age to sort out. It was found in 2014. I have seen it myself; it shows with remarkable clarity the female figure in monastic garb walking away in sorrow, her feet wreathed in flames.

42. When I visited the monastery in April 2015, he entered the Pokrov Central Church on the arm of his young cell orderly during matins. There was an audible sigh of delight from all present. The ninety-nine-year-old was walking without difficulty. He was stooped but otherwise seemed in fine fettle. To his death he was said never to have worn spectacles.

43. See fn. 2, chapter 8.

44. Afonsky tserkovny kalendar' 2017 (Athos: RPMA, 2017), pp. 175–8.

45. http://afonit.info/novosti/novosti-afona/patriarkh-bolgarskij-vstretilsya-s-delegat-siej-afonskikh-monastyrej-sv-panteleimona-i-ksenofont (accessed September 2018).

Conclusion

1. I. M. Hatzifotis, *Mones tou Agiou Orous, Tomos A'* (Athens: Hellandion, 2008), pp. 147–8.

2. The exemplary, mainly Greek workforce is paid good wages. The builders are mostly married men; the sooner they complete a job, the quicker they return to their families. I saw two workmen fitting out fifteen ceiling lights along a corridor on the second floor of the Preobrazhensky Korpus in the space of an afternoon. The kilometer-long wall linking the monastery's *arsanas* / harbor with the main vegetable gardens and the Church of Elijah the Prophet has been completed; during my five-day stay in October 2019, the last fifty meters of wall was finished.

3. Riley, p. 241.

4. Pilgrims are assigned to accommodation according to their status. The most important visitors are housed in the Tsarsky Arkhondarik / The Tsar's Guest Quarters, situated to the east of St Panteleimon Central Church. Even here the ultra-important guests, such as the patriarch himself, are assigned to the lower floors; less important VIPs go to the upper floors, the best rooms being with a balcony at the end of a corridor. The Preobrazhensky Korpus is divided into Arkhondarik I, for ordinary pilgrims, and the much more comfortable Arkhodarik II housing more valued guests. Those who come to help out with general obediences are housed in the Rabochy Korpus / the Workers' Building. There are probably several other grades of accommodation.

5. The Kiev dependency has recently closed, however, owing to lack of funds and ecclesiastical disagreements.

6. *SRA 6*, p. 735.

7. For many decades the Ecumenical Patriarchate had worked toward holding a Council of all the Orthodox Churches and an agreed date was finally set for 2016. But at the last minute the Russian Orthodox Church announced that it would not attend the gathering, citing the already announced non-participation of the Patriarchate of Antioch, the Patriarchate of Bulgaria, and the Patriarchate of Georgia.

8. Metropolitan Ilarion (Alfeev), head of the DECR, declared two days later: "The fact that the Patriarchate of Constantinople has recognized schismatic organizations means for us that it itself is now in schism." https://mospat.ru/en/2018/10/17/news165398/(accessed May 2019).

9. https://www.romfea.gr/agioritika-nea/26975-i-moni-agiou-panteleimonos-eklei-se-tis-portes-stous-ekprosopous-tis-oukranikis-ekklisias (accessed May 2019).

10. Even registering those who arrive by the Ouranoupolis–Daphne ferry is a laborious process. While pilgrims help themselves to tea, biscuits, and sweets, the guest master spends hours every morning checking everyone on his list and against assigned accommodation.

Assigning the accommodation is a separate and no doubt equally time-consuming procedure.

11. In his paper at the Friends of Mount Athos Madingley symposium, February 2015.
12. Lowther ClarkeW. K., *Translations of Christian Literature: Series I, Greek Texts*: "The Lausiac History of Palladius" (London: Society For Promoting Christian Knowledge, 1918), pp. 31 and 86.
13. https://www.youtube.com/watch?v=JFmVVCU_1Qo (accessed January 2017).
14. *SRA 10*, p. 776.
15. His address was on Sunday of the Myrrh-Bearing Women, April 13, 2015.
16. *SRA 16*, p. 25.
17. Many of the Russian pilgrims are thus clad. It seems that they have just finished military service or are retired military officers. On October 4, 2019, someone had left on the coffee table of the landing in the Preobrazhensky Korpus Arkhondarik II fresh copies of the patriotic special forces publication, *Spetsnaz Rossii*.
18. Mt Athos is known as *To Perivoli tis Panagias* or *Vertograd Bogoroditsy* / The Garden of the Mother of God. She is the Mountain's *Igumen'ya* / Abbess.
19. *SRA 1*, p. 499.
20. Ibid., p. 500.
21. Ibid., p. 501.
22. Ibid., p. 502.

Sources for Inset Photos and Illustrations

The following photos or illustration are from the archives of St Panteleimon's Monastery: Fig 1.1, Fig 1.3, Fig1.5, Fig 1.6, Fig 1.7, Fig 1.8, Fig 1.9, Fig 1.10, Fig 1.11, Fig 1.12, Fig 1.13, Fig 1.14, Fig 1.15, Fig 1.16, Fig 1.17, Fig 1.18, Fig 1.19, Fig 1.20, Fig 1.21, Fig 1.22, Fig 1.23, Fig 1.24, Fig 1.26, Fig 1.27, Fig 1.28, Fig 2.1, Fig 2.2, Fig 2.3, Fig 2.4, Fig 2.6, Fig 2.9, Fig 2.10, Fig 2.11, Fig 2.12, Fig 2.13, Fig 2.14, Fig 2.16, Fig 2.17, Fig 2.18, Fig 2.19, Fig 2.20, Fig 2.22, Fig 2.23, and Fig 2.25. © St Panteleimon's Monastery

The following photos or illustration belong to the author Nicholas Fennell: Fig 1.2, Fig 1.29, and Fig 2.15. © Nicholas Fennell

The sources for the other photos are as follows: Fig 1.4: 828096890 © Dmitri Kalvan | istockphoto.com; Fig 1.25: Photo 20294889 © Fotis Mavroudakis | Dreamstime.com; Fig 2.5: Photo 81149230 © Vasilis Ververidis | Dreamstime.com; Fig 2.7: Photo 81145025 © Vasilis Ververidis | Dreamstime.com ; Fig 2.8: Photo 81166113 © Vasilis Ververidis | Dreamstime.com; Fig 2.21: Photo By Harry Pot. Source: commons.wikimedia.org: Dutch National Archives, The Hague, Fotocollectie Algemeen Nederlands Persbureau (ANEFO), 1945-1989, Nummer toegang 2.24.01.05 Bestanddeelnummer 914-8680, CC BY-SA 3.0 nl; Fig 2.24: Photo 67809309 © Sergey Chaykovskiy | Dreamstime.com.

Glossary

abbot (Gr. *igoumenos*, Russ. *igumen*)—head or superior of one of the Twenty Ruling
    Monasteries

antiprosopos—Gr. representative of Ruling Monastery in Karyes

APA—*Außenpolitisches Amt*, Nazi Foreign Policy Office

archimandrite—honorary title conferred on senior Priest-Monk, usually head of monastery
    or skete

arkhondarik—Russ. guest reception rooms and quarters; Gr. *arhontariki*

Arkhiereysky sobor—The Hieratical Council of ROCOR, headed by Archbishop Anthony
    (Khrapovitsky), and based in Sremsky Karlovćy, Serbia, after the Bolshevik Revolution

arsanas—Athonite jetty

Athoniada—Athonite school, today based in the Serai

Batyshka—Affectionate Russian form of address of priest or elder; equivalent of Greek
    Pappous, Pappoulis

cenobium—plur. cenobia and adj. (subs. cenobium): monastic house in which the brethren
    give total obedience to the abbot (or prior), who is appointed for life; all monastic
    property and duties are shared; the brethren worship together at all services and eat
    together in the refectory

chrysobull / plur. chysobulla—seal and deed from the patriarch or crowned Orthodox
    patron; document bearing the patriarchal seal

civil governor of Mount Athos/ *Politikos Dioikitis*—Greek functionary, representative of
    the Hellenic State, responsible for the police and emergency services on the Mountain;
    resides in Karyes

Danubian Principalities—Wallachia and Moldavia, before the creation of unified Romania

Daphne—Main port of Mount Athos

Daskalos—Gr. title of respect for a learned elder; lit. "Teacher"

Decree 124—Issued by the military junta in Greece, 1967, aiming to subjugate Athos by
    giving control to the civil governor over the property of the Twenty Monasteries, the
    decisions of the Sacred Community, and over all Athonite legal matters

DECR / Department of External Church Relations—public relations department of the
    Moscow Patriarchate, Russ. *Otdel vneshnykh tserkovnykh svyazey* (*OVTsS*)

dekulakization—violent annihilation of the kulaks (qv.) and their property in the 1920s
    USSR

dependency—(Gr. *metochion*; Russ. *metokh* or *podvor'ye*) property belonging to Athonite
    house, but outside its monastic walls

diamonitirion—permit issued by Sacred Community outsiders to visit the Holy Mountain

227

DNB—Deutsches Nachrichtenbüro, the Nazi news agency

Double Synaxis—extraordinary meeting in Karyes of the representatives of the Twenty Monasteries and of the Twenty Abbots

dragoman—interpreter during Ottoman rule

dukhovnik—Russ. spiritual father; Gr. *pneumatikos*

EAM—political wing of ELAS, the Greek Liberation Army during the Second World War and the Greek Civil War

Ecumenical patriarch—Senior patriarch of all Orthodox Churches, resides in Constantinople

ekleziarkh—Russ. plur. *ekleziarkhi*, church orderly, looks after candles, lamps etc. and the smooth running of services

ekonom—(Russ.; Gr. *oikonomos*) steward, a senior position; representative of prior or abbot in a dependency

ELAS—Greek Liberation Army during the Second World War and the Greek Civil War

elder—(Russ. *starets*; Gr. *gerontas*) senior spiritually experienced monk, usually a father-confessor or spiritual father; in St Panteleimon's also a monk in charge of specialized workshop and chief craftsman

epigonation—A liturgical vestment worn by bishops, archimandrites, or senior priests

Epistasia, Iera—the executive committee of the Sacred Community (*Iera Koinotis*)

epitaphion—Gr. embroidered Holy Friday burial shroud

epitracheilion—Gr. stole

epitropos—Gr. plur. *epitropoi*, one of the elected leaders of an idiorrhythmic house

exarchate—body representative of or standing in the stead of patriarch, headed by exarch

father-confessor—Russ., *dukhovnik*, Gr. *pneumatikos*: the principal spiritual father and confessor of a monastery or skete

firman—Ottoman decree

fondarichny—Russ. guest-master, a corruption of Gr. *arhontaris*

Garden—The Garden of the Mother of God, i.e., Mount Athos, of which the Mother of God is the Abbess; *to Perivoli tis Panghias* Gr.

gospodar—princely title for rulers of the Danubian Principalities

grammatik—Russ. learned monk, chief secretary, translator, and interpreter to the abbot

Grand-Prince—Son or brother of the Russian tsar

Great Schema—A monk of the Great Schema in a Russian monastery has taken special vows and leads a stricter ascetic life than an ordinary monk

Gregorian Calendar—NS—Thirteen days ahead of the traditional Church Julian calendar (Old Style / OS); the Church of Greece is NS, but the Holy Mountain adheres to the (Old Style / OS) Julian Calendar

guest-master—Russ. *fondarichny*, in charge of guest reception and accommodation

Hagiorite—Athonite

harach—Ottoman head-tax

hesychasm—Quietism, meditative spirituality based on the recitation of prayers with the prayer rope, esp. the Jesus Prayer: prayer of the heart

Hierarchy—The immutable / *amevaliti* order of seniority of the Twenty Monasteries; St Panteleimon's is 19th

idiorrhythm /—adj. idiorrhythmic, describing loose-knit house or community of semi-independent monks who earn their keep and live according to their wealth; they do not eat together

igumen—Russ. for abbot

Igumen'ya—Abbess of the Holy Mountain, the Mother of God

isihastirion—hermitage, sub-kellion

Jesus Prayer, the—the main Hesychastic prayer

Julian Calendar—or Old Style (OS) calendar, thirteen days later than the Gregorian or Western Calendar

kaimakam—Turkish governor of Athos

kantselyariya —Russ. plur. *kantselyarii*, administrative office of St Panteleimon's

Karyes—Capital of Mount Athos

K.H.A.O, *Katastatikos Hartis Aghiou Orous*—Official Constitution of the Holy Mountain, enshrined in the Constitution of the Hellenic Republic

kathisma—small house, sub-kellion

katholikon—(Russ. sobor) central church of monastery; there are two at St Panteleimon's: the *Ano Katholikon* / Pokrovsky sobor or Upper Central Church of the Protecting Veil, and the *Kato Katholikon* or Lower Central Church of St Panteleismon

kavia—hut, sub-kellion

kellion—(Russ. kelliya) sub-skete; small Athonite house, often containing a chapel

kelliot—inhabitant of *kellion*

Koinotis, Iera—Sacred Community or Karyes governing body made up of the Twenty *antiprosopoi* / representatives

konaki—house in Karyes belonging to a Ruling Monastery or other Athonite house; accommodation for the house's *antiprosopos* (qv.)

Krumitsa—dependency of St Panteleimon's with vineyards, close to Novaya Fivaida and the Megali Vigla Athonite land border with mainland Greece

ktitor—founder and benefactor

kulak—private peasant landowner, liquidated by Bolsheviks in 1920s USSR

kyriakon—skete central church

kyriarchic—special independent status of monastery

Megali Vigla—Athonite land border with mainland Greece

Megalos Limos—The Great Greek Famine

metropolitan—senior bishop (whose see is in a metropolis)

Monahologion—descriptive list of a house's brethren

Morea—the Peloponnese

Name-Glorifier—adherent of the rebel faction believing in the special sanctity of the Name of Jesus; deported to Russia in 1913

Name-Hater—opponent of the rebel faction believing in the special sanctity of the Name of Jesus

namestnik (Russ.), *locum tenens*—deputy (of patriarch, abbot, prior); often designated as successor

non-possessor—an adherent of ascetic poverty and non-reliance on material possessions; a term originating in the sixteenth-century dispute in Russia with St Nil Sorsky and his followers, who opposed large-scale landowning by the monasteries

Novaya Fivaida—Dependency belonging to St Panteleimon's, on North-Westernmost shore of the Holy Mountain, close to Krumitsa. One of the centres of the Name-Glorifiers

obedience / *poslushanie (Russ)*, *diakonima (Gr)*—a job of work assigned to every monk in a cenobium

obschy dukhovnik—general or chief spiritual father of St Panteleimon's

ogorodnik—Russ. worker in vegetable *ogorod* / garden

oikonomos—Gr. for steward (Russ. *ekonom*)

Old (Mountain) Rusik—Stary (Nagorny) Rusik, Old Mountain St Panteleimon Monastery

omologon—Charter or deed, esp. between skete and monastery

Palestinskie Shtaty—arrangement of Empress Anne's, 1735, to provide money for the Holy Places and Orthodox East; superseded in 1882 by *Imperatorskoe Pravoslavnoe Palestinskoe Obschestvo*

Palomnicheskaya sluzhba RSPMA—Russ. St Panteleimon Pilgrims' Bureau

Pan-Orthodox—Orthodoxy embracing people of all ethnic origins

Pan-Slavism—nineteenth century. Russian ideological movement embracing Slav groups with Russia in preeminent position

panikhida—Russ. memorial service

Phanar—District of Constantinople where the ecumenical patriarch lives and has his cathedral

phelonion—Gr. cape—part of a priest's vestments

Philiki Hetaireia—secret Greek revolutionary society founded 1814

pneumatikos—(Gk.) father confessor

podvor'ye—dependency outside Athos, usually in a city

Pokrov—Protecting Veil of the Mother of God

Pokrovsky sobor—St Panteleimon Upper Central Church of Protecting Veil of the Mother of God

Pomestny Sobor—Local Church Council of 1917 at which Metropolitan Tikhon was elected patriarch of Moscow

Porte—/ Sublime Porte, the central government of the Ottoman Empire

prayer rope—knotted rope similar to Catholic rosary used for the Jesus prayer

Preobrazhensky Korpus—main *arkhondarik* / guest quarters of St panteleimon's

Priest-Monk—a monk who has been ordained priest

prior / Gr. *dikaios* Russ. *dikey*—superior or head of Athonite skete head of a skete

Prophet Elijah Skete—second Russian Athonite skete, belonging to Pantokratoros

Protepistatis, Protos—The Senior Council Representative, Head of *Iera Epistasia*

pustynnik—Russ. hermit, lit. desert dweller

ROCOR—Russian Orthodox Church Outside Russia

Rossikon—Gr. The Russian Monastery

RSNTO—Russian Steam Navigation and Trade Organization

Ruling Monastery—One of the Twenty, it owns and has absolute rights over all its sketes, *kellia*, hermitages, and *metochia*. E.g. Vatopedi is the Ruling Monastery of the Serai

Rus'—Ancient, Orthodox land before the fall of Kiev encompassing all the Russian-speaking people

Rusik—the Russian Monastery

Russik / Rossikon—the Russian Monastery of St Panteleimon

Sacred Community—Gr. *Iera Koinotis*, Karyes governing body made up of the Twenty *antiprosopoi* / representatives

schema—Monastic habit. In the Russian tradition the Great or Angelic Schema is conferred on monks professing the ultimate degree of asceticism. A great Schema-Monk adheres to a stricter regime of prayer and abstention; he devotes himself to prayer, silence, and seclusion within the monastery

Serai—the Russian Skete of St Andrew

siromakh—wandering beggar monk

skete—Athonite sub-monastery

skevophylax—keeper of precious ecclesiastical vessels

sobor—Russ. central church; the Council of Elders of skete; synaxis

Spiritual Father / *Dukhovnik* / *Pneumatikos*—senior monastery father who takes confessions and directs the conscience of brethren in his charge

St Andrew Skete—first Russian skete, the Serai, belonging to Vatopedi

starchestvo—system of complete obedience to *starets* / elder, to whom a spiritual child reveals, often daily, his innermost thoughts

starets—Russ. elder

Stary (Nagorny) (Old Mountain) Russik—Athonite dependency belonging to St Panteleimon's; the original site of the Russian Monastery

stavropegic—special status conferred on monastery by patriarch

synaxis—monastic meeting, esp. of Sacred Community

synaxis; double *synaxis*—meeting of the Twenty *antiprosopoi* / representatives and the Twenty abbots in karyes

syngilion—Gr. charter, seal

Troparion, plur. *troparia*—Gr., also *apolitykion*, dismissal hymn or verse chanted in commemoration of a feast or a holy figure

Tsarevich—Son of the tsar (cf. Grand-Prince)

Twenty, The—The Twenty Ruling Athonite Monasteries

ukaz—decree issued by the Russian government or tsar

Vasiliki—imperial title conferred on each of the Twenty Monasteries

velichaniya—Russ., sing. *velichnie*, hymn of praise

Xylourgou—oldest Russian monastery, both on Athos and elsewhere; now a St Panteleimon dependency

Zhurnal Moskovskoy patriarkhii—Journal of the Moscow Patriarchate

Župan—Ruler of Serbia

Bibliography

Bibliographical Abbreviations

ISRA 1   *Indrik: Seriya russky Afon, vol. 1*, P. Troitsky, "Istoriya russkikh obitieley Afona v XIX–XX vekakh" (Moscow: Indrik, 2009).

ISRA 3   *Indrik: Seriya russky Afon, vol. 3*, V. Mayevsky, "Afon i ego sud'ba" (Moscow: Indrik, 2009).

ISRA 4   *Indrik: Seriya russky Afon, vol. 4*, Ieromonakh Anikita, "Puteshestvie ieromonakha Anikity po svyatym mestam Vostoka v 1834–1836 godakh" (Moscow: Indrik, 2009).

ISRA 6   *Indrik: Seriya russky Afon, vol. 6*, A. A. Dmitrievsky, "Russkie na Afone: ocherk zhizni i deatel'nosti igumena svyaschennoarkhimandrita Makariya (Sushkina)" (Moscow: Indrik, 2010).

ISRA 7   *Indrik: Seriya russky Afon, vol. 7*, L. A. Gerd, "Russky Afon 1878–1914 gg." *ISRA 7* (Moscow: Indrik, 2010).

ISRA 8   *Indrik: Seriya russky Afon, vol. 8*, N. Fennell, P. Troitsky et al., "Il'insky skit na Afone" (Moscow: Indrik, 2011).

ISRA 9   *Indrik: Seriya russky Afon, vol. 9*, Boris Zaytsev, "Na Afon" (Moscow: Indrik, 2009).

ISRA 10   *Indrik: Seriya russky Afon, vol. 10*, Arkhimandrit Antonin (Kapustin), "Zametki poklonnika Svyatoy Gory" (Moscow: Indrik, 2013).

KNL 6/1   *Leont'ev, K. N.: Polnoe sobranie sochineniy i pisem v dvadtsati tomakh, vol. 6*, "Vospominaniya, ocherki, avtobiograficheskiye proizvedeniya 1869–1891 godov" (St Petersburg: Izdatel'stvo Vladimir Dal', 2003).

KNL 7/1   *Leont'ev, K. N.: Polnoe sobranie sochineniy I pisem v dvadtsati tomakh, vol. 7*, "Publtsistika 1862–1879 godov" (St Petersburg: Izdatel'stvo Vladimir Dal', 2005).

KS 16   *Al'manakh "K Svetu" N° 16, 1997 god*, "Novo-Afonsky Simono-Kananitsky Monastyr'."

KS 18   *Al'manakh "K Svetu" N° 18, 2000 god*, "Istoriya Russkogo na Afone svyato-Panteleimonova monastyrya."

SRA 1   *Seriya: Russky Afon XIX–XX vekov, vol. 1*, "Russky Afonsky otechnik XIX–XX vekov" (Athos: Izdanie RPMA, 2012).

SRA 2   *Seriya: Russky Afon XIX–XX vekov, vol. 2*, "Monakhalogy Russkogo svyato-Panteleimonova monastyrya na Afone" (Athos: Izdanie RPMA, 2013).

SRA 4   *Seriya: Russky Afon XIX–XX vekov, vol. 4,* "Istoriya Russkogo svyato-Pantelei-monova monastyrya na Afone s drevneyshikh vremyon do 1735 goda" (Athos: Izdanie RPMA, 2013).

SRA 5   *Seriya: Russky Afon XIX–XX vekov, vol. 5,* "Istoriya Russkogo svyato-Pantelei-monova monastyrya na Afone s 1735 po 1912 god" (Athos: Izdanie RPMA, 2015).

SRA 6   *Seriya: Russky Afon XIX–XX vekov, vol. 6,* "Istoriya Russkogo svyato-Pantelei-monova monastyrya na Afone s 1912 po 2015 god" (Athos: Izdanie RPMA, 2015).

SRA 7/1   *Seriya: Russky Afon XIX–XX vekov, vol. 7/1,* "Katalog slavyano-russkikh rukopisey" (Athos: Izdanie RPMA, 2013).

SRA 7/4   *Seriya: Russky Afon XIX–XX vekov, vol. 7/4,* "Katalog arkhivnogo fonda Russ-kogo svyato-Panteleimonogo monastyrya na Afone" (Athos: Izdanie RPMA, 2013).

SRA 9/1   *Seriya: Russky Afon XIX–XX vekov, vol. 9/1,* "Startsy-vozobnoviteli Russkogo Svyato-Panteleimonova monastyrya na Afone; chast' pervaya: Dukhovnik Ier-onim" (Athos: Izdanie RPMA, 2014).

SRA 9/2   *Seriya: Russky Afon XIX–XX vekov, vol. 9/2,* "Startsy-vozobnoviteli Russkogo Svyato-Panteleimonova monastyrya na Afone; chast' vtoraya: Igumen russ-kikh Afontsev—starets Makary ili zhizneopisanie i tvoreniya skhiarkhiman-drita Makariya (Sushkina)" (Athos: Izdanie RPMA, 2016).

SRA 10   *Seriya: Russky Afon XIX–XX vekov, vol. 10,* "Pis'ma vydayuschikhsya tserk-ovnykh i svetskikh deyateleiy Rossii startsam Russkogo Svyato-Panteleimon-ova monastyrya na Afone" (Athos: Izdanie RPMA, 2015).

SRA 12   *Seriya: Russky Afon XIX–XX vekov, vol. 12,* "Graf Ignat'ev i Russky Svyato-Pan-teleimonov monastyr' na Afone" (Athos: Izdanie RPMA, 2016).

SRA 15   *Seriya: Russky Afon XIX–XX vekov, vol. 15,* "Afonsky period zhizni arkhie-piskopa Vasiliya (Krivosheina) v dokumentakh" (Athos: Izdanie RPMA, 2016).

SRA 16   *Seriya: Russky Afon XIX–XX vekov, vol. 16,* "Dukhovniki Russkogo Svyato-Pan-teleimonova monastyrya na Afone otets Agafodor i otets Kirik" (Athos: Izdanie RPMA, 2016).

Printed Texts

Afonsky arkhiv XX veka: dokumenty Russkogo Svyato-Panteleimonobskogo monastyrya 1917-1941 (Moscow–Brussels: Arkhiv russkoy emigratsii, 2014).

Afonsky tserkovny kalendar' 2017 (Athos: RPMA, 2017).

Barsky, Vasily Grigorovich-, *Vtoroe Poseschenie svyatoy Afonskoy gory Vasiliya Grigorovi-cha-Barskogo im samim opisannoe* (Moscow: Indrik, 2004).

Bibikov, M. V., "Russkie monastyri na Afone i v Svyatoy Zemle v svete novykh i maloizvest-nykh istochnikov," *Rus'–Svyataya Gora Afon: tysyacha let dukhovnogo i kul'turnogo edinstva* (Moscow: Danilov monastyr', 2017).

Bobango, A. J., "The Emergence of the Romanian National State" (New York: East European Quarterly, 1979).

Clogg, Richard, *A Concise History of Greece* (Cambridge: Cambridge University Press, 1992).

Cyril, Patriarch of Bulgaria, *Contribution to the Bulgarian Church Problem (Documents from the Austrian Consulate in Salonika)* (Dublin–Vienna: Mosaic Publications, 1998).

Dakin, D., *The Greek Struggle in Macedonia 1897–1913* (Thessaloniki: Thessaloniki Institute for Balkan Studies, 1993).

Dmitrievsky, A. A., *Afon i ego novoe politicheskoe mezhdunarodnoe polozhenie* (St Petersburg: 1913).

Dölger, F., *Mönschland Athos* (Munich: F. Bruchmann, 1945).

Domrachov, Skhimonakh Ilarion, *Na gorakh Kavkaza* (St Petersburg: Voskresen'e, Dioptra, 2002).

Dorotheos Monahos (Vatopedinos), *To Aghio Oros, Miisi stin Istoria tou kai ti Zoi tou, Tomoi A' kai B'* (Katerini: Tertios, 1985).

Dostoevsky, F.M., *Polnoye sobranie sochineniy v tridtsati tomakh, vol. 15, Brat'ya Karamazovy*, vol. 1, "Startsy" (Moscow: Institut russkoy literatury AN SSSR, 1973).

Dragoumis, I., *Martyron kai Iroon Aima* (Athens: Malliaris-Paidia, 1903).

Dykstra, Tom, *Hallowed Be Thy Name: The Name-Glorifying Dispute in the Russian Orthodox Church and on Mount Athos, 1912–1914* (St Paul, Minnesota: OCABS Press, 2013).

Fennell, J. L. I., *A History of the Russian Church to 1448* (London: Longman, 1995).

Fennell, N., "The Garden of the Mother of God Revisited," *Friends of Mount Athos Annual Report* 2017.

Fotić, Alexandar, "From Mount Athos Stories: An Unusual 'Union' between Hilandar and St Panteleimon in the 16th and 17th Centuries," *Philosophy, Sociology, Psychology and History*, Vol 17, No. 2, 2018.

Gerasimos (Smyrnakis), Vatopedinos, *To Aghion Oros* (Mount Athos: Panselinos, 1988).

Gerd, L. A., *Konstatinopol'sky patriarkhat i Rossiya 1901/1914* (Moscow: Indrik, 2012).

Graham, Stephen, *With the Russian Pilgrims to Jerusalem* (London: Thomas Nelson, 1913).

Hatzifotis, I. M., *Mones tou Agiou Orous, Tomos A'* (Athens: Hellandion, 2008).

Il'f i Petrov, "Dvenadtsat' Stul'ev, chast' pervaya, glava XII, 'Rasskaz o gusare-skhimnike*****,'" *Il'ya Il'f, Evgeny Petrov: Sobranie sochineniy, Tom pervy* (Moscow: Gosudarstvennoe izdatel'stvo khudozhestvennoy literatury, 1981).

Ilarion (Alfeev), Episkop, *Svyaschennaya tayna tserkvi: vvedenie v istoriyu i problematiku imyaslavskikh sporov* (St Petersburg: Izdatel'stvo Olega Abyshko, 2007).

Ioakim (Sabel'nikov), Ieromonakh, *Velikaya Strazha, Book 1* (Moscow: Izdatel'stvo Moskovskoy Patriarkhii, 2001).

Ioanniky (Abernethy), Priest-Monk, "K Tysyacheletyu russkikh na Afone," unpublished typescript.

Kallistos (Ware), Metropolitan, "St Nil Sorsky: A Hesychast Bridge between Byzantium and Russia," *Mount Athos and Russia*, eds N. Fennell and G. Speake (Oxford: Peter Lang, 2018).

Kirion (Ol'khovik), Priest-Monk, "Istoriya svyatogorskikh monasheskikh traditsiy v Ksilourgou, Starom Rusike i Svyato-Panteleimonovom monastyre," *Rus'–svyataya gora Afon: tysyacha let dukhovnogo edinstva* (Moscow: Danilov Monastyr', 2017).

Kraskovsky, I. F., *Makary Afonsky igumen i svyaschennoarkimandrit svyatogo Panteleimonogo monastyrya* (Moscow: 1889).

Lowther Clarke, W. K., *Translations of Christian Literature: Series I, Greek Texts*: "The Lausiac History of Palladius" (London: Society for Promoting Christian Knowledge, 1918).

Metaxakis, Meletios, *To Agion Oros kai i rosiki politiki en anatoli* (Athens: P.D. Sakellariou, 1913).

Mylonakos, Nikiphoros, *Aghion Oros kai Slavoi* (Athens: Eisagoghi, 1960).

Natroev, A., *Iversky Monastyr' na Afone na odnom iz vysytupov Khalkidonskago poluostorova* (Tiflis: Tipografiya "Trud", 1909).

Nedosekin, Archpriest Pavel, "O nekotorykh prichinakh krizisa «russkogo Afona» v XX veke," *Afonsky Arkhiv XX veka. Dokumenty Russkogo Svyato-Panteleimonovskogo monastyrya 1917–1941* (Moscow–Brussels: Arkhiv russkoy emigratsii, 2014).

Nikodim (Rotov), Metropolitan of Leningrad, unpublished letter to Comrade Zelenkov.

Oakes, Sir Augustus, *The Great European Treaties of the Nineteenth Century* (Oxford: Clarendon Press, 1938).

Parfeny (Ageev), Inok, *Skazanie o stranstvii i puteshestvii po Rossii, Moldavii, Turtsii i Svyatoy Zemle*, vols 1 and 2 (Moscow: Novospassky monastyr', 2008).

Pavlovsky, A. A., ed., *Afonskiya Izvestiya, I i II* (Athos, 1915).

Pélagie, Moniale, "L'higoumène Misaël," *Buisson Ardent*, 19 (Penthalaz and Dijon: Diffusion CRF, Cahiers Saint- Silouane l'athonite, 2013).

Pigol', Pyotr, *Afonskaya tragediya. Gordost' i sataninskie zamysly* (Moscow: Institut Apostola Ioanna Bogoslova, 2005).

Pirogov, V. I. et al., *Rosikon: Afonsky russky paterik* (Mount Athos: Institut russkogo Afona, 2015).

Porfiry (Uspensky), Episkop, *Pervoe puteshestvie v Afonskie monastyri i skity arkhimandrita, nyne episkopa, Porfiriya Uspenskogo v 1845 godu* (Kiev, 1877).

Prousis, Theophilus C., "Eastern Orthodoxy Under Siege in the Ottoman Levant: A View from Constantinople in 1821" (2008), University of North Florida UNF Digital Commons,

History Faculty Publications, 13. <https://digitalcommons.unf.edu/cgi/viewcontent. cgi?article=1011&context=ahis_facpub>.

Réfutation du mémoire soumis par les moines russes kelliotes à la Conférence des Ambassadeurs de Londres et contenant des propositions anticanoniques et subversives de toute notre constitution (Karyes, 1913).

Reid, James J., *Crisis of the Ottoman Empire: Prelude to Collapse 1839–1878* (Stuttgart: Franz Steiner Verlag, 2000).

Riley, Athelstan L., *Athos, or: The Mountain of the Monks* (London: Longman, Green & Co, 1887).

Russky bigrafichesky slovar' (Moscow: Terra-Knizhny klub, 1999).

Russky monastyr' sv. Velikomuchenika i tselitelya Panteleimona na sv. Gore Afonskoy (Moscow: Podvor'e Russkogo na Afone svyato-Panteleimonova monastyrya v Moskve, 2005).

Russky na Afone Svyato-Panteleimonov monastyr': k 1000-letiyu russkogo monashestva na Svyatoy Gore Afon (RPMA: Izdatel'stvo Yulis, 2017).

Russky Obschezhitel'ny skit svyatago Proroka Ilii na Svyatoy Afonskoy Gore (Odessa: Tipografiya eparkhal'nogo doma, 1913).

Sentences arbitrales rendues par les membres neutres de la Commission Mixte en vertu de l'article 32 de la Convention signée à Ankara le 10 juin 1930 et relatives aux cas de certains moines et monastères du Mont Athos ayant demandé l'admission au bénéfice des articles 9 et 29 de la même Convention (Ankara: Tsitouris, 1930).

Serafim Svyatogorets / Skhieromonakh Sergy (Vesnin), *Pis'ma Svyatogortsa o svyatoy Afonskoy gore* (Moscow: 1895).

Sheshunova, S., "Parfeny Ageev" in "Russkiye pisateli 1800-1917," *Biografichesky slovar'*, vol. 4.

Shumilo, S. V., "The First Russian Monks on Mount Athos," *Mount Athos and Russia*, (New York: Peter Lang, 2018).

Smolitsch, I. K., "Le Mont Athos et la Russie," *Le Millénaire du Mont Athos* (Wetteren: Éditions de Chevetogne, 1963).

Soloviev, A., *Histoire du monastère russe au Mont-Athos* (Belgrade: Slavija, 1933).

Speake, Graham, *A History of the Athonite Commonwealth: The Spritual and Cultural Diaspora of Mount Athos* (Cambridge: Cambridge University Press, 2018).

Speake, Graham, *Mount Athos: Renewal in Paradise* (New Haven and London: Yale University Press, 2002).

St Sophrony (Sakharov), *Starets Siluan* (Essex: Stavropegic Monastery of St John the Baptist, 1990).

Tachiaos, A.-E., *To Georgianikon zitima (1868–1916)* (Thessaloniki: Institute for Balkan Studies, 1962)

Tachiaos, A.-E., *O Paisios Velitskofski kai i Askhitikophilologiki skholi tou* (Thessaloniki: Institute for Balkan Studies, 1964).

Tachiaos, A.-E., *Anekdota ellinika kai rossika eggrapha peri tou georganikou zitimatos* (Thessaloniki: Institute for Balkan Studies, 1972).

Taylor, A. J. P., *The Struggle for Mastery in Europe 1848–1918* (Oxford: Oxford University Press, 1971).

The London Times, November 22, 1877.

Yuvenaly (Poyarkov), Metropolit Kolomensky and Krutitsky, *Rossiya-Afon: tysyacheletie dukhovnogo edinstva*, "Vzaimootnosheniya Russkoy Pravoslavnoy Tserkvi i Afona v XX veke" (Moscow: Izdatel'stvo PSTGU, 2008).

Zabytye stanitsy russkogo imyaslaviya (Moscow: Izdatel'stvo Palomnik, 2001).

Internet Resources

http://afonit.info/biblioteka/knigi/afonskij-panteleimonov-monastyr-gotovit-k-izdaniyu-ne-imeyushchuyu-analogov-25-ti-tomnuyu-seriyu-russkij-afon-khikh-khkh-vekov

http://afonit.info/biblioteka/russkij-afon/prof-a-takhiaos-nachalo-dukhovnykh-svyazej-rusi-s-afonom-1000-let

http://afonit.info/novosti/1000-letie-russkogo-afona/glava-pravitelstva-rf-i-patriarkh-moskovskij-proveli-zasedanie-obshchestvenno-popechitelskogo-soveta-afonskogo-panteleimonova-monastyrya-video-i-foto

http://afonit.info/novosti/1000-letie-russkogo-afona/glava-pravitelstva-rf-i-patriarkh-moskovskij-proveli-zasedanie-obshchestvenno-popechitelskogo-soveta-afonskogo-panteleimonova-monastyrya-video-i-foto

http://afonit.info/novosti/novosti-afona/patriarkh-bolgarskij-vstretilsya-s-delegatsiej-afonskikh-monastyrej-sv-panteleimona-i-ksenofont

http://agioritikesmnimes.blogspot.com/2011/11/134.html?m=1

http://www.oinoxoos.net/oinos/3916/tsantali-ae-i-oinobiomichania-ton-15-ekatommurion-litron

http://www.orthedu.ru/ch-hist/14593-monasheskie-smuty-nachala-hh-veka-afon-optina.html

http://www.romfea.gr/epikairotita-xronika/6830-agnoia-apo-tous-agioreites-gia-episkepsi-patriarxi-mosxas

https://athosfriends.org/pilgrims-guide/

https://drevo-info.ru/articles/2463.html

https://korvet2.ru/ropit.html

https://mospat.ru/en/2018/10/17/news165398/

https://pravlife.org/ru/content/shiarhimandrit-ieremiya-alehin-podvizhnik-nashego-vremeni

https://pravoslavie.ru/28260.html

https://www.academia.edu/30994454/Secularization_of_Monastic_Estates_1863_._Some_Legal_Historical_Aspects

https://www.britannica.com/topic/kulak

https://www.cambridge.org/core/journals/journal-of-hellenic-studies/article/
monchsland-athos-by-f-dolger-pp-303-pl-184-munich-f-bruckmann-1943/3DCF3BE-
748D3E350D62DC6A4B53A7AD1

https://www.rocorstudies.org/2019/11/21/the-ever-burning-lamp-a-reassessment-of-the-
expulsion-of-the-last-russian-representatives-from-the-prophet-elijah-skete/

https://www.romfea.gr/agioritika-nea/26975-i-moni-agiou-panteleimonos-eklei-
se-tis-portes-stous-ekprosopous-tis-oukranikis-ekklisias

https://www.youtube.com/watch?v=JFmVVCU_1Qo

www.isihazm.ru/?id=2048

Index